AGRO-FORESTRY AND CLIMATE CHANGE

AGRO-FORESTRY AND CLIMATE CHANGE

Edited by

Dr. Pawan Kumar 'Bharti'
Centre for Agro-Rural Technologies (CART-India)
20, Jamaalpur Man, Raja Ka Tajpur
Bijnore (UP) - 246 735, (India)
E-mail: gurupawanbharti@rediffmail.com

&

Dr. Narayan Singh
Manager
CSR, Project - The Energy Resource Institute (TERI)
Dalash, Kullu, (Himachal Pradesh)
(India)

DPH

DISCOVERY PUBLISHING HOUSE PVT. LTD.
NEW DELHI-110 002

Published by:
Tilak Wasan
DISCOVERY PUBLISHING HOUSE PVT. LTD.
4383/4B, Ansari Road, Darya Ganj
New Delhi-110 002 (India)
Phone : +91-11-23279245, 43596064-65
Fax : +91-11-23253475
E-mail : discoverypublishinghouse@gmail.com
sales@discoverypublishinggroup.com
parul.wasan@gmail.com
web : www.discoverypublishinggroup.com

***First Edition:* 2014**

ISBN: 978-93-5056-514-8

Agro-Forestry and Climate Change

Printed at:
Aditi Fine Art Press
Delhi

Preface

Agroforestry is an integrated approach of using the interactive benefits from combining trees and shrubs with crops and/or livestock. It combines agricultural and forestry technologies to create more diverse, productive, profitable, healthy, and sustainable land-use systems. A simple and very small definition of agroforestry is 'trees on farms'.

The integration of agriculture or farming with forestry, so that the land can simultaneously be used for more than one purpose. This practice is meant to have both environmental and financial benefits. The presence of trees can provide benefits such as sheltering livestock from the elements and improving the soil so that crops will be more productive. The agroforestry system can also provide a more even income for landowners since all of their income is not tied to a few crops or a single season. Agroforestry can also make it easier for farmers to transition from one type of crop to another as market demand for their products changes.

Agroforestry does require more planning and know-how than simpler land uses because the system must take into consideration the diverse and sometimes contradictory needs of each component (the grazing needs of cattle versus a tree's need to have its roots undisturbed, for example). Examples of types of agroforestry practiced in the United States include alleycropping, silvopasture, windbreaks, riparian buffer strips and forest farming.

This book provides comprehensive coverage of the fundamental principles and current practices and trends in the field of environmental pollution, conservation, agriculture, ecology and environmental biotechnology. This book updates the subject matter, illustrations and problems to incorporate new concepts and issues related to Agro-forestry, environmental conservation, pollution, agriculture, ecology and biotechnology.

Particularly thanks are due to all contributors from Canada, Ethiopia, India; and publisher also for their contribution and assistance. I hope this book will be of benefit to both present and future colleagues, who teach, study and working in the field of Agroforestry, ecology, environmental conservation, agriculture, forest conservation and biotechnology.

Pawan Kumar 'Bharti'

Contents

1

Fuel-woods and Fodder Collection, Requirement and Scarcity in Central Himalayan Region of India

Bishan Singh Raikwal[1*]; Narayan Singh[2]
Arvind Kumar Bhandari[3]

ABSTRACT

A study of forest ecosystem, agro-ecosystem, livelihood and livestock conducted to understand the fuel and fodder status of Central Himalayan Region of Kumaun. Forest is the main source of fuel-wood and fodder for the local communities, which is mainly collected by local women. The availability of the fuel-woods and fodder on that study village was 5278.62 MT and 8461.79MT against the requirement of fuel-wood and fodder was 13889.58MT and 14677.69MT. The gross fuel-wood and fodder scarcity of 8610.94 MT and 5835.90MT has been observed in the study village.

Keywords: Fodder, Fuel-wood deficit, Central Himalayan, consumption and source, Van Panchayat and Focus group discussion and Participatory Rural Appraisal (PRA).

INTRODUCTION

In India, agricultural, along with animal husbandry is the main occupation of livelihood of their people, and that country has largest population of

1. **Researcher, Gene Campaign, Village-Simayal-Orakhan, Nainital - 263 158, Uttarakhand, India.**
2. **Manager, CSR, Project -The Energy Resource Institute (TERI), Dalash, Kullu, Himachal Pradesh, India.**
3. **Scientist, Biotechnology – Herbal Research and Development Institute, Mandal, Gopeshwar (Uttarakhand), India.**

livestock in the world (Palni, 1996). Most of the population directly and indirectly depends on forest ecosystem to fulfill their basic requirement of fuel-wood, timber, food, medicine, cloth and livelihood sustaining activity as well livestock also depend upon the forest. Forests meet up 40% of energy need in Indian (Dhyani, S. and Maikhuri, R.K, 2012) and Livestock meet about 30-50% their feed from the forest fodder and grassland (Bajracharya, 1999). Agro-forestry, in Central Himalayan region have been donating significant tangible (fuel-woods and fodder) and intangible resources (prevent soil erosion, to purify atmosphere oxygen, etc.) for the survival of hilly life. In Uttarakhand agroforestry being contributed 4.05 Lakh MT fodder (tree leaves) annually (Singh, K. and Singh, H.S. 2009).

Women of the Central Himalayan region of India have spent their lots of time and energy to the collection of the fuel-wood and fodder into the forest and they had added their drudgery (Dhyani, S and Maikhuri, R.K, 2012). In Himalayan region, agriculture and animal husbandry are primary occupation of their local people, generally every house-hold has one cow or buffalo and a single pair of bullock for the milking and farming purposes (Bajracharya, 1999; Negi, 1999 and Sati, 2005).

In Central Himalayan region, almost farmers have small land-holdings and farming system is mostly conventional, with lot of agricultural diversity, which also plays key role for ensuring fodder supply to the livestock. Fuel-wood and fodder have been collected through lopping or biomass collection. Introduction of stall feeding for ecological sustainability and conservation of natural resource has always been stressful to women, therefore, it's have increases proportion of fodder requirement as well as increases the drudgery of women. In Central Himalaya region every house-hold collected fodder and fuel-wood from the forest, some time two and three people of per house-hold have collected it, in frequently once and twice time in a day. Generally, every day women spent her 7 to 8 hours into fodder and fuel woods collection.

Unavailability of green forage results in low milk productivity in winter season, due to lack of vitamin and protein in forage, causing shortened breeding span and decrease in working capability of bullocks (Palni *et al.*, 1998). The main aim to the study are:

1. to address the fodder and fuel-wood availability in the study villages;
2. fuel-wood and fodder collection practices in the villages; and
3. list out fodder and fuel-wood species present in the villages.

STUDY AREA

The study was conducted in the 14 villages (Bakhali, Baralgaon, Chhitar, Chulerasim, Dantola, Ganai, Siroli, Bamangaon,Bashbhira, Chhana, Garshiyari, Mahatgaon, Mahalchora, and Naugaon) of Choukhutia block, district Almora, Uttarakhand state in the Central Himalayan region of India. Choukhutia block situated in-between N 029° 52′ 60 and E 079° 20′ 60 and study villages lies amid 1000 to 1500 meter from mean sea level height. The total population of these villages is 9951 in which female and male population is 4884 and 5067. The farmers have marginal land holding in the hill region and farming system is just for subsistence. Agricultural field of famers are too scattered so that they unable to manage it and also unable to protect crop from the popular destructive wild pig and monkey.

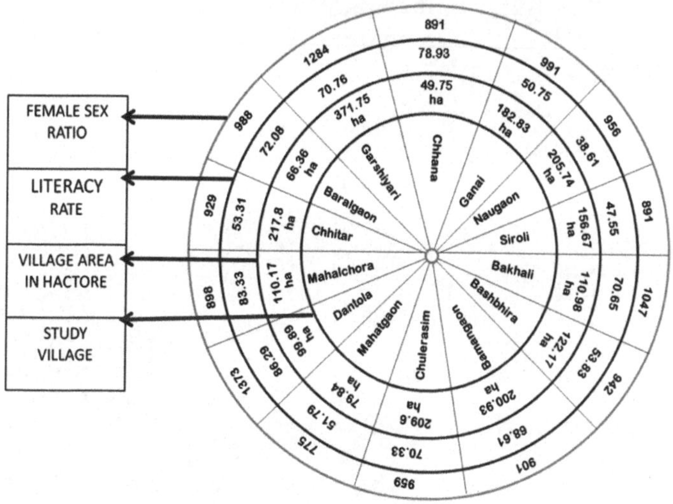

Fig. 1.1: Comprehensive Details of Study Area

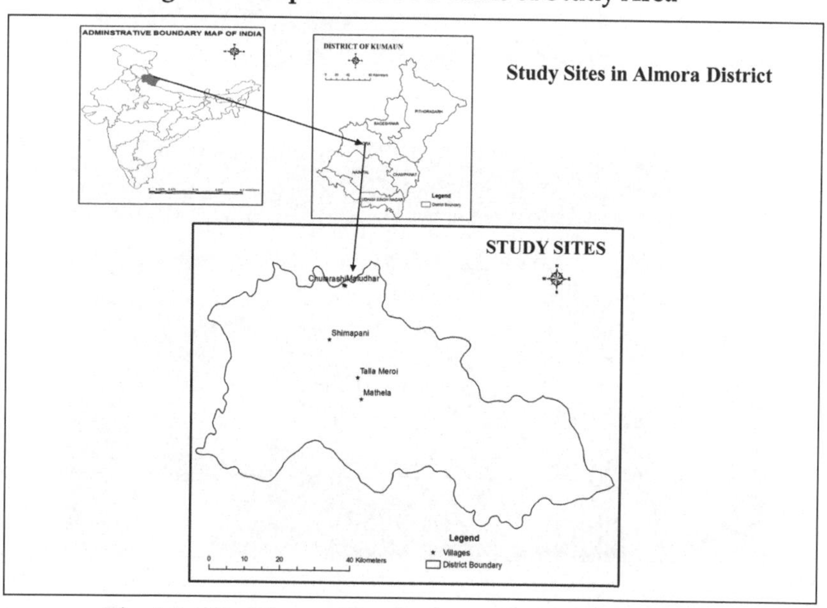

Fig. 1.2: Site Maps of Study Area of Almora District

A

B

C

Fig. 1.3 (A-C): General PRA (Public Rural Appraisal) for Resource Mapping

METHODOLOGY

The study and data collection was based on the house-hold survey, PRA and focus group discussion methods (FGD) by approaching different stake holders like self help group (SHGs), community-based organisation (CBOs), village representative, villager's different age groups man and women. Data was collected to understand the status of the fuel-wood and fodder in the different villages of Central Himalayan region. The detailed of demographical data of village were taken in PRA, FGD, Gram Panchayat, and Block level meeting. The estimation of the fodder and fuel-wood supply and its consumption was carried out through regular observation and interactions with the villagers. The fodder sources and supply determined as from forest, green grass, agro-byproduct, tree fodder, terrace fodder and agro-forestry. The estimated by daily observation of food supply and intake of the animal of some randomly selected house-holds. Fuel-wood source and consumption was determined as usage in cooking, room heating, and water heating and animal feed preparation in selected house-holds.

FUEL-WOOD CONSUMPTION

Forest are the primary and major source of fuel-wood, state have 64% forest natural resource, in which 70% forest is reserve forests and 11% forest lies with the Van Panchayat. At present 6777 Van Panchayat manage 5241 sq Km of the total forest 34662 sq Km of forested land in state (Pai, R., 2005).The fuel-wood used as the cooking, room heating in winter season purposes which is collected by women, men and children's near the forest and van panchayat forest. Fuel collection in the high elevation would be only in winter season and they have store it in using heap inside the house and in lower elevation fuel-wood has been collected throughout year. Regular collection or over collection of fuel-woods has resulted degradation of natural resource as well as the over collection of broad leaf firewood's causes pine tree or pine forest increases and dominant in Central Himalayan region. Forest are the primary sources of fuel to villagers but a tinny fractions of fuel also meet from the agriculture fields (Sundriyal *et al.*, 1994).

According to survey of fuel-wood requirement of all 14 villages are 13889.585 MT but the annual fuel-wood available was only 5278.62 MT. Hence, there is annual fuel-wood deficit of 8610.94 MT. For example, in the village of Naugaon there is less fuel-wood requirement then the collection so that the fuel-wood deficits are -747.6 MT. The details of fuel-wood requirement and consumption of entire 14 villages are given in Table:-1.About 20.26% of the total available fuel-wood requirement is met from the agro-forestry system of farmer's field or their private forest. Per day per family fuel-wood consumption varies with the season. In winter, the requirement of fuel-wood was 35-40 kg and in rainy season 15-20 kg per day per house-hold. The use of the kerosene is very low and the LPG required per family is 0.23 kg per day. The major fuel-wood species are *Quercus leucotricophora,Quercus floribunda, Grewia optiva, Quercus glauca, Bauhinia variegate, Pinus roxburghii* and Chhachari.

A

B

Fig. 1.4 (A-B): Agro-ecosystem and Human Habitation at Himalayan Villages

FODDER CONSUMPTION

Forests are also the main source of fodder. About 62.2% of fodder is extracted from the forest (tree, shrubs, leaves and herbaceous ground flora), the remaining 37.8% extracted from the agro-forestry system, low altitude grass lands, and crop residue (Singh et al., 1998). Fodder has been mainly collected by women and they are responsible for managing the dairy based economy in the Central Himalayan region. As per the livestock census 2003 of Uttarakhand, green and dry fodder deficit are about 43.13%, but gross deficit is higher than that due to poor feed system of dry fodder (Singh, K. & Singh, H.S. 2009).

A

B

Fig. 1.5 (A-B): Forests Surrounding the Villages are the Local Resource of Fuel and Fodder

Table 1.1: Fuel-Wood Position of Study Villages

Sl. No.	Name of GP	No of Household	Fuel-wood Requirement MT	Fuel-wood Collection from Forest Mt	Fuel-wood Meet from Agro-forestry Mt	Deficit of fuel-wood MT
1.	Bakhali	93	804.841	137.8	60.45	606.591
2.	Baralgaon	83	668.233	184.6	53.95	429.683
3.	Chhitar	166	1397.886	110.5	107.90	1179.486
4.	Chulerasim	71	607.378	292.5	46.15	268.728
5.	Dantola	197	1746.405	202.8	128.05	1415.555
6.	Ganai	219	1777.229	149.5	142.35	1485.379
7.	Siroli	140	1190.446	159.9	91.00	939.546
8.	Bamangaon	58	495.448	113.1	37.70	344.648
9.	Bashbhira	103	843.683	113.1	66.95	663.633
10.	Chhana	48	412.704	91.00	31.20	290.504
11.	Garshiyari	108	916.378	137.8	70.20	708.378
12.	Mahatgaon	68	547.468	110.5	44.20	392.768
13.	Mahalchora	116	976.836	267.8	75.40	633.636
14.	Naugaon	175	1504.65	2138.5	113.75	-747.6
	Total	1645	13889.585	4209.4	1069.25	8610.935

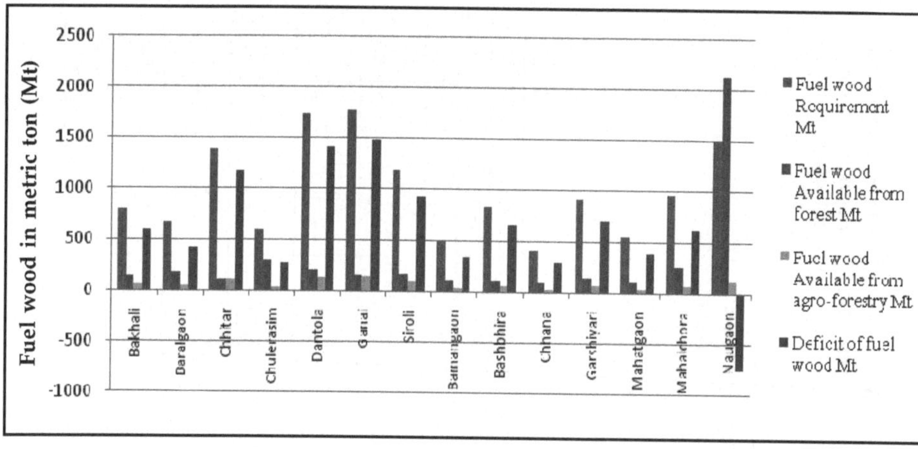

Fig. 1.6: Status of Fuel-wood of the Study Village, Choukhutia Block

Hence, forests have been facing much pressure of fodder extraction, resulting in degradation. Decline dense green forest cover before the ban on green felling accelerate soil erosion and siltation of water bodies (Valdiya., 1985) and water bodies and springs drying (Negi and Joshi, 2002) causes replacement and loss of species (Singh el al., 1984). This has increased the burden on women for fodder and fuel-wood collection (Pandey *et al.*, 1983). Fodder type, fodder availability, fodder production and fodder requirement was observed through regular surveys and focus group discussions with the villagers. The total fodder requirements was estimated to be 14677.69 MT, whereas the available fodder is 8841.79 MT (60.23%) and the deficit being 5835.90 MT (39.77%) (Table 1.2). of the total fodder collected, 70.54% fodder was collected from the grass (common lands, forest and personal lands), 21.94% fodder collected from agriculture residue (wheat, paddy, maize and millet residue and field terrace) and 7.50% fodder collected from the tree leaves (forest tree and agro-forestry tree leaves). The main fodder tree species in the villages were *Bauhinia variegate, Grewiaoptiva, Quercus leucotricophora,Quercus floribunda, and Quercus glauca.*

CONCLUSION SUSTANIABLE PROSPECT

The position of fuel-wood and fodder scarcity of study village of central Himalayan region is very bad. The annual fodder and fuel-wood scarcity of study villages are 5835.9MT or 39.77% and 8610.94MT or 61.99% of the total requirement. Due to the lack of fodder availability and lack of quality feed, livestock is in poor condition and dairy based economy is too low of villagers. Villagers have been left his livestock into forest region due to unable fulfill the requirement of fodder. Forest has been facing huge pressure for the fuel-wood requirement, leading towards extreme measures where sometime people have started felling green tree in the forest region for the full filling their fuel-wood requirement. Afforestration of socio-economic and fast growing species will resolve the problem of fuel-wood and also provide income to obtain al ternative fuel source to the villagers.

Table 1.2: Fodder Position of Study Village

Sl. No.	Name of GP	Fodder Require-ment MT	Fodder Collected from Grass MT	Dry Fodder of Agriculture Residues MT				Fodder from Forest and Agro-forestry Tree		Total Fodder Collected MT	Fodder Deficit MT
				Fodder Collected from Wheat Residue	Fodder Collected from Paddy Residue	Fodder Collected from Maize and Millets Residue	Fodder Collected from Field Terrace	Fodder Collected from Forest Trees Leaves MT	Fodder Collected from Agro-forestry Trees Tree MT		
1.	Bakhali	1170.3	292.32	59.15	67.45	10.45	9.5	28.79	1.2	468.86	701.44
2.	Baralgaon	583.77	133.41	45	55	8.25	1.2	10.38	5.45	258.69	325.08
3.	Chhitar	1969.14	582.03	80.22	88	30.45	24.5	32.23	36.89	874.32	1094.82
4.	Chulerasim	940.38	467.51	59.5	65	30.23	14.5	15.45	51.25	703.44	236.94
5.	Dantola	312.38	225.89	19.12	20.88	4.22	6.23	21.81	8.29	306.44	5.94
6.	Ganai	1245.66	356.18	45.56	90.22	20.85	15.75	44.51	36.89	609.96	635.70
7.	Siroli	1200.85	330.82	87.5	89.43	6.05	21.75	32.41	15.76	583.71	617.14
8.	Bamangaon	1377.37	1018.81	25.23	41.2	13.45	6.76	41.80	20.35	1167.6	209.77
9.	Bashbhira	637.24	435.47	34	35	29.35	14	31.46	23.45	602.74	34.50
10.	Chhana	586.77	121.35	42	60	3.67	4.25	14.49	10.25	256.01	330.76
11.	Garshiyari	1493.95	1379.32	21.34	23.44	11.67	5.65	26.33	12.87	1480.62	13.33
12.	Mahatgaon	538.53	351.98	40.66	34.44	12.25	7.5	18.72	9.67	475.22	63.31
13.	Mahalchora	1135.37	202.13	40.23	45.34	40	8.75	29.80	7.23	373.48	761.89
14.	Naugaon	1485.98	339.97	110.66	105.66	45	2.91	61.07	15.44	680.7	805.28
	Total	14677.69	6237.18	710.17	821.06	265.89	143.25	409.25	254.99	8841.79	5835.90

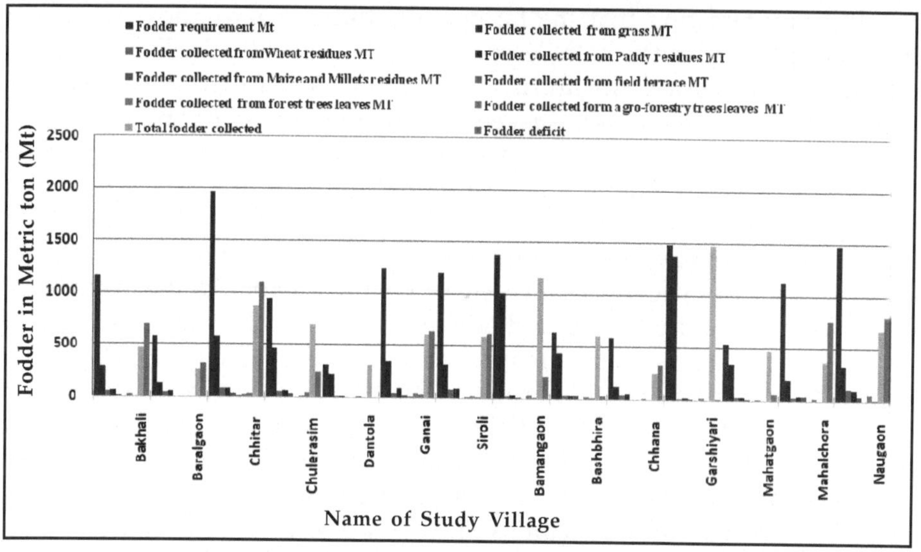

Fig. 1.7: Status of Fodder of the Study Village, Choukhutia Block

Efforts should be made to provide subsidize liquefied petroleum gas (LPG) and prevent in forest fire (which is very frequent into that villages twice and thrice time in a year) to reduce the fuel-wood problem. Promotion of sustainable fodder based programme cultivation of fodder tree in agro-forestry system and promote mineral mixture to the livestock will resolve livestock health problems.

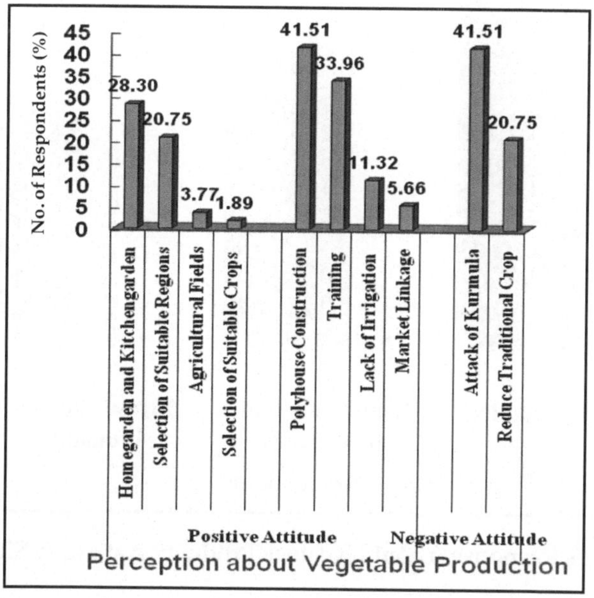

Fig. 1.8: Villager's Response About Vegetable Production at Study Sites in Almora District

It was interesting that the farmers of study sites to know what were their perception about vegetable production on their fields. For this it was appropriate to examine the attitude and options of farmers from vegetable belts. All the respondents were asked to share their opinions and experiences about vegetable production. It clearly depicts that the positive and negative attitude of the respondents. In positive attitude 28.30% farmers want to establish homegarden and kitchen garden for vegetables where as 20.75% farmer want to develop special suitable site on their fields. Only 3.77% farmers want to grow these vegetables on their agricultural fields. All the respondents were aware about the hybrid and advanced seeds which they were getting from govt agencies as well as market also so there was only 1.89% farmers want to know about suitable crops or seeds. The farmers or respondents were much aware about covered agriculture e.g. Polyhouse construction so in our study 41.51% farmers want polyhouses from concern agencies. 33.36% farmers want to develop their capacity building about advanced vegetable production. In agriculture facilities 11.32 and 5.66 & farmer want irrigation and market facilities. In negative attitude 41.41% farmer's fields was highly infected with 'Kurumula' a local harmful agricultural insect. According 20.75% farmer the agricultural production was decreasing day by day.

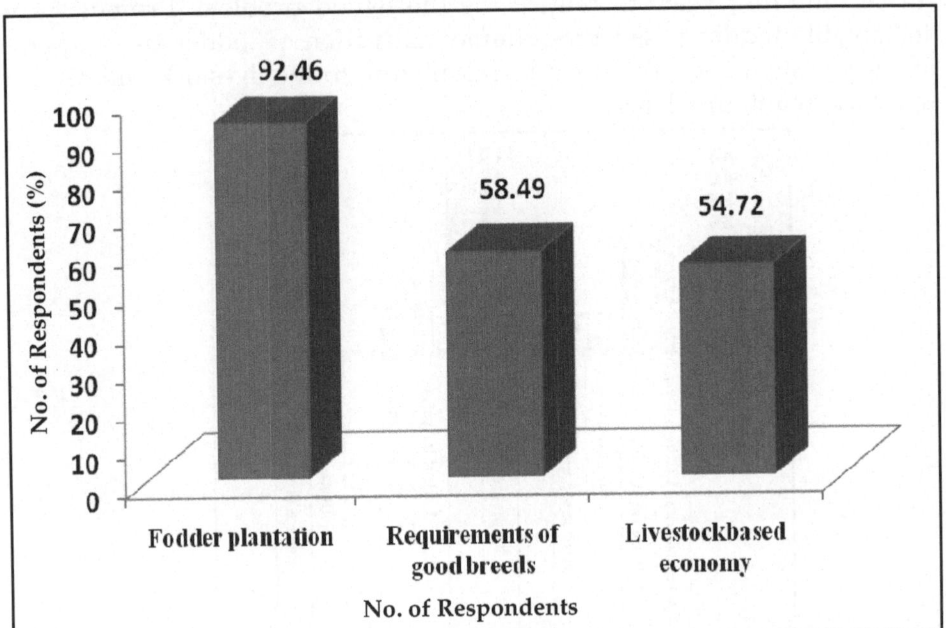

Fig. 1.9: Villager's Response About Livestock Production at Study Sites in Almora District

92.46% farmers/respondents want to plantation of fodder trees in their field bunds or other lands. The animal breeds about livestock were traditional in our study sites from 1000-1600 m so 58.49% farmers want to good and high yielding breeds of livestock and 54.72% farmers want to strengthen their economy through livestock.

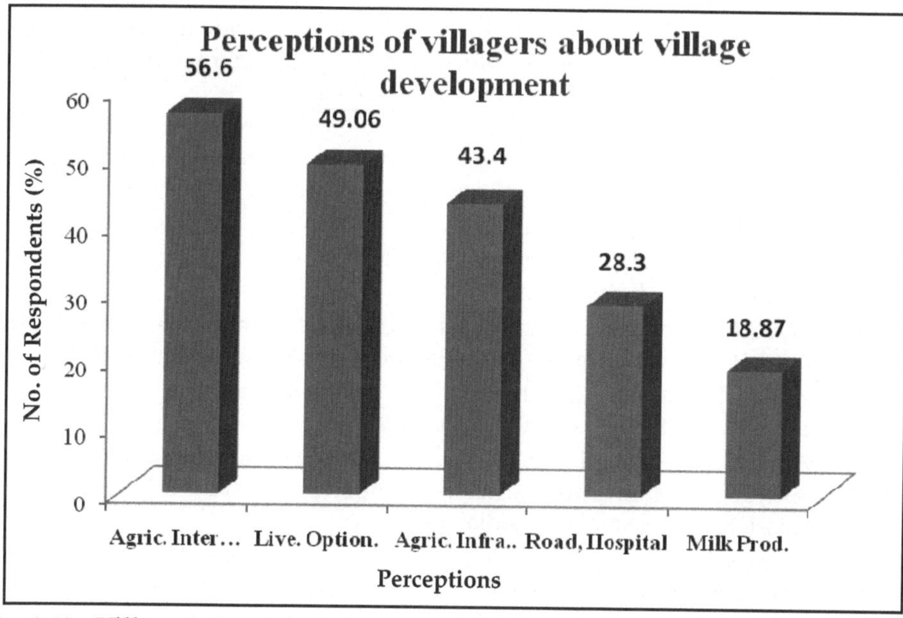

Fig. 1.10: Villager's Response About Livestock Production at Study Sites in Almora District

The farmers view about village development for various sectors in our study site from 1000 to 1600 m in Almora district. The response about various sectors was 56.6, 49.09, 43.4, 28.3 and 18.87 for agricultural interventions, various livelihoods options, agricultural infrastructure development, basic infrastructure development about road, hospital and milk production was 56.6, 40.06, 43.4, 28.3 and 18.87% respectively.

REFERENCES

1. Bajracharya, B. 1999.Sustainable Soil Management with Reference to Livestock Production System. ICIMOD, Kathmandu.
2. Dhyani, S. and Maikhuri, R.K, 2012. Fodder Banks can Reduce Women Drudgery and Anthropogenic Pressure from Forest of West Himalaya. G.B. Pant Institute of Himalayan Environmental and Development, Kosi-Katarmal, Almora, Current *Science,* Vol. 103, No. 7, October 2012.
3. Negi, G.C.S. and Joshi, V. 2002.Drinking Water Issues and Development of Spring Sanctuaries in a Mountain Watershed in Indian Himalaya. *Mt. Res. Dev.*, 22: 29-31.

4. Negi, Y.S. 1999. Sustainable Livestock Management in Mixed Crop-livestock Farming System of Himachal Pradesh, India. ICIMOD, Kathmandu, Nepal.
5. Pai. R., 2005.Evolution of Van Panchayat-Community Participation in Management and Protection of Forests. In M.L. Dewan and Jagdish Bahadur (Eds.*), Uttaranchal Vision and Action Programme* Concept Publishing Company, New Delhi, pp. 88-101.
6. Palni, L.M.S., Maikhuri, R.K.,and Rao, R.K. 1998. Conservation of the Himalayan Agro Ecosystem: Issues and Priorities. Report on the International Meeting on Himalayan Ecoregional Co-operation, pp. 263-291.
7. Palni, U.T. 1996. Cattle Feeds of Central Himalaya: Problems and Prospects. In: Ed. D.C. Pandey, Dimensions of Agriculture in the Himalaya, Almora: ShriAlmora Book Depot. pp. 345-60.
8. Pandey, A.N., Pathak, P.C. and Singh, J.S. 1983. Water, Sediment and Nutrient Movement in Certain *Forested and* Non-forested sites in Kumaun Himalaya. *Forest Ecol. Mgmt.*, 7: 19-29.
9. Sati, V. 2005, Natural Resource Condition and Economic Development in the Uttaranchal Himalaya, India. *Journal of Mountain Science* 2(4): 336-350.
10. Singh, J.S., Pandey, U. and Tiwari, A.K. 1984. Man and Forests: A Central Himalayan Case Study. Ambio, 13(2): 80-87.
11. Singh, J.S.,Singh, S.P., and Ram Jeet. Fodder and Fuel-wood Resources of Central Himalaya: Problem and Solution. Report Submitted to the Planning Commission, Government of India, 1998.
12. Sundriyal,R.C., Rai, S.C., Sharma, E., and Rai, Y.K. 1994. Hill Agro-forestry Systems in South Sikkim. Agro-forestry System 26: pp.215-235.
13. Valdiya, K.S. 1985. Accelerated Erosion and Landslide-prone Areas in the Himalayan Region. In: Singh, J.S. (Ed.) *Environmental Regeneration in the Himalaya: Strategies and Concepts*. Gyanodaya Prakashan, Nainital. pp. 12-38.
14. Singh, K. and Singh, H.S. 2009. Forage Resource Development in Uttarakhand: Experience and observations (http://www.uldb.org/pdf/Forage%20Resources_FDP_.pdf).

2

Diversity, Distribution Pattern and Status of the Threatened Plants in Murari Devi and Surrounding Areas of Mandi District in Himachal Pradesh, India

Pankaj Sharma[1*]; Pooja Patti Sharma[2]
Ajeet Agnihotry[3]; Hemant K Gupta[4]

ABSTRACT

The State Himachal Pradesh is famous for its specific topography, climate and unique vegetation. The present study has been carried out in Murari Devi and surrounding areas of Mandi district in Himachal Pradesh and covers the 'Sikandra Dhar' ranges of submontane Himalayas between 31° 37′30″ N latitudes and 76° 49′ 50″ E longitudes. A few studies are available on diversity, distribution pattern and status of the plants and no such studies available in the area. A total of 80 species (32 Trees; 28 Shrubs and 20 Herbs) belonging to 68 genera and 46 families have been identified as threatened from study areas. The area ranges in altitude between 700-2000m, and shady moist and forested habitats were identified as having the most vegetation. 09 species were identified as Critically Endangered, 16 species as Endangered; 24 species as Vulnerable; 31 species as Near Threatened

1. **Scientific Professional, State Centre on Climate Change, State Council for Science, Technology & Environment, B-34, SDA Complex, Kasumpti, Shimla-9, Himachal Pradesh, India.**
2. **Lecturer Biology, Govt. Senior Secondary School, Smaila - 175 034, Distt. Mandi, Himachal Pradesh, India.**
3. **Associate Professor, Department of Botany, NSCBM Govt. PG College, Hamirpur - 177 001, Distt. Hamirpur, Himachal Pradesh, India.**
4. **Chief Scientific Officer & Joint Member Secretary, Department of Environment, Science and Technology, State Council for Science, Technology & Environment, 34, SDA Complex, Kasumpti, Shimla-9, Himachal Pradesh, India.**

and remaining species as Least Concern based on threat categorization score. Among the habitats, dry (66 spp.), shady moist (60sp.), (58 spp.), bouldary (48 spp.), riverine (33 spp.), shrubbery (20 spp.), near crop field/cultivated field (18 spp.), waste places/road side (15 spp.), rocky (15 spp.) and water courses/marshy places (7 spp.) support maximum number of threatened species. These species and habitats represent the maximum part of the area, therefore, require adequate conservation measures. To develop an appropriate strategy for the conservation and management of all these threatened species and their habitats, population assessment and habitat monitoring using standard ecological methods are urgently required. Also, mass reproduction for ex situ conservation and to ensure availability of quality planting material for cultivation, together with education and awareness programmes for large-scale cultivation are suggested.

Keywords: Diversity, threat categorization, critically endangered, Murari Devi, Himachal Pradesh.

INTRODUCTION

The diversity of life exists on earth and each life form has its own needs for existence. Greater biodiversity leads to greater productivity and greater nutrient retention in ecosystem which leads to greater ecosystem stability (Tilman, 2000). Global biodiversity is being lost at an unprecedented rate, as a consequence of human induced environmental change (Pimm *et al.*, 1995). Since 1966 the International Union for Conservation of Nature and Natural Resources (IUCN) has evaluated species conservation status worldwide and today the IUCN Red Lists have become one of the most important information sources about the conservation status of world's flora and fauna worldwide. Evaluating species conservation status is one of the main tools for establishing conservation priorities and management policies (Mace & Lande, 1991). A species global conservation status, however, is not necessarily the same as the conservation status on a regional scale. Some species that are threatened on a global scale may not be threatened on a regional scale, and species that are not threatened on a global scale might be threatened in some part of their range (Gardenfors *et al.*, 2001). Some species may be declining fast across their ranges on average but may be locally stable or even increasing. Moreover, knowing the regional status of species is important for several reasons. Loss of population and genetic diversity is a major concern (Grammont & Cuaron, 2006). When a species is protected on a regional scale, conservation of its genetic diversity is promoted (Hunter & Hutchinson, 1994). Regional scale extinction of one species can provoke a cascade of extinctions, causing a change in species composition and in ecosystems processes (Lundberg *et al.*, 2000). The extinction of a species is the result of local extinctions of its populations. Clearly, conservation is in need of a method for the assessment of conservation priorities with small data demands, which combines the advantages of red lists and the assessment of international importance of a population. Degradation and fragmentation of >70% of the original habitats placed Himalaya in the list of Global Biodiversity Hotspots (Mittermeier *et al.*, 2004). In the IHR, attempts have been made to identify the threatened plants by various workers (Pangtey & Samant, 1988; Samant *et al.*, 1993, 2007; Pandey & Well, 1997; Badola & Pal, 2003; Singh *et al.*, 2009; Sharma, 2013; etc.). Under the current scenario, about 20% of all species are expected to be lost within 30 years and 50% or more by the end of 21st century (Myers, 1993&1998).

In the IHR, over exploitation and habitat degradation are the two major factors responsible for decrease in population of the species (Samant *et al.*, 1996). However, using different parameters of rarity *i.e.*, habitat preference, population size, distribution range and anthropogenic pressure, only few studies have been carried out in some of the protected areas (Samant *et al.*, 1996, 2001; Rawal & Dhar, 1997; Joshi & Samant, 2004; Singh, 2007; Singh *et al.* 2009) and unprotected areas (Pant, 2005; Sharma, 2013). In view of the ongoing threats, it is important to identify and prioritize biodiversity elements at local, regional and global levels. As such, threat assessment of all the species of a particular region has been carried out by a very few workers (Singh *et al.*, 2009; Sharma, 2013). Such studies are essentially required along the altitudinal and across the horizontal gradients of the IHR. Therefore, present attempt has been made to assess the threat categories of species in Murari Devi and surrounding areas and suggest conservation options.

STUDY AREA

The study has been carried out in Murari Devi and surrounding areas, situated at a distance of 40 Km in the south-west direction of Mandi on Mandi-Hamirpur highway. This covers the 'Sikandra Dhar' ranges of submontane Himalayas between 31° 37′ 30″ N latitudes and 76° 49′ 50″ E longitudes. Murari Devi temple is a beautiful place in the west of Sunder Nagar on the top of a sacred hill named Murari Dhar. It is believed that this temple was made by Pandvas during their "*Agyatwaas*". The study areas were fall in Suket, Bhambla and Nagrota Forest Division of Mandi District in Himachal Pradesh with an altitudinal range varies from 700 to 2,000 m amsl. Geographically, the area constitutes a part of Mandi (an area formed by the merger of the erstwhile princely states of Mandi and Suket on the formation of Himachal Pradesh on 15 April, 1948). The area is inhabited by a large number of villages *i.e.*, Ukhla, Smaila, Plassi, Kot, Baldwara, Bhambla, Sikandra, Bachawan, Kasmela, Math, Bhated, Balra, Alsogi, Chowk, Ambla galu, Kalkhar, Katoh, Badoun, Dabhoi, Trifalghat, Ropadi, Leda, etc. The area is well known for its diverse habitats and rich biodiversity being dominated by tropical, sub-tropical, temperate and sub-alpine broad leaved and coniferous forests, and supports a large number of sensitive biodiversity elements including medicinal and aromatic plants, wild edibles, rare endangered, native and wild relatives of crop plants. Agriculture and Horticulture are the amongst major livelihood options of the villages. However, to a considerable extent, the villagers augment their income from agriculture, by rearing sheep and goats for wool and meat and by extracting medicinal plants. Extraction of medicinal herbs and collection of wild edibles has been their traditional source of income generation.

The geology of the area is varied. The area comprises of Granite Gneiss, Leucogranite, Phyllite, Quartazenite, Minor Limestone, Pebbly Quartzite, Slate, Grit, Streaky and Banded Gneisses, and Schists. The two chief types of rocks of the area are Gneissic rocks, Shales and Slates which fall under Mandi Granitoid Complex and are composed of granites of varied compositions and textures. These are Prophyroblastic Granite Gneiss, Biotite Granite, Muscovite Granite and Leucogranites. These granites are mainly composed of Quartz, Feldspar and Mafics (*Source:* Himachal Pradesh Forest Department).

CLIMATE

The district represents a subtropical highland climate under the Koppen climate classification. The climate of the district is composite having hot summers and cold winters. Usually, four different seasons represent the area, i.e., winter (Mid-December to February), summer (March to June), rainy (July to Mid September), autumn (October to November). Winter is calm in low down areas, while it snows on high peak ranges. Springs are warm and fair. Rainy season is the wettest part of the year and characterized by high humidity. Summers are itchy and hot throughout the monsoon periods (Sood & Thakur, 2004). Temperature typically ranges from 6°C to 41°C over the course of a year. The average temperature during summer is between 18.9°C and 39.6°C and between 6.7°C and 26.2°C in winter. Monthly precipitation varies between 25.4 mm in November to 228.6 mm in August. It is typically around 58.3 mm per month during winter and spring and around 101.6 mm in June as the monsoon approaches. The average total annual precipitation is 1,092.2 mm, which is much less than most other hill stations but still greatly heavier than on the plains. Snowfall in the region, which historically has taken place few years back is now very rare or no due to increasing temperature and global warming.

VEGETATION: FLORA & FAUNA

The altitudinal sprawls, as well as climatic and pedological conditions of this area have resulted into highly diversified vegetation. The distribution of different species follows fairly regular altitudinal stratification. The vegetation comprises of tropical, sub-tropical, temperate and sub-alpine broad leaved and coniferous forests and supports a large number of sensitive biodiversity elements including medicinal and aromatic plants, wild edibles, rare, endangered, native, endemic and wild relatives of crop plants. The subtropical forests (1300-1800m) are characterized by; *(i)* evergreen coniferous forests mainly of *Pinus roxburghii*; and *(ii)* evergreen broad leaved forests of *Myrica esculenta, Quercus leucotrichophora, Q. glauca* and *Rhododendron arboreum.* The temperate forests (1800-2800m) are characterized by; *(i)* broad leaved deciduous forests comprising of *Acer cappadocicum* and *A. acuminatum, etc.*; *(ii)* evergreen forests dominated by coniferous forests *i.e., Cedrus deodara* and *Pinus wallichiana*; and *(iii)* evergreen broad leaved forests of *Ilex diyprena* and *Ilex excelsa, etc.* Sub-alpine forests (>2800m) are characterized mainly by; *(i)* evergreen broad leaved forests mainly of *Quercus semecarpifolia;* and *(ii)* coniferous forests of *Abies pindrow* and *Taxus baccata* subsp. *wallichiana*. The forest types support a large number of biodiversity elements.

Besides, the area is bestowed with varied landscape features that provide large number of habitats to a diverse group of faunal types, there is a good diversity of mammals, reptiles and avian fauna, including the Indian National Bird, *Pavo cristatus* L. The main animals are Leopard (*Panthera pardus* L.), Himalayan Black Bear (*Selenarctos thibetanus* Cuvier), Jungle cat (*Felis chaus* Guld.), Wolf (*Canis lupus* L.), Indian Fox (*Vulpes bengalensis* Shaw), Himalayan Pine Martin (*Martes flavigula* Bodd.) and Indian Porcupine (*Hystrix indica* Kerr.) Amongst the birds, Blue Rock Pigeon (*Columba intermedia* Srickl.), Dove (*Streptopelia decaocto* Lath.), Jungle Myne (*Acridotheres fuscus* Wangl.), Kaleej Pheasant (*Lophura leucomelanos* Lath.), Cheer Pheasant (*Catreus wallichii* Hardw.), *etc.* Besides these, Woodpeckers, Parakeets and in reptiles, snakes are of common occurrence (Source: Himachal Pradesh Forest Department).

MATERIALS AND METHODS

Different attributes such as habitat specificity, population size, distribution range, use values, extraction, nativity and endemism of the taxa have been used for the threat categorization of the floristic diversity (Ved *et al.*, 2003, 2005; Singh, 2007; Singh *et al.*, 2009; Goraya, 2011; Sharma 2013). The attributes used were divided into three grades; highest (10 marks); subsequent (6 marks) and least (2 marks). The species fulfilling all the attributes in highest grade resulted in highest cumulative values and one which falls in least grade for every attribute resulted in least cumulative values. The species having >70% score were considered as Critically Endangered; 60-69% as Endangered; 50-59% as Vulnerable; and 40-49% as Near threatened, whereas <45% were considered as Least Concern.

Table 2.1: Parameters Used for the Threat Categorization of Floristic Diversity

Points/Scores	Parameters					
	Altitudinal Range (m)	H/Hs	Use Values	Population Size	Native & Endemic	Extraction
10	<500	2	>4	250 Ind/2 locations	Native & Endemic	Commercial
6	500-1000	3-4	3-4	1000 Ind/3-5 location	Native/Endemic	Self Use
2	>1000	>4	<3	>1000 Ind/>5 location	Non-native	No Extraction

Abbreviations Used: H/Hs=Habitat/(s); and **m**=Meter

Categorization of these species for the State and globally as Critically Endangered, Endangered, Vulnerable, *etc.*, has also been done following Singh *et al.* (2009); Ved *et al.* (2003). The species, which occurred in the area but not cited in the sampled sites have also been considered for categorization.

RESULTS

Diversity of Threatened Species

From the total 384 species recorded, 80 species (32 Trees; 28 Shrubs & 20 Herbs) belonging to 68 genera and 46 families have been identified as threatened from Murari Devi and surrounding areas. Thirty one (31) species have been found to be Near Threatened. The remaining species fall under the Least Concern category.

ALTITUDINAL DISTRIBUTION

Along an altitudinal gradient, the maximum rare endangered species (71 spp.) were distributed in 700-1300m zone, followed by 1301-1800m (09 spp.) zone (Fig. 2.1).

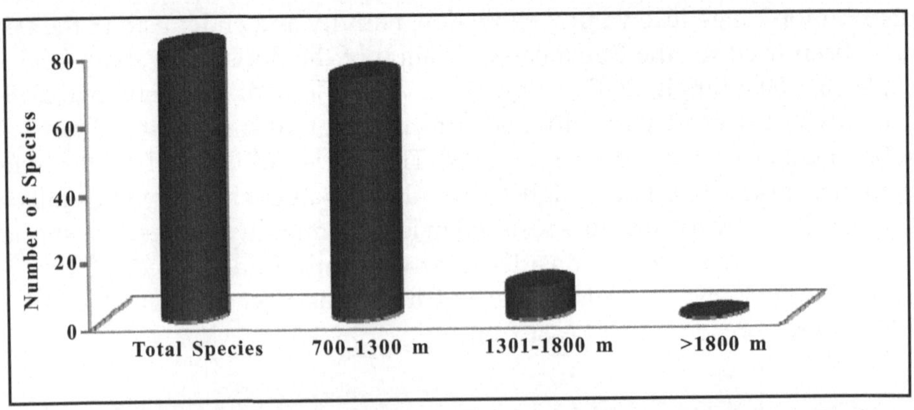

Fig. 2.1: Altitudinal Distribution of Threatened Plants in Murari Devi and Surrounding Areas of Mandi District in Himachal Pradesh, India

THREAT CATEGORIZATION

In the present study, of the total species, 09 species were identified as Critically Endangered, 16 species as Endangered; 24 species as Vulnerable; 31 species as Near Threatened and remaining species as Least Concern based on threat categorization score. Some of the notable Critically Endangered species are *Azadirachta indica, Pistacia integerrima, Terminalia bellirica, T. chebula, Elaeagnus conferta, Juglans regia, Zanthoxylum armatum, etc.*, Endangered, *Acorus calamus, Asparagus adscendens, Justicia adhatoda, Deeringia amaranthoides, Bauhinia vahlii, Melothria heterophylla, Dioscorea deltoidea, Albizia julibrissin, Butea monosperma, Ougeinia oojeinensis, Cinnamomum tamala, Morus alba, Syzygium cumini, Habenaria marginata, Rosa brunonii, Valeriana jatamansi, etc.*, Vulnerable, *Asparagus racemosus, Inula cappa, Bombax ceiba, Rhododendron arboretum, Emblica officinalis, Lespedeza gerardiana, Mucuna pruriens, Quercus leucotricophora, Hedychium spicatum, Hypericum oblongifolium, Salvia lanata, Nepeta hindostana, Acacia catechu, Ficus nemoralis, Myrica esculenta, Cedrus deodara, Plantago ovata, Zizyphus oxyphylla, Murraya koenigii, Aegle marmelos, Murraya paniculata, Bergenia ligulata, Vitex negundo, etc.*, Near Threatened, *Lannea coromandelica, Sauromatum venosum, Phoenix humilis, Elephantopus scaber, Berberis lycium, Buddleja crispa, Bauhinia racemosa, Cyanotis cristata, Dioscorea bulbifera, Euphorbia royleana, Millettia auriculata, Dalbergia sissoo, Flacourtia indica, Salvia nubicola, Roylea cinerea, Reinwardtia indica, Osbeckia stellata, Tinospora cordifolia, Albizia chinensis, Pinus roxburghii, Pyrus pashia, Leptodermis lenceolata, Boenninghausenia albiflora, Helicteres isora, Symplocos chinensis, Grewia asiatica, etc.*, for Murari Devi and surrounding areas.

Also using new IUCN criteria, 05 species have been categorized as Endangered; Vulnerable (05 spp.) and Least Concern (01 sp.) for Himachal Pradesh and total 03 species; Endangered and Vulnerable (01 sp.) were under global threat categories, whereas 02 species *i.e., Berberis aristata* (Rare) and *Dioscorea deltoidea* (Vulnerable) have been recorded in the Red Data Book of Indian Plants (Nayar & Sastry 1987, 1988, 1990) (Table 2.2).

HABITAT WISE DISTRIBUTION

In general, 66 species were reported from the dry, 60 species in shady moist, 58 species degraded, 48 species in bouldary, 33 species in riverine, 20 species in shrubbery, 18 species in near crop field/cultivated field, 15 species in waste places/road side, 14 species in rocky and 07 species in Water courses/ marshy places. Habitat wise distribution of species in the study area showed that one species i.e., *Sauromatum venosum* was distributed in one habitat only, 09 species in two habitats, whereas 17 species were distributed in three habitats and 53 species in >3 habitats. Among the species, *Syzygium cumini, Berberis lycium* (08 habitats); *Emblica officinalis, Juglans regia, Roylea cinerea* and *Zanthoxylum armatum* (07 habitats); *Aegle marmelos, Vitex negundo, Murraya koenigii* and *Murraya paniculata* (06 habitats); *Albizia chinensis, Buddleja crispa,*

Euphorbia royleana, Phoenix humilis, Hedychium spicatum, Hypericum oblongifolium, Helicteres isora, Pinus roxburghii, Tinospora cordifolia, Quercus leucotricophora, Pistacia integerrima, Symplocos chinensis, Rosa brunonii, Pyrus pashia Terminalia bellirica, T. chebula, Reinwardtia indica, Bauhinia vahlii, Dioscorea deltoidea, Butea monosperma, Asparagus racemosus and *Rhododendron arboreum* (05 habitats, each); *Boenninghausenia albiflora, Berberis aristata, Elaeagnus parviflora, Azadirachta indica, Albizia julibrissin, Morus alba, Mucuna pruriens, Nepeta hindostana, Acacia catechu, Cedrus deodara, Plantago ovata, Zizyphus oxyphylla, Z. rugosa, Lannea coromandelica, Elephantopus scaber, Millettia auriculata, Dalbergia sissoo, Flacourtia indica* and *Salvia nubicola* (04 habitats, each) represented the maximum habitats (Table 2.2).

DISCUSSION

The Himalayas covers eight countries (i.e., Afghanistan, Bangladesh, Bhutan, China, Myanmar, Nepal, Pakistan, and India) and are supposed to be a rich storehouse of valuable threatened plant species. The Himalayas cover 18% of the Indian subcontinent, account for more than 50% of India's forest, and contain 40% of India's endemic species (Maikhuri *et al.* 2000). The area harbors about 8000 species of angiosperms of which 1748 are used for medicinal purposes (Samant *et al.* 2007). In the present scenario, biodiversity crisis is being experienced throughout the globe. Therefore, appropriate conservation actions need to be set up in the most efficient way possible to optimally use limited resources. Unfortunately, none of the available methods of conservation priority setting are widely accepted as their data requirements are too stringent, scientifically unsound, or are too complex for the usage by decision makers. In most of the studies, identification of threatened species has been carried out using qualitative attributes/observations, only. However, assessment of the status of species using standard format including qualitative as well as quantitative attributes has been suggested by few workers (Airi *et al.*, 1997). Knowing the importance of floristic diversity for the human being, threat categorization at local, regional and global levels are essentially required. Threat categorization at local level would help in developing adequate management plans. In view of this, threat categorization of floristic diversity at local level along an altitudinal and horizontal gradients has been initiated in the IHR. So that based on grass root level information adequate management plan could be developed for the entire IHR and globe. Habitat specificity, population size, distribution range and use pattern play an important role in identification of status of the species. In the present study, threat assessment of floristic diversity for a particular region has been carried out. On the basis of Threat Categorization Score (TCS), species have been categorized. The more TCS indicates the need for a greater level of attention to local strategies for conservation and management. Categorization of 09 species as Critically Endangered, 16 species as Endangered; 24 species as Vulnerable and 31 species as Near Threatened indicates the high degree of anthropogenic pressure.

Table 2.2: Diversity, Distribution Pattern and Status of the Threatened Plants in Murari Devi and Surrounding Areas of Himachal Pradesh, India

Taxa/Threat Category	Family	AR (m)	Habitat/s	HF	Status			Threat
					HP	GB	RD	
Critically Endangered								
Pistacia integerrima Bin	Anacardiaceae	700-1800	1, 2, 3, 4, 5	T	-	-	-	OE, HD
Berberis aristata DC.*	Berberidaceae	1000-2000	1, 2, 3, 4	Sh	EN	EN	R	OE, HD
Terminalia bellirica (Gaertn.) Roxb	Combretaceae	700-1300	1, 2, 3, 4, 5	T	-	-	-	OE, HD
T. chebula Retz.	Combretaceae	700-1500	1, 2, 3, 4, 5	T	-	-	-	OE, HD
Elaeagnus conferta Roxb. *	Elaeagnaceae	1200-1900	3, 4, 7	Sh	-	-	-	HD
E. parviflora Wall. Ex Royle	Elaeagnaceae	1400-2000	1, 3, 4, 5	Sh	-	-	-	HD
Juglans regia L.*	Juglandaceae	700-2000	1, 2, 3, 4, 5, 8, 9	T	-	-	-	OE, HD
Azadirachta indica L.	Meliaceae	700-1100	1, 3, 4, 5	T	-	-	-	OE, HD
Zanthoxylum armatum DC.	Rutaceae	900-1900	1, 2, 3, 4, 5, 7, 9	Sh	EN	-	-	OE, HD
Endangered								
Justicia adhatoda L.	Acanthaceae	700-1300	1, 3, 5	Sh	-	-	-	OE, HD
Deeringia amaranthoides (Lam.) Merr.	Amaranthaceae	700-1200	3, 4, 5	Sh	-	-	-	HD
Acorus calamus L.	Araceae	1000-1800	1, 10	H	-	-	-	OE, HD
Asparagus adscendens Roxb.	Asparagaceae	700-1400	1, 2	H	-	-	-	HD
Bauhinia vahlii (Wt. & Arn.) Benth.	Caesalpiniaceae	700-1200	1, 2, 3, 4, 5, 6, 9	Sh	-	-	-	OE, HD
Melothria heterophylla (Lour.) Cogn.	Cucurbitaceae	1100-1700	1, 3, 4	H	-	-	-	HD
Dioscorea deltoidea Wall. ex Kunth	Dioscoreaceae	800-2000	1, 4, 5, 6, 7	H	EN	EN	VU	OE, HD
Albizia julibrissin Durazz	Fabaceae	700-1500	3, 4, 5, 9	T	-	-	-	OE, HD
Butea monosperma (Lamk.) Taub.	Fabaceae	700-1200	1, 3, 4, 8, 9	T	-	-	-	OE, HD

(Contd...)

Taxa/Threat Category	Family	AR (m)	Habitat/s	HF	Status			Threat
					HP	GB	RD	
Ougeinia oojeinensis (Roxb.) Hochr.	Fabaceae	700-1200	3, 4, 5	T	-	-	-	HD
Cinnamomum tamala Nees & Ebern*	Lauraceae	700-1500	1, 2, 9	T	VU	-	-	OE, HD
Morus alba L.	Moraceae	700-1000	1, 3, 4, 5	T	-	-	-	HD
Syzygium cumini Skees	Myrtaceae	700-1500	1, 3, 4, 5, 6, 7, 8, 9	T	-	-	-	OE, HD
Habenaria marginata Hk.f. ex Collett	Orchidaceae	700-2000	1, 2	H	EN	EN	-	HD
Rosa brunonii Lindl.	Rosaceae	700-2000	1, 2, 4, 5, 7	Sh	-	-	-	HD
Valeriana jatamansi Jones	Valerianaceae	1500-2000	1, 2	H	VU	-	-	OE, HD
Vulnerable								
Asparagus racemosus Willd.	Asparagaceae	700-2000	1, 2, 3, 4, 9	Sh	-	-	-	HD
Inula cappa (Buch.-Ham. ex D.Don) DC.	Asteraceae	1000-1900	1, 7, 9, 10	Sh	-	-	-	HD
Bombax ceiba L.	Boraginaceae	700-1700	2, 3, 4, 5, 6, 9	T	-	-	-	HD
Rhododendron arboreum Sm.	Ericaceae	1600-2000	1, 2, 4, 5, 6	T	-	-	-	OE, HD
Emblica officinalis L.	Euphorbiaceae	700-2000	1, 3, 4, 5, 6, 8, 9	T	-	-	-	OE, HD
Lespedeza gerardiana Grah. ex Maxim.*	Fabaceae	1200-2000	3, 4, 5	H	-	-	-	HD
Mucuna pruriens (L.) DC.	Fabaceae	700-1100	3, 4, 5, 7	Sh	-	-	-	HD
Quercus leucotricophora A. Camus	Fagaceae	1200-2000	1, 2, 4, 5, 6, 7, 8	T	-	-	-	OE, HD
Hypericum oblongifolium Choisy*	Hypericaceae	1000-2000	1, 2, 4, 5, 9	Sh	VU	-	-	OE, HD
Salvia lanata Roxb.*	Lamiaceae	1500-2000	1, 2, 4	H	-	-	-	HD
Nepeta hindostana B.Heyne	Lamiaceae	700-1100	1, 3, 4, 5	H	-	-	-	HD
Acacia catechu (L.f.) Willd.	Mimosaceae	700-1000	3, 4, 5, 6	T	-	-	-	OE, HD

(Contd…)

Taxa/Threat Category	Family	AR (m)	Habitat/s	HF	Status			Threat
					HP	GB	RD	
Ficus nemoralis Wall. ex Mir	Moraceae	1500-2000	4, 5, 7	T	-	-	-	OE, HD
Myrica esculenta Buch.-Ham. ex Don	Myricaceae	1400-2000	1, 2, 4	T	-	-	-	OE, HD
Cedrus deodara (Roxb. ex D. Don) G. Don*	Pinaceae	1600-2000	1, 3, 4, 5	T	-	-	-	OE, HD
Plantago ovata Forssk.	Plantaginaceae	1600-2000	1, 3, 4, 5	H	-	-	-	OE, HD
Zizyphus oxyphylla Edgrew.	Rhamnaceae	700-1100	3, 4, 5, 7	Sh	-	-	-	OE, HD
Z. rugosa Lamk.	Rhamnaceae	700-1000	2, 3, 4, 7	Sh	-	-	-	HD
Murraya koenigii (L.) Spr.	Rutaceae	700-1400	1, 3, 4,5, 7, 8	Sh	-	-	-	HD
Aegle marmelos (L.) Corr.	Rutaceae	700-1200	2, 3, 4, 5, 8, 9	T	-	-	-	HD
Murraya paniculata (L.) Jack	Rutaceae	700-1000	1, 3, 4, 6, 7, 9	Sh	-	-	-	HD
Bergenia ligulata (Wall.) Engl. *	Saxifragaceae	1000-1800	1, 6, 10	H	-	-	-	HD
Vitex negundo L.	Verbenaceae	700-1600	2, 3, 4, 7, 8, 9	Sh	-	-	-	HD
Hedychium spicatum Sm.*	Zingiberaceae	700-2000	1, 2, 8, 9, 10	H	VU	-	-	OE, HD
Near Threatend								
Lannea coromandelica (Houtt.) Merr.	Anacardiaceae	700-1400	1, 3, 4, 5	T	-	-	-	HD
Sauromatum venosum Kunth.	Araceae	1000-2000	1	H	-	-	-	HD
Phoenix humilis Royle	Araceae	700-1700	2, 3, 4, 5, 6	Sh	-	-	-	HD
Elephantopus scaber L.	Asteraceae	700-1600	1, 3, 4, 5	H	-	-	-	HD
Berberis lycium Royle*	Berberidaceae	700-2000	1, 3, 4, 5, 6, 7, 8, 9	Sh	EN	-	-	OE, HD
Buddleja crispa Benth.	Buddlejaceae	1400-1900	3, 4, 5, 7, 8	Sh	-	-	-	HD
Bauhinia racemosa Lamk.	Caesalpiniaceae	700-1000	1, 3, 4	T	-	-	-	OE, HD
B. retusa Roxb.	Caesalpiniaceae	700-1000	1, 3	T	-	-	-	HD

(Contd...)

Taxa/Threat Category	Family	AR (m)	Habitat/s	HF	Status			Threat
					HP	GB	RD	
Cyanotis cristata (L.) Don	Commelinaceae	700-2000	1, 2, 4	H	-	-	-	OE, HD
Cyperus compressus L.	Cyperaceae	700-2000	3, 10	H	-	-	-	OE, HD
C. squarrosus L.	Cyperaceae	700-1700	9, 10	H	-	-	-	HD
Dioscorea bulbifera L.	Dioscoreaceae	700-2000	1, 4	H	-	-	-	HD
Euphorbia royleana Boiss.	Euphorbiaceae	700-2000	1, 2, 3, 4, 5, 8	Sh	-	-	-	HD
Millettia auriculata (Benth.) Baker	Fabaceae	700-1100	1, 3, 4, 5	Sh	-	-	-	HD
Dalbergia sissoo Roxb.	Fabaceae	700-1300	3, 4, 5, 8	T	-	-	-	OE, HD
Flacourtia indica (Burm.f.) Merr.	Flacourtiaceae	700-1000	1, 3, 4, 5	T	-	-	-	HD
Salvia nubicola Wall.*	Lamiaceae	1300-2000	1, 3, 4, 5	H	-	-	-	HD
Roylea cinerea Baill.	Lamiaceae	700-2000	1, 2, 3, 4, 5, 7, 8	Sh	VU	VU	-	OE, HD
Reinwardtia indica Dum.*	Linaceae	700-2000	1, 2, 4, 7, 10	Sh	-	-	-	HD
Osbeckia stellata Buch.-Ham. ex D. Don	Melastomataceae	1200-2000	1, 3, 4	Sh	-	-	-	HD
Tinospora cordifolia (L.) Merr.	Menispermaceae	700-1300	1, 2, 3, 4, 5	Sh	-	-	-	HD
Albizia chinensis (Osb.) Merr	Mimosaceae	700-1300	2, 3, 4, 5, 8	T	-	-	-	OE, HD
Pinus roxburghii Sarg.*	Pinaceae	700-2000	1, 3, 4, 5, 6	T	-	-	-	OE, HD
Pyrus pashia Buch.-Ham. ex D. Don	Rosaceae	700-2000	1, 2, 3, 4, 7	T	-	-	-	HD
Leptodermis lenceolata Wall.	Rubiaceae	700-2000	1, 3, 4	Sh	-	-	-	HD
Wendlandia heynei (Roem. & Schult.) Sant. & Merch.	Rubiaceae	700-1600	1, 3, 4	T	-	-	-	HD
Limonia acidissima L.	Rutaceae	700-1000	1, 6	T	-	-	-	HD

(Contd...)

Taxa/Threat Category	Family	AR (m)	Habitat/s	HF	Status			Threat
					HP	GB	RD	
Boenninghausenia albiflora (Hk.f.) Reichb. ex Meissn.	Rutaceae	1300-2000	1, 3, 4, 7	H	-	-	-	HD
Helicteres isora L.	Sterculiaceae	700-1000	1, 2, 3, 4, 5	Sh	-	-	-	OE, HD
Symplocos chinensis (Lour.) Druce	Symplocaceae	1300-2000	1, 2, 3, 4, 5	T	LC	-	-	OE, HD
Grewia asiatica L.	Tiliaceae	700-1100	3, 4, 5	T	-	-	-	OE, HD

Abbreviations used: **=Endemic; *=Near endemic; **AR**=Altitudinal Range; **LF**=Life Form; **HP**=Himachal Pradesh; **GB**=Global; **RD**=Red Data Book; **T**=Tree; **Sh**=Shrub; **H**=Herb; **Fn**=Fern; **R**=Rare; **CR**=Critically Endangered; **EN**=Endangered; **VU**=Vulnerable; **LC**=Least Concern; **1**=Shady Moist; **2**=Riverine; **3**=Degraded; **4**=Dry; **5**=Bouldary; **6**=Rocky; **7**=Shrubbery; **8**=Waste Places/Road Side; **9**=Near crop field/Cultivated field; **10**=Water courses/ marshy places.; **OE**=Over Exploitation; and **HD**=Habitat Degradation

Some species such as *Azadirachta indica, Pistacia integerrima, Terminalia bellirica, T. chebula, Elaeagnus conferta, Juglans regia, Zanthoxylum armatum, Acorus calamus, Bauhinia vahlii, Dioscorea deltoidea, Cinnamomum tamala, Syzygium cumini, Valeriana jatamansi, Asparagus racemosus, Rhododendron arboretum, Emblica officinalis, Quercus leucotricophora, Hedychium spicatum, H. oblongifolium, Acacia catechu, Myrica esculenta, Cedrus deodara, Plantago ovata, Zizyphus oxyphylla, Aegle marmelos, Murraya koenigii, M. paniculata, Bergenia ligulata, Vitex negundo, Berberis lycium, Dalbergia sissoo, Flacourtia indica* and *Tinospora cordifolia* showed high threats in the study areas, Himachal Pradesh and throughout the Globe hence have high conservation importance. Land use, climate change, nitrogen deposition, biotic exchange and atmospheric carbon dioxide have been the major cause of changes in biodiversity. Moreover, the climate change is not, at the moment, the major threat affecting plants and it is less important than the change in the land use. Two factors *i.e.*, overexploitation and habitat degradation have been causing decrease in the population of a species throughout globe. 38 species were severely affected by both the factors and 41 species were suffering from habitat degradation. Over exploitation of underground parts *i.e.*, roots/rhizomes/barks/tubers/bulbs of *Acorus calamus, Dioscorea deltoidea, Zanthoxylum armatum, Juglans regia, Hedychium spicatum, H. oblongifolium, Acacia catechu, Murraya koenigii, Vitex negundo, Berberis lycium, Tinospora cordifolia, etc.* may lead to extinction of these species from their natural habitats. Listing of species like *Berberis aristata* and *Dioscorea deltoidea* in the Red Data Book of Indian Plants indicated priority attention for conservation.

Among the species, *Syzygium cumini, Berberis lycium* (08 habitats); *Emblica officinalis, Juglans regia, Roylea cinerea* and *Zanthoxylum armatum* (07 habitats); *Aegle marmelos, Vitex negundo, Murraya koenigii* and *Murraya paniculata* (06 habitats); *Albizia chinensis, Buddleja crispa, Euphorbia royleana, Phoenix humilis, Hedychium spicatum, Hypericum oblongifolium, Helicteres isora, Pinus roxburghii, Tinospora cordifolia, Quercus leucotricophora, Pistacia integerrima, Symplocos chinensis, Rosa brunonii, Pyrus pashia Terminalia bellirica, T. chebula, Reinwardtia indica, Bauhinia vahlii, Dioscorea deltoidea, Butea monosperma, Asparagus racemosus* and *Rhododendron arboreum* (05 habitats, each); *Boenninghausenia albiflora, Berberis aristata, Elaeagnus parviflora, Azadirachta indica, Albizia julibrissin, Morus alba, Mucuna pruriens, Nepeta hindostana, Acacia catechu, Cedrus deodara, Plantago ovata, Zizyphus oxyphylla, Z. rugosa, Lannea coromandelica, Elephantopus scaber, Millettia auriculata, Dalbergia sissoo, Flacourtia indica* and *Salvia nubicola* (04 habitats, each), *etc.*, showed wide range of distribution and habitat preferences but due to over exploitation for various purposes, and also due to habitat degradation, some of these species are facing high degree of threats. Promotion of mass scale propagation through conventional and *in vitro* methods of such species and their rehabilitation in the *in-situ* conditions or akin habitats may help in conservation and management. Amongst habitats,

66 species were reported from the dry, 60 species in shady moist, 58 species degraded, 48 species in bouldary, 33 species in riverine, 20 species in shrubbery, 18 species in near crop field/cultivated field, 15 species in waste places/road side, 14 species in rocky and 07 species in Water courses/marshy places support maximum number of threatened species, hence merit conservation attention. These species and habitats represent the maximum part of the area, therefore, require adequate conservation measures. Altitudinal zone, 700-1300m showed the richness of threatened species. This may be due to heavy biotic pressure on this zone leading to habitat degradation and ultimately to extinction of the species. To develop an appropriate strategy for the conservation and management of all these threatened species and their habitats, population assessment and habitat monitoring using standard ecological methods are urgently required.

Elaeagnus conferta

Vitex negundo

Juglans regia

Hedychium spicatum

Acorus calamus

Butea monosperma

Bergenia ligulata

Berberis aristata

Asparagus racemosus

Acacia catechu

Dioscorea deltoidea

Syzygium cumini

Myrica esculenta

Rhododendron arboreum

REFERENCES

Airi, S., Rawal, R.S., Dhar, U. and Purohit, A.N. (1997). Population Studies on Podophyllum Hexandrum Royle-a Dwindling Medicinal Plant of the Himalaya. Plant Genet. Resour. 110: 29-34.

Badola, H.K. and Pal, M. (2003). Threatened Medicinal Plants and Their Conservation in Himachal Himalaya. Ind. For. 129: 55-68.

Gardenfors, U., Taylor, C.U., Mace, G.M. and Rodriguez, J.P. (2001). The Application of IUCN red List Criteria at Regional Levels. Conserv. Biol. 15: 1206-1212.

Goraya, G.S. (2011). Conservation Concern Medicinal Plants for Himachal Pradesh. Medplant - ENVIS Newsletter on Medicinal Plants, Vol. 3. Ministry of Environment and Forests, Government of India, New Delhi.

Grammont, P.C.D. and Cuaron, A. D. (2006). An Evaluation of Threatened Species Categorization Systems Used on the American Continent. Conserv. Biol. 20(1): 14-27.

Hunter, M.L., and Hutchinson, A. (1994). The Virtues and Shortcomings of Parochialism: Conserving Species that are Locally Rare, but Globally Common. Cons. Biol. 8: 1163-1165.

Joshi H.C. and Samant, S.S. (2004). Assessment of Forest Vegetation and Conservation Priorities of Communities in a Part of Nanda Devi Biosphere Reserve, West Himalaya. Part 1. Int. J. Sustain. Dev. World Ecol. 11(3): 326-336.

Lundberg, P., Ranta, E. and Kaitala, V. (2000). Species Loss Leads to Community Closure. Ecol. Letters 3: 465-468.

Mace, G.M. and Lande, R. (1991). Assessing Extinction Threats: Towards Reevaluation of IUCN Threatened Species Categories. Cons. Biol. 5: 148-157.

Maikhuri, R.K., Nautiyal, S., Rao, K.S., Chandrasekhar, K., Gavali, K. and Saxena, K.G. (2000). Analysis and Resolution of Protected Area–people Conflicts in Nanda Devi Biosphere Reserve, India. Environ. Cons. 27(1): 48-53.

Mittermeier, R.A., Gil, P.L., Hoffman, M., Pilgrim, J., Brooks, T., Mittermeier, C.G., Lamoreux, J. and Fonseca, G.A.B.D. (2004). Hotspots Revisited: Earth's Biologically Richest and Most Endangered Terrestrial Ecoregions, Conservation International, Washington.

Myers, N. (1988). Threatened Biotas: 'Hotspots' in Tropical Forests. Environmentalist 8 (3): 1-20.

Myers, N. (1993). Biodiversity and the Precautionary Principle. Ambio 22 (2-3): 74-79.

Pandey, S. and Well, M.P. (1997). Eco-development Planning at India's Great Himalayan National Park for Biodiversity Conservation and Participatory Rural Development. Biod. & Cons. 6: 1277-1292.

Pangtey, Y.P.S. and Samant, S.S. (1988). Observation on the Threatened, Rare-endangered Flowering Plants and Ferns in the Flora of Kumaun Himalaya. Advances For. Res. Ind. 3: 65-74.

Pant, S. (2005). Assessment of Plant Diversity and Ethnobotany of Mornaula Reserve Forest in Kumaon, West Himalaya. Ph.D. Thesis, Kumaon University, Nainital.

Pimm, S.L., Russell, G.L., Gittleman, J.L. and Brooks, T.M. (1995). The Future of Biodiversity. Science 269: 347-350.

Rawal, R.S. and Dhar, U. (1997). Sensitivity of Timberline Flora in Kumaun Himalaya, India: Conservation implications. Arctic and Alpine Research 29 (1): 112-121.

Samant, S.S. and Pangtey, Y.P.S. (1993). Rediscovery of Some Rare and Endangered Shrubs and Climbers of Kumaun Himalaya. J. Econ. & Taxon. Bot. 17(3): 509-512.

Samant, S.S., Dhar, U. and Palni, L.M.S. (2001). Himalayan Medicinal Plants: Potential and Prospects. Gyanodaya Prakashan, Nainital.

Samant, S.S., Dhar, U. and Rawal, R.S. (1996). Conservation of Rare Endangered Plants: The Context of Nanda Devi Biosphere Reserve. In: Ramakrishnan, P.S., Purohit, A.N., Saxena, K.G., Rao, K.S. & Maikhuri, R.K. (eds.) Conservation and Management of Biological Resources in Himalaya. Oxford & IBH Publishing Company Private Limited, New Delhi. pp. 521-545.

Samant, S.S., Pant, S., Singh, M., Lal, M., Singh, A., Sharma, A. and Bhandari, S. (2007). Medicinal Plants in Himachal Pradesh, North Western Himalaya, India. Int. J. Biod. Sci. & Mangnt. 3: 234-251

Sharma, P. (2013). Ecological Assessment of Floristic Diversity and Possible Impacts of Hydropower Projects in Kullu District of Himachal Pradesh, North Western Himalaya. Thesis Submitted to Kumaun University, Nainital.

Singh, A. (2007). Assessment of Plant Diversity and Conservation Status of Forest Vegetation in a Cold Desert Biosphere Reserve of the Western Himalaya. Thesis Submitted to Kumaun University Nainital.

Singh, A., Lal, M. and Samant, S.S. (2009). Diversity, Indigenous Uses and Conservation Prioritization of Medicinal Plants in Lahaul Valley, Proposed Cold Desert Biosphere Reserve, India. Int. J. Biod. Sci. & Mangmnt., 5(3): 132-154.

Sood, S. K. and Thakur, S. (2004). Ethnobotany of Rewalsar Himalaya. Deep Publications, New Delhi.

Tilman, D. (2000). Causes Consequences and Ethics of Biodiversity. Nature 405: 208-211.

Ved, D.K., Kinhal, G.A., Ravikumar, K., Prabhakaran, V., Ghate, U., Vijaya Shankar, R. and Indresha, J.H. (2003). Conservation Assessment and Management Prioritization for the Medicinal Plants of Jammu & Kashmir, Himachal Pradesh & Uttaranchal. Foundation for Revitalisation of Local Health Traditions, Bangalore, India.

Ved, D.K., Kinhal, G.A., Ravikumar, K., Vijaya Shankar, R. and Haridasan, K. (2005). Conservation Assessment and Management Prioritization (CAMP) for the Wild Medicinal Plants of North-East India. Med. Plant Cons. 11: 40-44.

3

Carbon Sequestration Potential of Dry Afromontane Chilimo Forest Dendi District, Oromia, Ethiopia

Bayissa Dida[1]; Wekene Negessa[2]; Akhila S. Nair[1*]

ABSTRACT

Understanding carbon sequestration potential of both natural and plantation forests can help to develop appropriate forest conservation strategies, thereby mitigating climate changes and uplifting carbon trade. This study was to estimate carbon sequestration potentials of above and below ground masses of dry afromontane Chilimo forest. Pre-field works, field works and post field works were conducted. Results show that the carbon stock of Chilimo forest depends on the density of forest. The total 4476.74ha of the forestland comprises of dense forest (15.1%), moderately dense forest (32.7%), less dense forest (11.7%) and shrub/scrubland vegetation (40.5%). The highest carbon stock (347.35t ha^{-1}) is observed in the dense forest strata, whereas the lowest (15.31t ha^{-1}) in the shrub land vegetation. The highest proportion of shrub land vegetation indicated degradation of the Chilimo forest. Three pixels of canopy density and eight homogenous strata were observed. High and moderately homogeneity maps were found in interior forest due to human interferences. The study determined a total of 5065106.3 tonnes of CO_2 as removed by Chilimo forest. The highest (5.07%) and lowest (2.24%) soil organic carbon concentration were observed in dense forest and shrub land vegetation, respectively. This implies that not only forest but also soils under

1. **Department of Biology, College of Natural and Computational Science, Ambo University, Ambo, West Shoa, Ethiopia.**
2. **Michigan State University, East Lansing, MI 48824, USA.**

forest play significant role in carbon sequestration. In general, the results of the present study is encouraging forest conservation and designing appropriate carbon trading in international market as a strategy to mitigate climate changes in Ethiopia.

Keywords: Afromonatane, Biomass, Canopy, Carbon sequestration, Carbon stock, Chilimo.

INTRODUCTION

Climate change is the single biggest environmental and humanitarian crisis of the current time. The earth's atmosphere is overloaded with heat-trapping carbon dioxide, which threatens large scale disruptions in climate with disastrous consequences. Carbon emission, through different sources, is a perturbing factor of global warming. Over the past century, human activities like burning of fossil fuels, deforestation and urbanization have resulted in high concentration of Carbon-dioxide (CO_2) and other greenhouse gases (GHG) in the atmosphere. CO_2 is one of the most common GHG resulting in global warming which in turn brings about drought, flood and other calamities. Global warming is a complex phenomenon, and its full-scale impacts are hard to predict far in advance. But each year scientists learn more about how global warming is affecting the planet, and many agree that certain consequences are likely to occur if current trends continue. Melting glaciers, early snowmelt and severe droughts will cause more dramatic water shortages, rising sea levels will lead to coastal flooding, warmer sea surface temperatures will fuel more intense hurricanes, forests, farms and cities will face troublesome new pests and more mosquito-borne diseases, disruption of habitats such as coral reefs and alpine meadows could drive many plant and animal species to extinction are the main consequences experienced by the world out of global warming. However, to tackle the problem of global warming, carbon sequestration with forest or vegetation and soil are some of the strategies to be encouraged.

In 2000, approximately 30% (3,869 Mha) of the earth's land area was covered by forest. Almost half of forested lands are in the tropics, a third are in the boreal region, and approximately 10% are in each of the sub-tropical and temperate forest regions. The proportion of the world's terrestrial surface that is forested has been changing as a result of anthropogenic activities. For instance, during the decade 1990 to 2000, the forested area within the tropics decreased by 14.2 Mha per year, primarily because of deforestation. Forested ecosystems function through interaction among the carbon, nutrient and hydrological cycles. In turn, these cycles vary as a result of natural environmental shifts that operate on a scale of centuries to millenia. In historical times, human influences have imposed another set of factors in the Carbon balance of forests through deforestation and forest management.

More recently, this is occurring due to human modification of atmospheric chemistry and climate change. The net terrestrial flow of carbon is the difference between uptake (sinks) and sources. During the 1990s, the terrestrial biosphere (of which forests are a major part) was absorbing carbon at a rate of approximately 1.4 Gt per year. Forest trees and soils have been estimated to contain 1,146 Gt of Carbon. Approximately 37% of this Carbon is held in low-latitude forests; 14% in mid-latitude forests; and, the remaining 49% at high-latitudes. Carbon density (mass of C per unit forest area) is greatest in high-latitude forests owing to large stocks of soil carbon. Carbon density is lowest in mid-latitude forests. In the absence of human intervention, the CO_2 balance of forests (uptake versus emission) is in dynamic equilibrium with long-term environmental changes and cycles. Harvesting in excess of growth reduces landscape-level carbon. Conversion of forests for agriculture results in a rapid net loss of carbon to the atmosphere. On the other hand, when agricultural land reverts back to forest, carbon pools can be increased. Retention time of carbon in forests varies from days for fast decomposing tissues to centuries or millennia for the slower carbon pools. Retention times vary by forest type and climatic zone and are affected by natural and non-natural disturbances (http://iufro.boku.ac.at/iufro/taskforce/hptfcs.htm).

Carbon sequestration is a method for overseeing the quantity of carbon dioxide that is emitted to the atmosphere by burning carbon based fuels, mainly carbon rich petroleum fuels. It is comparatively a new idea brought about by the concern that high concentrations of atmospheric carbon dioxide contribute to global warming. In principle, carbon sequestration refers to storage of carbon that would or else be liberated into the atmosphere. Three main methods which favours carbon sequestration include: (a) Near term storage in the terrestrial biosphere where vegetation would soak up the CO_2 and store it in biomass and soil; (b) Long term storage in the earth's soil by pumping CO_2 into existing or drilled/excavated sub-surface reservoirs; and (c) Long term storage in the earth's oceans where CO_2 would be injected thousands of feet deep and trapped by the water. Three factors are important consideration of forest management options for carbon storage. These are: (a) Carbon pool size: Forest ecosystems are the largest terrestrial carbon pool. They store more than 80% of all terrestrial aboveground carbon and more than 70% of all soil organic carbon. (b) Carbon dynamics: Net-growing forests cause sequestration of carbon. After harvesting the life-cycle of the wood products is decisive. Forest management and societal decisions both have significant influence on the carbon balance. (c) Chemical form of carbon: Carbon is stabilized in terrestrial ecosystems to different degrees. The stable carbon form in biomass is wood, whereas many carbohydrates and proteins are quickly recycled. Soil carbon is comprised of a complex array of compounds. Stable forms are organic molecules that are chemically tied to the mineral soil. Stabilized soil carbon has a residence time of many decades.

Carbon accumulated on the surface (forest floor material) has a much shorter residence time and is more vulnerable following disturbance (http://www.iufro.org/science/task-forces/carbon-sequestration/).

The use of vegetation, especially forests to address climate change is understandably appealing, from both a political and environmental perspective. Carbon mitigation through forests has recently been recognized as one of the most important ecosystem services with specific reference to global warming and implication of the Kyoto-Protocol. Forests are crucial for ecological functions such as regulating climate change and nourishing water resources. Forests possess significant potential to capture and hold carbon thereby playing an important role in global carbon cycle. Forests' ecosystem stores nearly two third of terrestrial carbon making the amount of carbon density (carbon per hectare) huger than any other land uses (Zhou *et al.*, 2008). Photosynthesis, respiration, decomposition and biomass combustion make the terrestrial ecosystems important components of the global carbon budget. Forest biomass is the largest terrestrial carbon sink, comprising 90% of all living biomass (Zhao and Zhou 2005). Substantial carbon is transferred from terrestrial reservoir to the atmosphere as a result of change in biomass due to deforestation and degradation. Anthropogenic actions and natural disturbances such as pests, fire and climate change cause forest degradation and reduction in the productivity that inevitably deteriorate the carbon sequestration potential. Carbon density is a critical parameter in determining the extent of human activity on ecosystem.

The United Nations Framework Convention on Climate Change (UNFCCC) has agreed to study and consider a new initiative led by forest-rich developing countries. It calls for economic incentives to help facilitate 'Reductions in Emissions from Deforestation in Developing countries' (REDD).Under these, countries are required to estimate and report CO_2 emissions and removals by forests. The developing global carbon markets require accurate and reliable methods to quantify the sources and sinks of carbon in forests. The REDD concept at its core is a proposal to provide financial incentives to help developing countries voluntarily reduce their national deforestation rates and associated carbon emissions below a baseline (based either on a historical reference case or future projection). Countries demonstrating a reduction in emissions can sell those carbon credits on the international carbon market or elsewhere. These emissions reduction could simultaneously combat climate change, conserve biodiversity and protect other ecosystem goods and services. Accurate estimation and mapping of the forest biomass distribution are prerequisites in answering a long debate on the role of forest vegetation in the local, regional and global carbon cycle (Lu 2006). For this, key factors are selection of appropriate biomass estimation method and use of reliable forest inventory data (Zhao and Zhou 2005).

In the late nineteenth century, about 30% of Ethiopia was covered with forest. The clearing of land for agricultural use and the cutting of trees for fuel gradually changed the scene, and today forest areas have dwindled to less than 4% of Ethiopia's total land. The northern parts of the highlands are almost devoid of trees. However, about 45,000 square kilometres of dense forest exist in the southern and southwestern sections of the highlands. Some of these include coniferous forests, found at elevations above 1,600 meters, but a majority of the forestland consists primarily of woodlands found in drier areas of the highlands and in the drier areas bordering the highlands. Reforestation programmes resulted in the planting of millions of seedlings in community forests throughout Ethiopia. A variety of Non Governmental Organisations, which had to organize their activities through the local peasant association, supplemented government efforts to rehabilitate Ethiopia's forests. However, critics maintain that both systems caused communal resources to be developed at the expense of private needs. As a result, reforestation programs did not perform well. Seedling survival rates varied from as low as 5 to 20% in some areas to 40% in others, largely because of inadequate care and premature cutting by peasants. In late 1990, Addis Ababa was in the process of launching the Ethiopian Forestry Action Plan (EFAP) to improve woodland conservation, increase public participation in reforestation projects, and prevent further depletion of existing forest resources. It is estimated that in 2000 Ethiopia had 4,344,000 ha of natural forest area, which is 4% of its total land area. Compared to other East African countries Ethiopia's deforestation rate is about average. However, the deforestation rates in East Africa are second highest of the continent. Moreover, it has the smallest fraction of its forest area designated primarily for conservation. Apart from Northern Africa, East African countries show the second highest decline rates of conservation forests in the continent.

At this point, this study has mainly focused on biomass and carbon stock estimation at landscape level afromontane Chilimo forest and tried to reveal the role of Chilimo forest in carbon sequestration.

MATERIALS AND METHODS

Study Area

Chilimo forest is found in Western Shoa Zone close to Ginchi town, Capital of Dendi District, about 90 km west of Addis Ababa (9°5′ North 38°10′ East) and covers an area of about 5000ha. Altitudinal range of this area is between 2250m-3000m. This area is located at the western end of a chain of hills and ridges that stretches 200 km from north of Addis Ababa west wards up to the Gedo highlands. River valleys and gorges cut through the hills. The general physiograghy of Chilimo forest is presented in Fig. 3.1 and the map of Afromontane forests in the East Africa is shown in Fig 3.1(a).

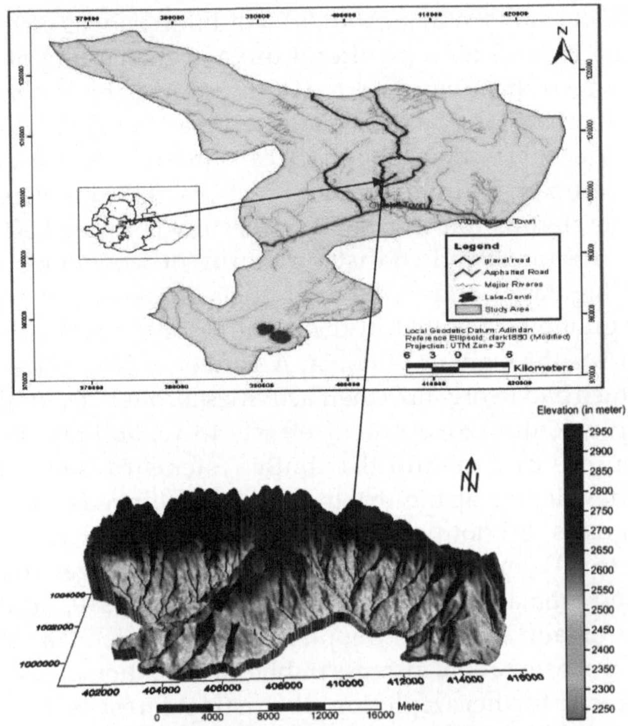

Fig. 3.1: Physiography of Chilimo Forest

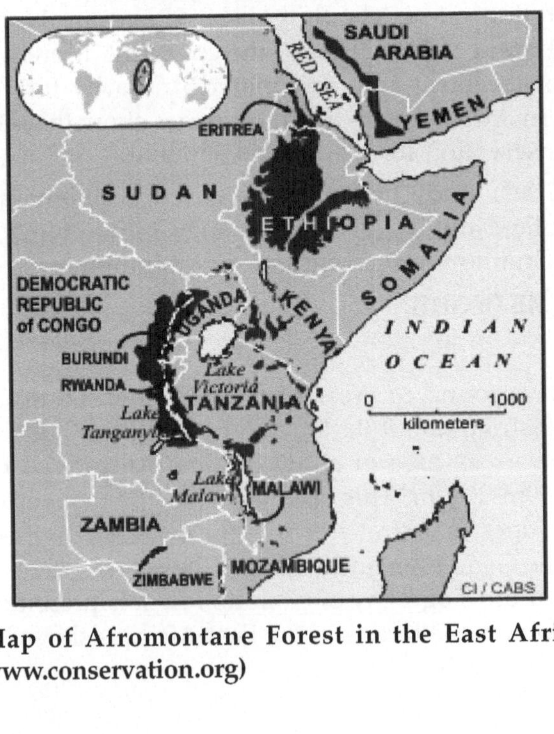

Fig 3.1 (a): Map of Afromontane Forest in the East Africa (*Source:* http://www.conservation.org)

Chilimo forest is one of the few remnants of dry afromontane forest on Ethiopian Central Plateau. The forest is montane mixed broadleaf-coniferous, predominated by conifers. The vegetation throughout this area has been subject to human impact and the rate of deforestation has been extremely high, with significant changes in forest cover observed even since the 1970s. The main species in the canopy are *Juniperus procera, Podocarpus falcatus, Prunus africana, Olea europaea cuspidata, Apodytes dimidiata* and *Ficus* species. Historically; this entire upland area was covered by *Juniperus-Podocarpus* forest. Selective cutting of trees for commercial use stopped about 1973, but illegal cutting by the local people has continued. Various types of scrublands now dominate the landscape. Grasses in the forest is used for grazing by smallholder farmers settled around the forest. A few shrub species dominate such as *Myrsine africana, Maytenus arbutifolia* and *Rubus apetalus* are indicators of forest disturbance. Small patches of plantation forests initiated by the Forestry Department of the State in 1976 are present within the forested lands indicating that the indigenous species were replaced by exotic species like *Eucalyptus saligna, E. camaldulensis, Pinus patula* and *Cupressus lusitanica*. The predominant indigenous species were *Juniperus procera, Hagenia abyssinica* and *Podocarpus falcatus*. The species compositions of Chilimo forest revealed that it has been threatened by excessive exploitation and conversion to other land-uses.

The research work was divided in to three phases: pre-field work, field work, and post field work. The overall research frame work for this study is shown in Figure 3.2.

Sampling Design and Dimensions of Sample Plots

Stratified random sampling with probability proportion to size to the homogenous strata was followed for sampling design (Husch *et al.*, 1972). The sampling strategy was mainly based on the accessibility of locations and density of populations. A nested sampling strategy, plot and subplots were employed to collect field data in the form of quadrate shape layout. Five main plots (20m×20m) were allocated on the basis of stratified random fashion for the estimation of tree biomass. Within each such plot one subplot (4m×4m) was nested at the centre for estimating shrubs.

Forest Sub-types Density and Homogenous Strata Mapping

Different sub-strata, density and homogeneity were examined for gathering and verifying ground truth. Until establishing permanent maps, temporary maps of the field were verified, and corrected. Forest cover type map and density map data could be obtained during ground truth collection. Finally, different strata cover types and density maps were generated using image elements. Base map of canopy density was prepared by ERADS IMAGINE by computing remote sensing reflectance values of vegetation.

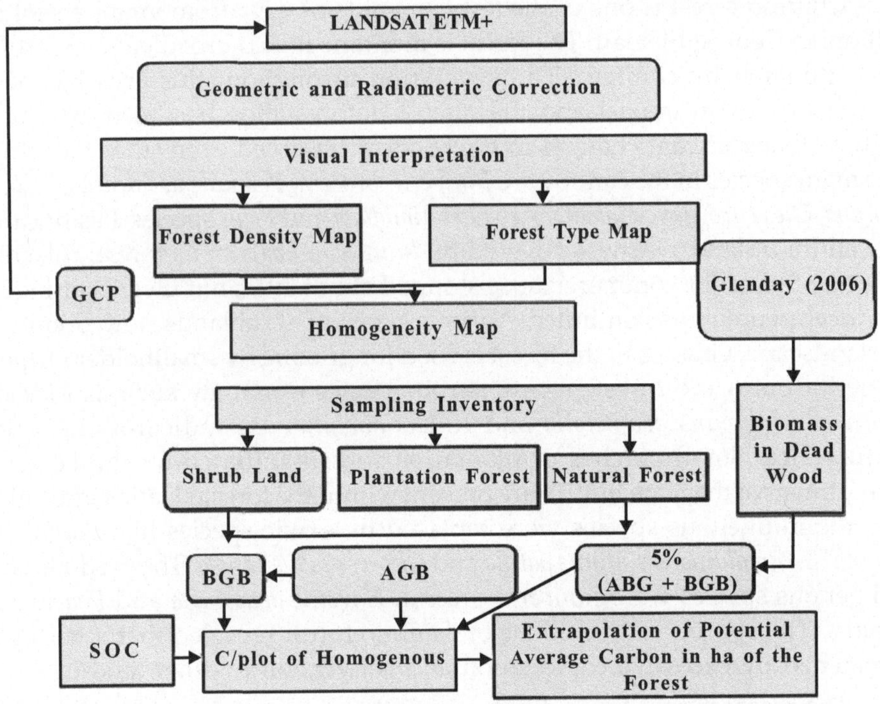

Fig. 3.2: The Research Frame Work Adopted for the Current Study

Subsequently, all the corresponding attributes or signatures were assigned to each cover classes in ERDAS IMAGINE and ArcGIS. Relatively dominated homogenous Chilimo forest cover types map and forest density map were then overlaid in GIS domain to generate dominated Chilimo forest in terms of pixel value into their adjacent strata. Consequently, the homogenous type and density strata map (homogeneity map) were generated. The strata were given attributes, proper colors and legends and stored in GIS for further analysis.

Forest Canopy Density Mapping Model

Forest Canopy Density (FCD) Model is one of the time-and-cost saving methods to detect and estimate the canopy density over large area (JOFCA, 1996). The remote sensing data used in FCD model is Landsat TM data. The FCD model comprises bio-physical phenomenon modelling and analysis utilizing data derived from four indices: Advanced Vegetation Index (AVI), Bare Soil Index (BI), Shadow Index or Scaled Shadow Index (SI, SSI) and Thermal Index (TI). FCD is then determined by modelling operation using these indices. The degree of forest density is expressed in percentages for each pixel (Rikimaru *et al.*, 2002).

BIOMASS ESTIMATION

Above Ground Biomass (AGB) Estimation

The above ground biomass for different components (trees, shrubs and dead wood) was estimated and calculated for each relatively homogenous stratum. The AGB of trees within each class was estimated by measuring diameter at breast height (dbh) of all live trees for each plot inventory. The dbh was measured at 1.3m above ground. The biomass per average tree of each class was estimated directly by sampling tree diameter of the area and applying allometric equations. The above ground biomass has been estimated as per the equation put forward by Brown (1997) as follows.

$$AGB= 42.69 - 12.8 \times (dbh) + 1.242(dbh)^{2} \text{ for trees 5cm - 138cm dbh} \quad (1)$$

$$AGB= AGB=10\wedge \{-0.535+\log (BA)\} \text{ for trees <5cm dbh} \quad (2)$$

Where, dbh in cm; basal area in cm^2 and AGB is above ground biomass per tree in kilogram.

Total above ground biomass (AGB) and below ground biomass (BGB) estimation.

The sum of tree, shrubs, and deadwood biomass (t/ha) was taken as total AGB of the plot and strata-wise. Measurements of root biomass are indeed highly uncertain and the lack of empirical values for this type of biomass has for decades been a major weakness in ecosystem models. So, the belowground biomass (BGB) was calculated from the value obtained for AGB according to Cairns *et al.*, (1997).

Biomass in Deadwood

Glenday (2006) reported that the amount of deadwood biomass was 5% of the sum of AGB and BGB.

Vegetation Carbon Stock Density Estimation

The multiplication of biomass with the conversion factor of 0.47 represents the average carbon content in biomass (Westlake, 1963). Aboveground carbon (AGC) and belowground carbon (BGC) for each substrata class were calculated by multiplication factor with corresponding AGB and BGB for substrata class. After careful comparison of the different international standards to be followed for forest carbon estimation, the carbon fraction (CF) default value (IPCC, 2006) was used to convert the biomass value into carbon stock.

The carbon stock density of Chilimo forest was calculated by summing the carbon stock densities of the individual carbon pools of each stratum. Finally, the total carbon stock was simply converted into tons of CO_2 equivalent by multiplying it by 44/12 (Pearson *et al.*, 2007).

Soil Organic Carbon (SOC) Estimation

Near the centre of all plots or sub-plots, a single pit of up to 30 cm in depth was dug to best represent forest types in terms of slope, vegetation density and vegetation cover. Soil bulk density is determined from the weight of dry soil divided by the total soil volume. Soil organic carbon (SOC) was estimated using standard method of Walkley and Black (1934). The carbon stock density of soil organic carbon in tons per hector (t/ha) and the carbon stock per unit area (t ha^{-1}) were calculated by the methods suggested by Pearson *et al.,* (2007).

RESULTS AND DISCUSSION

Forest Cover Sub-types Mapping

After extensive ground truth verification and assessing spectral accuracy with sample plots verification; the dominant strata were further classified. Based on their density, the forest was classified into four major subtype classes: dense forest, moderate forest, less dense forest, and shrub land. The map is given in Fig. 3.3. Area of different Chilimo forest cover subtypes mapping is given in table 3.1. The dominated Chilimo forest covers an area of about 4476.74ha, out of which dense forest occupies 15.1%, moderately dense forest occupies 32.7%, less dense forest occupies 11.7% and shrub land occupies 40.5%. From this result and actual ground truth, it becomes vivid that shrub land occupies the greatest of all Chilimo forest land cover. The change of forest to shrub land indicates an overall destruction of forests, mainly by human interventions. Plates 3.1-3.3 show the various anthropogenic activities around Chilimo forest. The need for fuel wood, arable land and grazing areas are the main causes of forest degradation, frequently leading to loss of forest cover and biodiversity, erosion, desertification and reduced water resources. Role of forests on climate change adaptation study by Ministry of Forests and Soil Conservation in Nepal, reported similar results (MOFSC, 2011).

Forest Canopy Density Mapping

Chilimo forest canopy density map was generated by constructing algorithms of three indices of graphical models with Model Maker. The Chilimo forest canopy density map was generated from the three indices of Landsat ETM+ Mapper of Chilimo forest (i.e. by addition of advanced vegetation index, shadow index and advanced bare soil index). Assisted by a forestry expert, the pixels of canopy density were classified into below 60% density classes, 60-80% density classes, and above 80% density classes. The map of Chilimo forest density classes are shown in the Fig 3.4.

Homogeneity Map

The sample plots were distributed and laid in all classes considering probability, proportion and size. The homogeneity was considered and described as having same forest density and type in each stratum of the study area. The forest homogeneity map was generated by overlaying forest type map and forest density map as shown in Fig 3.5. Further processing of the image could gain the final map with eight relatively homogenous strata; through merging insignificant classes with their neighbouring classes. Areas of different homogenous strata are presented in Table 3.2.

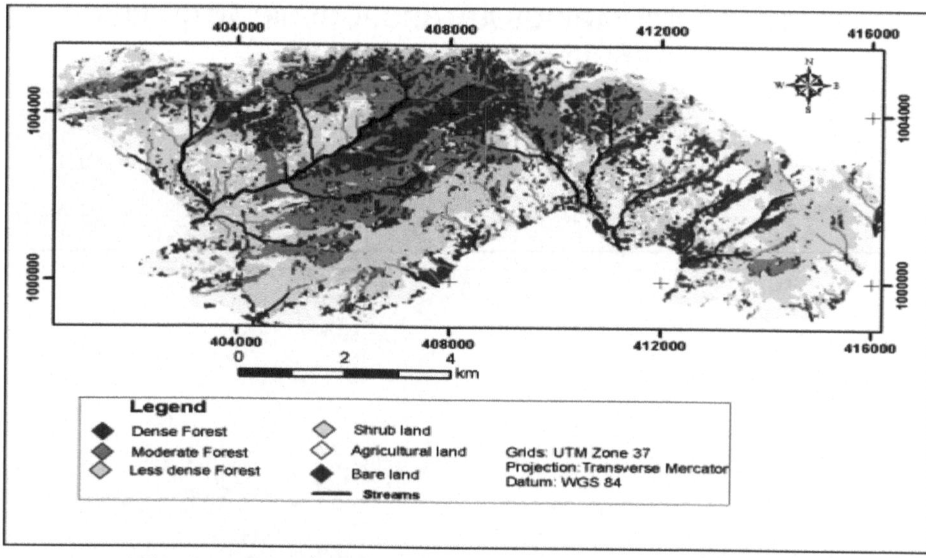

Fig. 3.3: Map of Chilimo Forest and Dominated Subtypes

Table 3.1: Area of Different Chilimo Forest Cover Subtypes Mapping

Sl. No.	Land Cover Type	Area (in ha)	Area (%)
1.	Dense Forest	675.66	15.1
2.	Moderate Forest	1465.87	32.7
3.	Sparse Forest	523.58	11.7
4.	Shrub Land	1811.63	40.5
	Total	4476.74	100.0

In the homogeneity map, *dense forest (canopy density>80%) and moderate forest (with canopy density 60-80%) were mostly found in* interior of the forest region, far from settlements and agriculture. Hence the biotic pressure is lesser there compared to other classes. Sparse forest (with canopy density <60%) and shrub/scrublands (with canopy density <60%) were sharing borders with settlements and agriculture. This can be attributed to more biotic pressure on coastal forests resulting to forest degradation and canopy opening. However, each sector of the forest is controlled by participatory forest management. Strict management policies prompt local people abstain from cutting trees of Chilimo forest. Yet illegal attempts are there to meet commercial, house construction and firewood demands. Sengota and Mesalema sectors proximate to Ginchi town were covered mostly by shrub types indicating a probable interference by local population.

PLATES 3.1-3.3: VARIOUS ANTHROPOGENIC ACTIVITIES AROUND CHILIMO FOREST

Plate 3.1: Potato Farm Near the Chilimo Forest

Plate 3.2: Juniperus Trees out Skirted by Road Under Construction

Plate 3.3: Soil Erosion is a Curse to the Sites Near Chilimo Forest

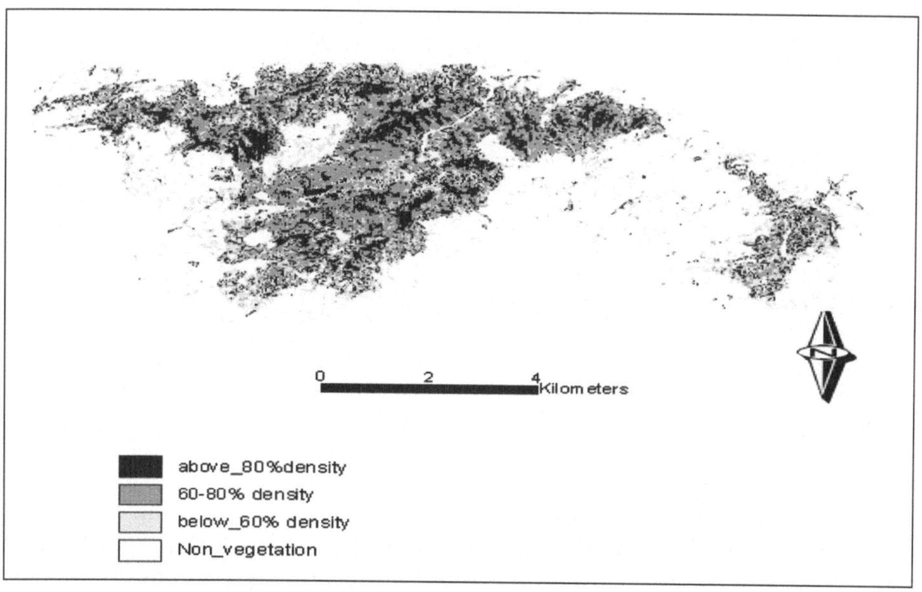

Fig. 3.4: Map of Chilimo Forest Canopy Density Classes

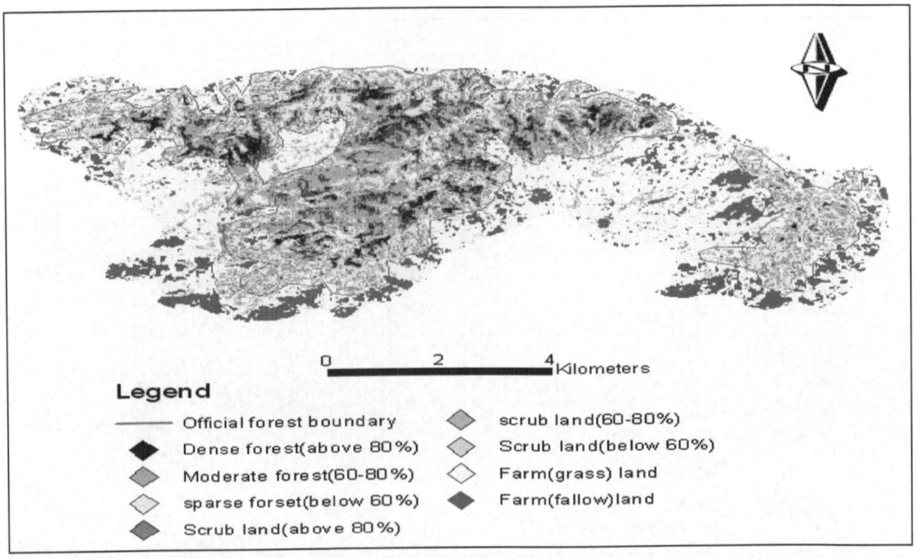

Fig. 3.5: Homogenous Strata Map of Chilimo Forest

Table 3.2: Area (ha) of Different Homogenous Strata

Sl. No.	Forest Strata	Code	Density (%)	Area(ha)	Area (%)
1.	Dense forest (>80)	D_F (>80%)	>80	675.66	15.1
2.	Moderate forest (60-80)	M_F (60-80%)	60-80	994.87	22.2
3.	Plantation type-A (60-80%)	P_A (60-80%)	60-80	366	8.2
4.	Plantation type-B (60-80%)	P_B (<60%)	60-80	105	2.3
5.	Sparse forest (<60)	S_F (<60%)	<60	523.58	11.7
6.	Shrub/scrubland (>80)	S_L (>80%)	>80	683.5	15.3
7.	Shrub/scrubland (60-80)	S_L (60-80%)	60-80	641.0	14.3
8.	Shrub/scrubland (<60)	S_L (<60%)	<60	484.1	10.8
	Total	4473.71	100		

BIOMASS

Biomass of Tree Layer

The main carbon pools in forest ecosystems are the living biomass of trees and understory vegetation and the dead mass of litter, woody debris and soil organic matter. The carbon stored in the aboveground living biomass of trees is typically the largest pool. And thus, estimating aboveground forest biomass carbon is the most essential step in quantifying carbon stocks. The nature of biomass accumulation may vary in the same species under different locality factors such as accumulation of nutrient in the soil, management practices and availability of light and other environmental factors. Glenday (2006) reported that the above ground biomass of trees layers of tropical moist forests ranges between 328 and 472 t ha^{-1}. According to Getachew (2007), the above ground biomass of trees layers of dry afromontane tropical forests ranges between 403.08–754.32 t ha^{-1}. The above ground biomass reported in the present study (30.31–694.69 t ha^{-1}) was higher than most tropical dry forests but within the range of tropical rain forests. In this study, highest aboveground plant biomass was recorded at Dense forest (>80%), followed by Plantation Type B (60-80%) and the lowest aboveground plant biomass was recorded for Scrub/shrub land (<60%). The largest AGB vegetation was 694.69 t ha^{-1} estimated from natural dense forest, and the minimum was 30.31 t ha^{-1} estimated from scrub/shrub land with density <60%. Table 3.3 presents detailed information about the mean AGB density in (t ha^{-1}) of tree layers in different strata.

Table 3.3: Average AGB Density (t ha^{-1}) of Vegetation in Different Forest Strata

Sl.No.	Forest Strata	AGB(t ha^{-1})
1.	Dense forest (>80%)	694.69
2.	Moderate forest (60-80%)	586.67
3.	Sparse forest (<60%)	372.25
4.	Plantation type A (60-80%)	230.62
5.	Plantation type B (60-80%)	662.99
6.	Scrub/shrub land (>80%)	81.98
7.	Scrub/shrub land (60-80%)	68.75
8.	Scrub/shrub land (<60%)	30.31

Below Ground Biomass

The belowground biomass was estimated from root/shoot ratio for tree layer (IPCC 2006). The maximum BGB was 180.62 t ha^{-1} for dense forest, followed by 172.38 t ha^{-1} for P_B and the minimum was 7.88 t ha^{-1} for S_L(<60%). The result showed that trend of BGB density was analogy with tree layer of AGB (Fig 3.6).

Biomass in Deadwood

Negligible herbaceous layer in the forest was due to the bigger trees inhibiting the growth of herbs by competing for nutrients, water and sunlight. Glenday (2006) reported the amount of deadwood biomass was 5% of the sum of AGB and BGB. Results are presented in Table 3.4. The highest biomass of deadwood (180.2 t ha^{-1}) was found in dense forest, whereas the lowest (7.9 t ha^{-1}) in shrub land.

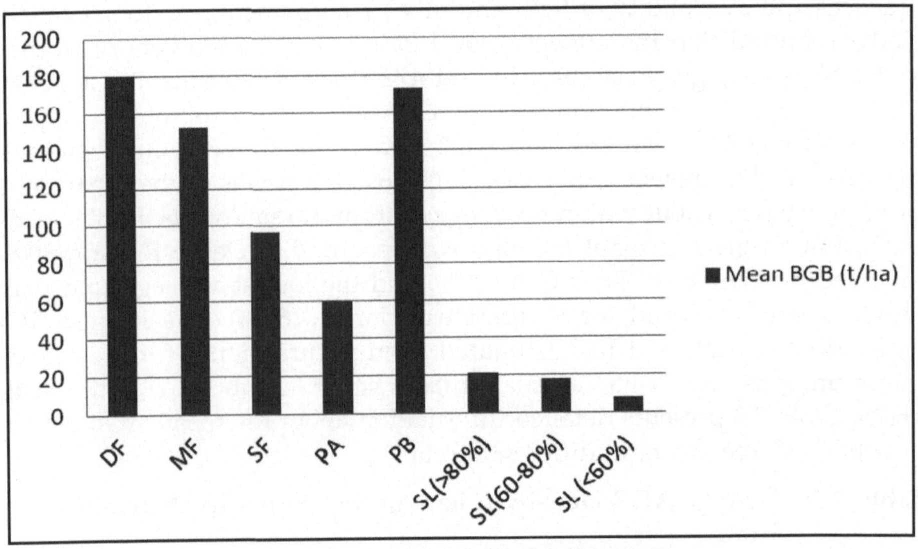

Fig. 3.6: BGB as Affected by Different Strata

Table 3.4: Average Biomass of Deadwood of Different Homogenous Strata

Sl. No	Forest Strata	MB Trees ($t\ h^{-1}$)	BGB ($t\ h^{-1}$)	BM Deadwood ($t\ h^{-1}$)
1.	Dense forest (>80%)	694.69	180.62	43.77
2.	Moderate forest (60-80%)	586.67	152.53	36.96
3.	Sparse forest (<60%)	372.25	96.79	23.45
4.	Plantation type A (60-80%)	230.62	59.96	14.53
5.	Plantation type B (60-80%)	662.99	172.38	41.77
6.	Scrub/shrub land (>80%)	81.98	21.31	5.16
7.	Scrub/shrub land (60-80%)	68.75	17.88	4.33
8.	Scrub/shrub land (<60%)	30.31	7.88	0.38

Total Biomass Density

The total biomass (AGB, BGB and deadwood) showed an increasing trend with higher canopy density classes as in Table 3.5. This is because of impacts on various components of AGB variability such as location, species composition, age and types of anthropogenic pressures.

ABOVE GROUND CARBON STOCK (AGC) OF VEGETATION

The above ground carbon (AGC) density of vegetation was calculated from above ground biomass of vegetation in each stratum. The mean AGC densities ($t\ ha^{-1}$) in different strata are presented in Table 3.6. The highest AGC density (347.35 $t\ ha^{-1}$), was obtained in Dense forest, whereas the lowest AGC (15.31 $t\ ha^{-1}$), in scattered shrub land with canopy density <60%.

According to Moll and Moll, (1994) wood is comprised of four basic materials namely: cellulose accounting for 50% or more of the bulk; hemi-cellulose-20%; lignin-25% and resin or oils accounting for the remainder. Brown, (1997) reported that carbon quantities are about 50% of the aboveground woody biomass weight. Woody plants are characterized by secondary growth and a continuous conversion of structural tissue into non-living, therefore non-respiring biomass. This leads to the increase in girth of a plant due to the lateral meristem action of the vascular cambium producing the secondary xylem popularly known as wood. This dry matter remains an integral part of an individual tree essential to its functioning. As Costa, (1996) reported, plant tissues vary in their carbon storage with stems and fruits having more carbon per gram of dry weight than leaves and that longer-lived trees with high-density wood store more carbon per volume than short-lived, low-density, fast-growing ones.

Table 3.5: Average Total Biomass of Different Homogenous Strata

Sl.No.	Forest Strata	AAGB+deadwood (t ha^{-1})	BGB (t ha^{-1})	Total-BM (t ha^{-1})
1.	Dense forest (>80%)	738.46	180.62	919.08
2.	Moderate forest (60-80%)	623.63	152.53	776.16
3.	Sparse forest (<60%)	395.70	96.79	492.49
4.	Plantation type A (60-80%)	245.15	59.96	305.11
5.	Plantation type B (60-80%)	704.76	172.38	877.14
6.	Scrub/shrub land (>80%)	87.14	21.31	108.45
7.	Scrub/shrub land (60-80%)	73.08	17.88	90.96
8.	Scrub/shrub land (<60%)	30.91	7.88	38.57

Table 3.6: Mean AGC Stock of Vegetation in Different Strata

Sl.No.	Forest Strata	AGC Vegetation (t ha^{-1})
1.	Dense forest (>80%)	347.35
2.	Moderate forest (60-80%)	293.34
3.	Sparse forest (<60%)	186.13
4.	Plantation type A (60-80%)	115.31
5.	Plantation type B (60-80%)	331.49
6.	Scrub/shrub land (>80%)	40.99
7.	Scrub/shrub land (60-80%)	34.38
8.	Scrub/shrub land (<60%)	15.19

BELOW GROUND CARBON (BGC) STOCK

The trend of carbon density was similar with tree layer of AGC. Similarly, the results of total vegetation carbon were also in accordance with tree layer and BGC. This implies that tree layer contributed more to the carbon stock (Table 3.7).

Table 3.7: Mean AGC Stock of Vegetation in Different Strata

Strata Type	AGC Veg.	BGC (t ha^{-1})
Dense forest (>80%)	347.35	90.31
Moderate forest (60-80%)	293.34	76.18
Sparse forest (<60%)	186.13	48.39
Plantation type A (60-80%)	115.31	29.98
Plantation type B (60-80%)	331.49	86.19
Scrub/shrub land (>80%)	40.99	10.66
Scrub/shrub land (60-80%)	34.38	8.94
Scrub/shrub land (<60%)	15.19	3.95

CARBON STOCK IN DEADWOOD

The carbon stock in deadwood was calculated from the above and below ground carbon stock values. Hence, the highest and lowest carbon stock in deadwood was observed in dense forest, and scrubland respectively. The average carbon densities of deadwood are depicted in Table 3.8. Finally, carbon stock in biomass of different forest stratum was obtained by adding carbon density in AGB, BGB and deadwood. Hence, the maximum carbon stock in biomass was found in dense natural forest (459.54 t ha^{-1}) and the lowest, in scrub/shrub land with density< 60% (20.1 t ha^{-1}).

Table 3.8: Mean Carbon Stock of Deadwood in Different Homogenous Strata

Sl.No.	Forest Strata	AGC veg. (t ha^{-1})	BGC (t ha^{-1})	Deadwood (t ha^{-1})
1.	Dense forest (>80%)	347.35	90.31	21.88
2.	Moderate forest (60-80%)	293.34	76.18	18.48
3.	Sparse forest (<60%)	186.13	48.39	11.73
4.	Plantation type A (60-80%)	115.31	29.98	7.26
5.	Plantation type B (60-80%)	331.49	86.19	20.88
6.	Scrub/shrub land (>80%)	40.99	10.66	2.28
7.	Scrub/shrub land (60-80%)	34.38	8.94	2.17
8.	Scrub/shrub land (<60%)	15.19	3.95	0.96

Soil Organic Carbon (SOC)

Among all strata, the highest total SOC was estimated in Dense forest (>80%), and the lowest was estimated in Shrub land (<60%) as presented in Table 3.9. This indicates a decreasing trend in SOC with decrease of forest density classes in each subtype. On the other hand, the average SOC density recorded in Moderate forest (60-80%) was 103.52 t ha^{-1} and 80.92 t ha^{-1} in Plantation type B (60-80%). For land use change involving re-establishment of woody vegetation (e.g. forest to plantation, reversion to agriculture), effect on soil carbon depended on vegetation type, age of new vegetation, decomposability of litter and vertical distribution of carbon inputs throughout the soil profile by the roots (Guo & Gifford 2002; Kasel & Bennett 2007). The global soil carbon pool, composed of both organic and inorganic carbon, is approximately three times the size of the atmospheric pool and four times the size of the biotic pool. Soils are generally acknowledged as the largest store of terrestrial carbon that can be further increased by proper land management practices, particularly on agricultural and forest lands. Accumulation of carbon in the soil could serve as an important carbon sink. The rate of soil organic carbon sequestration depends on the complex interaction between climate, soils, tree species, and management practices. About 60% of soil organic matter is carbon (Amundson 2001). This study indicates that the amount of carbon sequestered underneath of vegetation or forest varies depending upon the tree density and species composition. The soil organic carbon stored in forest soils depends upon the type and age of the soil. The soil organic carbon concentration can range from 0% in very young soils to as much as 50% in some organic or wetland soils, with most soils containing between 0.3% and 11.5% in the top 20 cm of soil (Lal 2005).

Table 3.9: Soil Organic Carbon in Different Forest Strata

Sl.No.	Strata Type	SOC (%)	SOC (t ha^{-1})
1.	Dense forest (>80%)	5.07	108.63
2.	Moderate forest (60-80%)	4.26	103.52
3.	Sparse forest (<60%)	2.69	66.98
4.	Plantation type A (60-80%)	2.96	75.48
5.	Plantation type B (60-80%)	3.69	86.35
6.	Scrub/shrub land (>80%)	2.91	72.17
7.	Scrub/shrub land (60-80%)	2.81	73.34
8.	Scrub/shrub land (<60%)	2.24	69.89

ASSESSMENT OF THE POTENTIAL OF CARBON STOCK

The highest density was 568.17 tons of carbon per hectare in dense forest whereas the lowest was 89.99 tons per hectare observed in natural forest (Table 3.10). The carbon stock of natural forest and plantation forest across the study area were estimated respectively as 1242818.1 t carbon in 4002.7 ha and 138574.5 t carbon in 471 ha. The total carbon stocks were then multiplied by 44/12 to estimate GHG (CO_2) removals. Hence, about 4556 999.7 t and 508 106.5 t of CO_2 were removed, respectively by natural forest and plantation forest of the study area whereas a total of 5 065 106.3 tones of CO_2 were removed by Chilimo forest site.

Table 3.10: Mean Carbon in Biomass, Soil Carbon and Total Carbon of Different Strata

Sl.No.	Forest Strata	Biomass-C ($t\ ha^{-1}$)	SOC ($t\ ha^{-1}$)	Total-C ($t\ ha^{-1}$)
1.	Dense forest (>80%)	459.54	108.63	568.17
2.	Moderate forest (60-80%)	388.00	103.52	491.52
3.	Sparse forest (<60%)	246.26	66.98	313.24
4.	Plantation type A (60-80%)	152.55	75.48	228.03
5.	Plantation type B (60-80%)	438.56	86.35	524.91
6.	Scrub/shrub land (>80%)	53.93	72.17	126.10
7.	Scrub/shrub land (60-80%)	45.49	73.34	118.83
8.	Scrub/shrub land (<60%)	20.10	69.89	89.99

CONCLUSION

Chilimo forest sequesters significant amount of Carbon/GHG. About 5065106.3 tons of GHG (CO_2) was removed by Chilimo forest. The carbon stock potentials of both plantation trees and natural forests in the study area show vital economic benefit contributed by these vegetation strata with respect to carbon trade. The present study findings provide baseline information for further studies to ascertain the status of forest carbon stock and prudently plan forest management. This is important in two ways: first, forest degradation is currently aggravating problems associated with climate; second, developing carbon trading can not only safeguard the remnant Ethiopian forests but also encourage plantation forestry.

REFERENCES

Amundson, R. 2001. The Carbon Budget in Soils. Annual Review of Earth and Planetary Sciences, 29: 535-562.

Brown, S. 1997. *Estimating Biomass and Biomass Change of Tropical Forests: A Primer.* A Forest Resources Assessment Publication, FAO, Rome, 55p.

Cairns, M.A., S. Brown, E.M. Helmer & G.A. Baum Gardener. 1997. Root Biomass Allocation in the World's Upland Forests. *Oecologia.* 111: 1-11.

Costa, P.M. 1996. Tropical Forestry Practices for Carbon Sequestration: A Review and Case Study from Southeast Asia. *Ambio* 25: 279-278.

Getachew Tesfaye, 2007. Structure, Biomass and Net Primary Production in a Dry Tropical Afromontane Forest in Ethiopia. *Ph.D.Thesis*. University of Bayreuth, Germany.

Glenday, J. 2006. Carbon Storage and Emissions Offset Potential in an East African Tropical Rainforest. *Forest Ecology and Management*. 235: 72-83.

Guo, L.B. & R.M. Gifford. 2002. Soil Carbon Stocks and Land Use Change: A Meta Analysis. *Global Change Biology*. 8: 345-360.

http://www.conservation.org

http://www.iufro.org/science/task-forces/carbon-sequestration/

Husch, B., Miller & T.W. Beers. 1972. *Forest Mensuration*. The Ronald Press Company, New York, 55-60.

IPCC, 2006. *Good Practice Guidelines for National Greenhouse Gas Inventories. Switzerland: Intergovernmental Panel on Climate Change*. 4. from www.ippc.ch/Publications_and_data/publications_and_data_reports.html accessed on 22/02/2011

JOFCA, 1996. *Proceedings of the Workshop on Utilization of Remote Sensing in Site Assessment and Planning for Rehabilitation of Logged-over Forests*. Bangkok, Thailand.

Kasel, S. & T.L. Bennett. 2007. Land Use History, Forest Conversion and Soil Organic Carbon in Pine Plantations and Native Forests of South Eastern Australia. *Geoderma*. 137: 401-413.

Lal R. 2005. Forest Soils and Carbon Sequestration. Forest Ecology and Management 220: 242-258.

Lu, D. The Potential and Challenge of Remote Sensing-based Biomass Estimation. 2006. *International Journal of Remote Sensing* 27(7-10): 1297-1328.

Ministry of Forests and Soil Conservation (MOFSC). 2011. *Role of Forests on Climate Change Adaptation*. MOFSC, Kathmandu, Nepal.

Moll, E., and G. Moll. 1994. Struik Pocket Guide-Common Trees of Southern Africa Struik Publishers (Pty), Cornelis Struik House, 80 McKenzie Street, Cape Town-South Africa.

Pearson, T.R., S.L. Brown & R.A. Birdsey. 2007. *Measurement Guidelines for the Sequestration of Forest Carbon*. Department of Agriculture. Northern research Station. U.S.

Priyanka Bohre, O.P. Chaubey and P.K. Singhal. 2012, Biomass Accumulation and Carbon Sequestration in *Dalbergia sissoo* Roxb, *International Journal of Bio-Science and Bio-Technology* 4(3), 29-44.

Rikimaru, A., P.S. Roy & S. Miyatake. 2002. Tropical Forest Cover Density Mapping. *Tropical Ecology*. 43(1): 39-47.

Walkley, A. & I.A. Black. 1934. An Examination of Degatjareff Method of Determining Soil Organic Matter and a Proposed Modification of the Chromic Acid Titration Method. *Soil Science*. 37: 29-37.

Westlake, D.F. 1963. Comparisons of Plant Productivity. *Bio. Rev*. 38: 385-425.

Zhao, M. & G.S. Zhou. 2005. Estimation of Biomass and Net Primary Productivity of Major Planted Forests in China Based on Forest Inventory Data. *Forest Ecology and Management*. 207(3): 295-313.

Zhou, C., X. Wei, G.Y.J. Zhou, X. Wang, C. Wang, Liu, X. Tang & Q. Zhang. 2008. Impact of a Large Scale Reforestation Programme on Carbon Storage Dynamics in Guangdong, China. *Forest Ecology and Management*. 255: 846-854.

4

Cassia Fistula - A Medicinal Plant *Review of its Phytochemical and Medicinal Properties*

Vijay Laxmi[1]; A.K. Bhatia[2]
Govind Sharma[3]; Anubhuti Sharma[1*]

ABSTRACT

Cassia fistula (Leguminosae) is a medium size tree with beautiful bunches of yellow flowers used in the traditional medicines in tropical and sub tropical countries. Various phytochemicals are reported from this plant such as anthraquinones, flavonoids, tannins, glycosides, steroids and phenolic compounds. Due to presence of these phytochemicals different parts of Cassia fistula have been used in the treatment of various diseases and showed high therapeutic values. The objective of this paper to review all the experimental studies performed about Cassia fistula and have all valuable information on designing future research plan and its utilization in herbal medicines.

Keywords: *Cassia fistula,* phytochemicals, medicinal properties, laxative Properties, antibacterial property.

INTRODUCTION

Cassia fistula Linn (Leguminosae) is an ornamental tree commonly known as Golden shower, have become extensively distributed in various countries including Mauritus, India, S. Africa, Maxico, China, West Indies, East Africa and Brazil (Trease & Envas, 1985). *Cassia fistula* is first mentioned in *Sushruta*

1. **Banasthali University, Rajasthan, India.**
2. **HOD, Biotech Deptt., GLA University, Mathura, U.P., India.**
3. **NRDC, New Delhi, India.**

Samhita and *Charaka Samhita*. In the Indian literature different parts of *Cassia fistula* have been described to be useful in the treatment of skin diseases, liver troubles, tuberculous glands, haematemesis, pruritus, leucoderm and diabetes (Bahorun *et. al.*, 2005). Ayurveda recognizes the *Cassia fistula* plant as- *Aragvadha* – meaning "disease killer".

Sramsana: *Amaltas* expels the aggravated *doshas* out of the body.

Jwaranuta: It is useful in management of any type of fever.

Hrudaroganuta: It manages all types discomfort in the heart region.

Mridu Virechana: It reduces soft purgation.

Phytochemicals in different parts of *C. fistula*

Fruit

Modi and Khorana, (1952) identified anthraquinone derivative 'rhein' in the pulp. They also confirmed the compound 1, 3-dihydroxy-3-anthraquinone carboxylic acid from the pods. Kapadia and Khorana (1966) confirmed that free rhein are complexed with sennidin like compounds in *C. fistula* pods. A fistulic acid, an anthraquinone acid has been reported from the pods (Agrawal *et. al.*, 1972). Vasi and Kalintha,(1980) indicated that fruit as an important source of nutrients and energy due to presence of protein and carbohydrate contents. The fruit was reported to be a rich source of potassium, calcium Iron, and manganese, also contain 15.3, 13 and 7.8% of aspartic acid, glutamic acid and lysine of the total amino acids respectively in the pulp (Barthakur *et. al.*, 1995). Misra *et. al.*, (1996) isolated a polar compounds including 5- nonatetracontanone, 2-hentriacontanone, triacontane, 16-hentriacontanol and â ?sitosterol along with an oil probably an isoprenoid compound in *C. fistula* pods. 3-formyl-1-hydroxy-8-methoxy-anthraquinone was isolated from the pods (Rani and Kalidhar, 1998). Luximon-Ramma *et. al.*, (2002) studied that pod contained the highest level of phenolic compound.

Leaves

Kaji *et. al.*, (1968) confirmed the presence of free rhein, rhein glucoside and sennosides A and B in leaves. Morimoto *et. al.*, (1988) isolated (-) epiafzelechin 3-O-B-D glucophranoside, 7 biflavanoids and two triflavanoids together with (-) epiafzelechin, (-) epicatechin and procyanidin B-2 from the leaves. Mahesh *et. al.*, (1984), Khanna & Chandra (1996) studied the anthraquinones chrysophanol, rhein and physcion in the leaves, Lohar *et. al.* (1975), Asseleih *et. al.*, (1990), Chowdhury *et. al.*, (1996) reported the characterization of sennosides and their contents in leaves. Luximon-Ramma *et. al.*, (2002) showed that young and old leaves contain highest total phenolic flavanoid and proanthocyanidin contents. Two new aliphatic compound heptacosnyl-5-hydroxypentadic-2 enoate and octacosan-5, 8-dial have been reported from the leaves (Singh *et. al.*, 2005). Evaluation of phytochemicals such as alkaloids, flavonoids, carbohydrates, glycosides, protein and aminoacids, saponins and triterpenoids in polar extracts compared with non polar extracts (Panda *et. al.,* 2011).

Seed

Sen and Shukla (1968), Niranjan and Katiyar (1979) noted 31% of crude proteins comprising mainly globulin and albumin in the wild seed and also found that seeds were rich sources of cephalina and lecithin phospholipids and contained carbohydrates. A major carbohydrates galactomannan consisting of eight different types of sugar moieties was reported by Lal and Gupta, 1976. Abusayeed *et. al.,* (1999) revealed that seeds were rich in glycerides with linoleic, oleic stearic and palmitic acids together and traces of caprylic and myristic acids. Kuo *et. al.,* 2002 identified four new compounds, 5-(2-hydroxyphenoxymethyl) furfural (1), (2′S)-7-hydroxy-5-hydroxymethyl-2-(2′-hydroxypropyl) chromone (2), benzyl 2-hydroxy-3, 6-dimethoxybenzoate (3) benzyl 2beta-O-D-glucopyranosyl-3, 6-dimethoxy-benzoate (4), together with four known compounds, 5-hydroxy-methylfurfural, (2′S)-7-hydroxyl-2-(2′-hydroxyprpyl)-5-methylchromone and two oxyanthraquinones, chrysophanol and chrysophanein were isolated and identified from seeds of *C. fistula.* Aspertic acid, glutamic acid and lysine constituted 16.6, 19.5 and 6.6 respectively of the total amino acids (Barthakur *et. al.,* 1995)

Flowers

Kumar *et. al.,* (1966) isolated a bianthraquninone glycoside, fistulin, together with Kalmpheral and rhein from ethanol extracts of *C. fistula* flower. Narayanan and Seshadri (1972) reported the presence of kaempferal and a proanthacyanidin tetramer having a free glycol in the acetone extract of flowers. Asseleih *et. al.,* 1990 studied a certain amount of alkaloids in the flowers. Traces of triterpenes have been observed in flowers, (Gurib-Fakim *et. al.,* 1994). Mondal *et. al.,* (1998) identified free aminoacids such as phenylalanine, methionine, glutamic acid and proline. Aurantiamide acetate (0.011), â sitosterol (0.006) and its â D glucoside (0.02%) have been isolated from flowers (Rastogi and Mahrotra 2004).

Roots

Vaishnav and Gupta (1996) isolated a compound rhamnetin 3-0-gentibioside in *C. fistula* roots. Root bark besides tannins contain phlobaphenes and oxyanthraquinone substances (Chopra *et. al.,* 2006; Agrawal and Paridhavi 2005). Two new compounds 7-methylphyscion, betulinic acid and â sitosteral have been isolated from the roots (Vaishnav *et. al.,* 1993; Rastogi and Mehrotra 2004).

Other Parts

Padmanabha Rao and Venkateswarlu (1965) extracted fistucacidin, an optically inactive leucoanthocyanidin (3, 4, 7, 8, 4-pentahydroxyflavan) from the heart wood. The stembarks have been shown to contain lupeol, beta sitosterol and hexacotanal (Gupta *et. al.*, 1989). Rani and Kalidhar (1998) have shown the presence of oxyantroquinone and dihydroxyanthroquinone from bark. Luximan – Ramma *et.al.*, (2002) observed proanthocyanidin and flavonoid in vegetative and reproductive organs of *C. fistula*. Priya *et.al.*, (2010) isolated an anthraquinonen derivative, 6-9 dimethyl-3-methyl, 1, 4, 5-trihydroxy-anthraquinone-2-carboxylic acid. It is an antifungal constituent.

Medicinal properties of *C. fistula*

Laxative Properties

Both the leaves and pods widely used in traditional medicines as laxatives suitable for children and pregnant woman (Satyawati and Sharma, 1989; Van, 1976). It is also of purgative and a tonic for many other intestinal disorders like healing ulcers (Biswas and Ghose 1973; Kirtikar and Basu 1975). Akanmu *et. al.*, (2004) concluded that *C. fistula* pod infusion could be safely utilized as laxative drugs and substitute for the *Official Senna*. Sakulpanich and Gritsanapan (2009) studied that the central and North-East dried leaf sample contained about 0.5% w/w of total anthaquinone glycosides and thus they had ability to be developed as an optional herbal laxative drug. Karthikeyn and Gobianand (2010) compared antiulcer activity of ethanolic leaf extract with ranitidine treatment against pylorus legation-induced gastric ulcer and found better recovery in attenuation of gastric volume, pH, free acidity, and total acidity in the gastric juice by ethanolic leaf extract (750 gm/Kg body wt.).

Antibacterial Properties

Patel and Patel (1956) studied the antibacterial potential of alcohol and aqueous extracts of *C. fistula* fruit and seed and observed that the dealcoholized extract of the pulp showed greater effect on gram-positive bacteria than aqueous extract, while in the case of gram negative bacteria both kind of extract exhibited similar effect. Perumal *et. al.*, (1998) tested antibacterial activity of aqueous, diethyl ether, ethylacetate dichloromethane and methanol extract of *C. fistula* leaves against *E. coli, Klebsella aerogenes, Protious vulgaris and Pseudomonas aerogense* at 1000-5000 ppm using the disc diffusion method and reported significant inhibitory effect against of said microorganisms. Abbas (2004) using 30 µg/disc and found to be active against all of the bacterial strains and showed strong activity against *Bacillus megaterium, Streptococcus â-haemolyticus* and *Shigella boydii*. Yogesh and Mohan (2006) observed that methanol extract more effective against *Salmenella paratyphi* and *S. aureus*. Kumar *et. al.* (2006) studied that dichloromethane and methanol extracts were effective against *B. cereus, B. pumilus, Bordefella bronchiseptica, Micrococeus luteus S. aureus, S. epidermids, E.coli, Klelebsiella pneumonie*. Duraipandiyan and Ignacimutu (2007) reported that hexane, chloroform, ethyl acetate, methanol and water extracts of flower of *C. fistula* exhibited activity against gram positive organisms and among the gram negative bacteria only *Pseudomonas aeruginosa* was susceptible to the extracts.

Ali *et. al.*, (2007) successfully formulated new, cost effective antimicrobial combination for Multi Drug Resistant (ADR) *Salmonella enterica, Serover Typhi (SETS)* based on the synergistic activity of amoxicillin with *C. fistula*. Sangetha *et. al.*, (2008) reported that methanolic extracts of different parts of *C. fistula* showed effect against *S. typhi, E.coli, Azospirillum lipoferum, K. pneumonicae, S. aureus, E. aerogenes and B. subtilis*. Vimalraj *et. al.*, (2009) tested antibacterial activity of aqueous and alcoholic extract of stem bark against pathogenic bacteria of veterinary importance and observed activity against only *S. aureus*. Vasudevan *et. al.*, (2009) showed that alcoholic extract of leaves have significant antimicrobial activity against *S. aureus, P. aeruginosa, E. coli* and Group A *Streptococci*. Awal *et.al.*, (2010) studied antibacterial activity of ethanol extracts of leaf and roots of *C. fistula* and found that the leaf extract was comparatively better antibacterial property against five gram positive bacteria namely *Sarcina lutea, Bacillus megaterium, Bacillus subtilis, Streptococcus* β-*haemolyticus, Staphylococcus aureus* and nine gram negative bacteria – *Salmonella typhi, Shigella dysenteri, Shigella boydii, Shigella sonni, Shigella flexneri, Shigella shag, E. coli, Pseudomonas aeruginosa* and *Klebsiella pnumoniae*. Venkatesan *et. al.*, (2010) observed that alcoholic extract of aerial parts of *C. fistula* showed activity against *S. aureus and E. coli*. Growther & Janardhanan (2010) found that ethanol, methanol and petroleum ether extract of *C. fistula* effective against MRSA (Methicillin resistant *Staphylococcus aureus*) and MSSA (Methicillin sensitive *Staphylococcus aureus*). Bhalodia *et. al.*, (2011) found that hydroalcohol and chloroform extract of flowers were effective against *Staphylococcus aureeus, Streptococcus pyogenes, E. coli* and *P. aeruginosa*. Both extracts showed dose dependent activity. Singh *et. al.*, (2011) showed that alcohol extract of flower materials of *C. fistula* exhibited activity against *B subtilis, K. pneumonia, Pseudomonas aeruginosa* and *S. aureus*. Aneja *et. al.*, (2011) evaluated anti microbial potential of *C. fistula* against the pathogens causing otitis externa and found that organic extracts of flowers, stembark and leaves produced significant inhibition zones against tested bacteria.

Antifungal Activity

C. fistula plant has been widely used by tribal people to treat various ailments including ringworm and other fungal skin infections (Rajan *et. al.*, 2001). Phongpaichit *et. al.*, 2004) investigated that *C. fistula* was the most potent inhibitor of *P. marneffei* and methanol extracts of *C. alata, C. fistula* and *C. tora* inhibited the hypal growth of *Trichophyton rubrum, Peniclillium marneffli* and *Microsperum gypseum*. Kumar *et. al.*, (2006) found that dichloromethanolic and methanolic extract of pod exihibited activity against *Aspergillus niger*. Singh *et. al.*, (2006) observed that methanol extract of leaves exhibited highest activity (21 mm) for *C. albicans*. A crystal was isolated, which was confirmed as 4-hydroxy benzoic acid hydrate and it exhibited antifungal activity against *Trichophyton mentagraphytes* and *Epidermophyton floccosum* (MIC 0.5 mg/ml) (Drudiphandiyan and Ignqcimuthu 2007). Methanolic extracts of different parts (leaves, flowers, stem and pods) of *C. fistula* showed inhibition zone against *C. albicans* and *A. niger* (Sangetha *et. al.*, 2008). Panda *et. al.*, (2010) studied that petroleum ether, chloroform, ethanol, methanol and aqueous extracts of *C. fistula* leaves exhibited antifungal activity against *Candila albicans* (12.6 mm), *C. krusei* (13.3 mm), *C. parapsilosis* (14 mm) and *C. tropicalis* (14.3 mm). Petroleum ether and ethnol extract also showed zone of inhibition for *A. niger* (12.0 mm). Priya *et. al.*, 2010 found that methanol extract of bark showed good antifungal activity than other extracts of different parts due to presence of antifungal constituent anthraquinone derivative. Hydroalcohol and chloroform extracts of flowers and found both extracts effective against *Aspergillus niger, A. clavatus,* and *C. albicans*. Bhalodia *et. al.*, (2011)

Antiviral Activity

Ethanolic extract of pod and stem bark of *C. fistula* were found active against Ranikhet disease virus (RDV) and *Vaccinia* virus (Dhar *et. al.*, 1968). Narong *et. al.*, (2007) found that *C. fistula* fruit have activity against foot and mouth disease virus (FMD virus). Sharma *et. al.*, 2010 studied that hot aqueous extract of pods of *C. fistula* have antiviral activity against IBR virus in dose dependant manner.

Antiparasitic Activity

Sartorelli *et. al.*, (2007) isolated Clerosterol compound from methanolic extract of fruit which infer 50% inhibitory concentration of 10.03 μg/ml against promastigot of *Leishmamia chagasi* and 18.10 μg/ml for intracellular amenstigotes. In another study Sartorelli *et. al.*, (2009) isolated biochanin-A an isoflavone compound from dichloromethane extract of fruits of *C. fistula* which infer 50% effective concentration value of this compound 18.96 μg/ml against promastigot of *Leishmamia chagasi*. They also studied that biochanin-A showed anti Tripanosama-cruzi activity with effective concentration value of 18.32 μg/ml and 2-4 fold more containers then benznidizole.

Antioxidant Activity of *C. fistula*

Jawahar and Gupta (1972) reported that stem bark and leaf extracts exhibited highest superoxide radical scavenging and reducing power than other parts in a dose-dependent manner. It contacts a 4 ortho postion hydroxyl which provides active hydrogen to take part in reaction to scavenge O_2. Gupta *et. al.*, (1990), Kashiwada *et. al.*, (1990) showed that some of the bioactive compounds like exanthones flavonols and pro anthocyanidins present in the stem bark and leaf extract, should performed as good singlet oxygen quenchers, they also noted DPPH radical scavenging ability of the stem bank and leaves extract might be due to the presence of high concentration of tannins, proanthocynidins flavonols and xanthones indicated the ability of *C. fistula* extract to act as radical scavenger and metal quencher thereby, protecting free radical mediated damage. Sunil and Muller (1998) showed that methanolic extract of fruit has been reported to inhibit 2,2-azo-bis(2-amidinopropane)-dihydrochloride (AAPH) induced lipid peroxidation in bovine brain phospholipids. Chaminda *et. al.,* (2001) reported that in *vitro* 1, 1-diphenyl-2-picrylhydrazyl-2-picrylhydrazyl (DPPH) radical scavenging and deoxyribose damage protection properties by using aqueous extract of root. Siddhuraju *et. al.,* (2002) calculated DPPH readical scavenging activities in order, stem bark 93%, leaves 74.9%, butylated hydroxytoluene BHT 37.8%, flowers 33.2%, pulp 15.7% and noted that it was directly proportional to total phenolic content in its extract. Suresh *et. al.,* (2008) also reported lipid peroxidation inhibition of leaves extract. Luximon – Ramma *et. al.,* (2002) found that reproductive organs of *C. fistula* have highest antioxidant properties compare to vegetative part, the antioxidant properties were found in the following order: pod > flower > stem > bark > leaves and it was also directly proportional to the content of total phenols, proanthocyanidins and flavanoids in it extract. Raju *et. al.,* (2005) studied, bark extract found to have radical scavenging capacity also by inhibiting lipid peroxidation in CCL_4 and $FeSO_4$ induced liver homogenate. Bhalodia *et. al.,* (2011) investigated that the hydroalcoholic extract of *C. fistula* showed antioxidant activity of inhibiting DPPH and hydroxyl radical, total phenol content and reducing power activities.

Hepatoprotective Acivity

Bhakta *et. al.,* (1999) found that n-heptane extract of *C. fistula* leaves at a dose of 400 µg/ml showed significant hepatoprotective activity against CCl_4 and liquid paraffin induced hepatic damage in rats, which was comparable to that of a standard hepatoprotective agent. Kannampalli *et. al.,* (2005) showed that ethyl extracts of leaves in CCl_4 induced hepatotoxicity in rats, restored three fold elevated malondialdehyde (MDA) level. Kannampalli *et. al.,* (2007) again investigated that oral administration of ethyl extract of leaves restored the normal values of aspatate, alanine tranaminase, alkaline phosphatase, γ-glutamyl tranferase, lactate dehydrogenase and serum billirubine of serum in diethylenitrosamine (DEN) induced hepatic damage. Das *et. al.,* (2008) showed significant hepatoprotective activity of aqueous extract of fruit pulp of *C. fistula* against CCl_4 induced liver damage in albino rats. Patwardhan *et. al.,* (2009) investigated heptoprotective activity of ethanolic extract of bark against hepatotoxicity induced by CCl_4 with olive oil (1:1), and noticed significant decrease in AST, ALT, ALP, tryglycerides, bilirubin and protein levels in comparison to CCl_4 control group. Wasu and Mully (2009) found that daily oral consumption of an aqueous extract of the

C. fistula leaves and bark reduced the CCl_4 toxicity. Chaudhari *et. al.,* (2009) observed that the methanolic extract of seeds marked reduction in the elevated level of SGOT, SGPT, SALP and serum billurubin. Jahangir *et. al.,* (2010) observed that co-treatment of *C. fistula* leaf extract preventive INH and RIF (Isoniazed and Rifampicin) induced hepatotoxicity in rats and showed both biochemically and morphologically hepatoprotective effect of *C. fistula* due to counteraction of free radicals by its flavonoids acting as antioxidant.

Anti-inflammatory, Analgesic and Antipyretic Potential of *C. fistula*

Patel *et. al.,* (1965) reported analgesic and antipyretic action. Mazumdar *et. al.,* (1998) also observed sedative and analgesic action of *C. fistula* seeds. Raju *et. al.,* (2005) showed that aqueous and methanol extract of stem bark reduced the weight of cotton pellet granuloma and paw oedima in rats at significant level. The anti-inflammatory activities of aqueous and alcoholic extracts of *C. fistula* bark were found to posses anti-inflammatory effect in both air pouch granuloma and cotton pallet granuloma models and reduce biomarker enzymes, acid phosphates in serum (Rajeswari *et. al.,* 2006). Patel *et al.,* (2010) reported that methanol extract at a dose of 300 mg/Kg body weight showed maximum antipyretic activity amongst other extracts which was statistically significant as a the value of $p < 0.05$. Anwikar *et al.,* (2010) investigated that aqueous extract of fruit showed maximum anti-inflammatory activity at 500 mg/Kg dose against carragenan-induced pow edema model in rats. Gobianand *et. al.,* (2010) found ethanolic extract of *C. fistula* significantly inhibited both the carrageenan induced hind paw odema and cotton-pellet granuloma, ethanolic extract at 250 and 500 mg $Kg^{-1b\ wt}$; reduced TAB vaccine induced pyredia in rats after 60 minutes, where as at 750 mg $Kg^{-1\ wt}$; it reduced the vaccine induced elevated body temperature post 30 minutes of its administration. Sheikh *et. al.,* (2010) studied analgesic activity of *C. fistula* methyl alcohol extract in wistar albino rats and it showed significant inhibition in pain response induced by thermal, mechanical and writhing stimuli in dose dependant manner.

Wound Healing Property

Kumar *et. al.,* (2006) observed that *C. fistula* treated rats exhibited; better wound closer, improved tissue regeneration at the wound site. The ethanolic extracts of leaves have been found to have wound healing activity by tissue regeneration at the site of wound (Muthusamy *et. al.,* 2006; Bhakta *et. al.,* 1998).

Hypoglycemic and Hypocholesterolaemic Potentials of *C. fistula*

Singh and Bhardwaj (1975) preliminary examined hypoglycemic effect of seed in normal rat. el Saadany *et.al.,* (1991) investigated hypochloesterolaemic potential of the legume of *C. fistula* in hypercholesterolaemic rats and showed that administration of extract significantly reduced blood and liver total lipids. They also noted that it induced a significant decrease in the serum GOT, CPT, alkaline and acid phosphatase values. Espasito *et. al.*, (1997) showed that aqueous extract of leaves significantly decreased glycemia. Bhakta *et. al.*, (1997) reported that methanol extract of leaves significantly reduced blood glucose level up to 25.2% and 45.7% at the dose of 400 mg/Kg and 600 mg/Kg respectively at the end of 10 h in alloxan diabetic rats.

Nirmala *et. al.*, (2008) studied that hexane extract of *C. fistula* bark at doses 0.15, 0.30, 0.45 Kg $^{-1}$ weight for 30 days suppressed the elevated blood glucose levels in diabetic rats. The ethyl acetate fraction exhibited significant reduction in blood glucose levels than alcoholic extract and found effective in restoring blood lipids to normal levels against in alloxan induced diabetic rats (Malpani *et. al.*, 2010).

Other Bioefficacies of *C. fistula*

Bhakta *et. al.*, (1998) studied dose dependant antitussive activity of *C. fistula leaf* extract (400, 600 mg/Kg, body weight) showed maximum inhibition of cough in mice induced by sulfur dioxide gas.

Gupta *et. al.*, (2000) studied antitumor activity of methanolic extract (ME) and showed an increase of life span and a decrease in the tumar volume and viable tumar cell count in the Ehrlich ascites carcinoma (EAC) tumar hosts.

Yadav and Jain (1999) reported that aqueous extract of seeds of *C. fistula* prevented pregnancy in all the treated female rats by virtue of anti-implantation property with antiestrogenic activity. In another experiment it is concluded that its antiestrogenic nature alters the biochemical milieu of the reproductive tract and produce significant antifertility effect (Yadav and Jain, 2009).

The fruit of *C. fistula* combination with amoxicillin (Amoxy-Cassia) have been reported to have immunomodulatory effect on humoral immune system in BLB/C mice (Ali *et. al.*, 2008). Das *et. al.*, (2008) evaluated that *C. fistula* has significant kusthaghna activity and also in systemic and local therapy for skin disorders in general and vicharchika (enzyme).

Govindrajan *et. al.*, (2009) tested the leaf extract of *C. fistula* for the larvicidal, ovicidal and repellent activity against *Aedes aegypti* and showed that the crude extract of *C. fistula* served as a potential larvicidal, ovicidal and repellent agent against Chikungunya vector mosquito, *Aedes aegypti*. Mehdi *et. al.*, (2010) studied larvicidal property of leaf extract of *C. fistula* mosquito along with delayed morphogenetic effects that exhibited IGR activity pertaining to its effect on growth and development.

Khatib *et. al.*, (2010) reported cardio protective effect of the methanolic extract of *C. fistula* bark against doxorubicin induced cardio toxicity and showed that treated rats significantly decreased the elevated levels of serum enzymes histological disturbances and electrocardiogram changes to normal myocardium functioning.

Hernandez and Leonido *et. al.,* (2010) showed that tannins present in methanolic extract of C. *fistula* can significantly and effectively reduced the body weight of paramaterial fat in diet induced lipidemia in mice.

Kalantri and Zsuga *et. al.,* (2011) found that bromobenzene induced nephrotoxicity in mice reflected by the hydro-alcoholic extract of fruit of C. *fistula* and nephroprotective, effect was confirmed by the histological examination of the kidneys.

Ziyaurrahman *et. al.,* (2011) investigated that hydroalcoholic extract of C. *fistula* leaf extract were found to possess significant neuropathy activity. C. *fistula* leaf was unable to protect the animals from acrylamide while it was able to reverse alcohol induced peripheral neuropathy in dose dependant manner in the rats and showed that C. *fistula* could be of immense importance in the amelioration of the mono neuropathy in the human beings.

Hanif *et. al.,* (2006) studied that C. *fistula* biomass act as naturally occurring biosorbent for the batch removal of Ni (II) and this sorption ability tends to be in the order: leaves < stem bark > pods bark.

Ramesh *et. al.,* (2010) evaluated anti-urolithiatic activity of the wood bark extracts of C. *fistula* in sodium oxalate induced urolithiasis in rats and found methanolic and aqueous extracts were significantly increased urine output and elimination of sodium and chlorides.

CONCLUSION

C. *fistula* is rich source of phenolic compounds, tannins, flavanoids and glycosides. Various bioactive phenolic compounds present in both *in vivo* and *in vitro* extracts may prove to be very important antioxidants. Extracts prepared from different parts may be used in protecting against a number of diseases; thus the plant C. *fistula* has a lot of therapeutic value in folk and herbal medicine. This paper is likely to be an important source on designing any future research on C. *fistula* for their other utilization in herbal medicine.

REFERENCES

1. Abbas AM, Abu-sayeed M, Bhuiyan MSA, Sohel FI, Sarmina Y, Antimicrobial Screening of *C. fistula* and *Mesua ferrea,*. J of Med. Sci, 4 (2004) 24-29.
2. Abu Sayeed M, Abbas Ali M, Astaq Mohal Khan GRM, Rahman MS, Studied on the Characterization and Glyceride Composition of *Cassia fistula* Seed Oil, Bangladesh J. Sci. Indust. Res., 34(1999) 144-148.
3. Agarwal GD, Rizvi SAI Gupta PC, Tewari JD, Structure of Fistulic Acid a New Colouring Matter from the Pods of *Cassia fistula,* Planta Med., 2 (1972) 150-155.
4. Agrawal SS, Paridhavi M, Clinicallly Useful Herbal Drugs, Ahuja Pub. House, (2005) 281-282.

5. Akanmu MA, Iwalewa EO, Lujoba AA, Adelusola KA, Toxicity Potentials of *Cassia fistula* Fruits as Laxative with Reference to Senna. African J. of Biom. Res. 7 (2004) 23-26.
6. Ali NH, Kazmi SU Faizi S (2007). Activity of Synergistic Combination Amoxy-Cassia against *salmonella*. Pak. J. Pharm. Sci. 20: 140-145.
7. Ali NH, Kazmi SU, Faizi S (2008). Modulation of Humoral Immunity by *Cassia fistula* and Amoxy-Cassia. Pak. J. Pharm. Sci. 21: 21-23.
8. Aneja KR, Sharma CS, Joshi R (2011) *In vitro* Efficacy of *C. fistula* L. Against the Pathogens Causing Otitis Externa. Jundishapur J. Microbiology, 4(3), 175-183.
9. Anwikar S, Bhitre M (2010). Study of the Synergistic Anti-inflammatory Activity of *S. xanthocarpum, C. fistula* L. Inst J. Ayrveda Res. 1: 167-171.
10. Asseleih LMC, Hernandez OH, Sanchez JR (1990). Seasonal Variation in the Content of Sennosides in Leaves and Pods of Two *Cassia fistula* Populations. Phytochemistry 29: 3095-3099.
11. Awal MA, Ahsan SM, Haque E, Asghar QH, Ahmad M (2010). *In-vitro* Antibacterial Activity of Leaf and Root Extract of *C. fistula*. Dinajpur med. Clg. J, 3: 10-13.
12. Bahorun T, Neergheen VS, Aruoma OI (2005). Phytochemical Constituents of *Cassia fistula*. Afr. J. Biotechnology 4: 1530-1540.
13. Barthakur NN, Arnold NP, Alli I (1995). The Indian Labernum (*Cassia fistula* L.) Fruit: An Analysis of its Chemical Constituents. Plant Foods Human Nutr. 47: 55-62.
14. Bhakta T, Mukharjee PK, Mukharjee K, Banerjee S, Mandal SC, Maity TK, Pal M, Saha BP (1999). Evaluation of Hepatoprotective Activity of *Cassia fistula* Leaf Extract. J. Ethnopharmacol. 66: 277-282.
15. Bhakta T, Mukharjee PK, Pal M, Saha BP (1998a). Studies on Antitussive Activity of *Cassia fistula* (Leguminosae) Leaf Extract. Pharm. Biol. 36: 140-143.
16. Bhakta T, Mukharjee PK, Pal M, Saha BP (1998b). Studies on *In vivo* Wound Healing Activity of *Cassia fistula* Linn. Leaves (Leguminosae) in Rats. Nat. Prod. Sci. 4: 84-87.
17. Bhakta T, Mukharjee PK, Saha K, Pal M, Saha BP (1997). Hypoglycemic Activity of *Cassia fistula* Linn. (Leguminosae) Leaf (Methanol Extract) in Alloxan-induced Diabetic rats. J. Ethnobot. 9: 35-39.
18. Bhalodia N, Nariya PB, Acharya RN, Shukla VJ (2011) Evaluation of *In vitro* Antioxidant Activity of Flowers of *C. fistula* Linn. Int. J. Pharma Tech. Res. 3(I) 589-599.
19. Bhalodia NR, Nariya PB, Shukla VJ (2011). Antibacterial and Antifungal Activity from Flower Extracts of C. *fistula*. L. Inst. J. Pharm Tech. Res. 3 (1) 160-168.
20. Biswas K, Ghose AB (1973). In Bharatia Banawasadhi, Calcutta University, Advertisement of Learning, Calcutta 2: 336.
21. Chaminda T, Munasinghe J, Seneviratne CK, Thabrew MI, Abeysekera AM (2001). Antiradical and Anti Lipoperoxidative Effects of Some Plant Extracts Used by Sri Lankan Traditional Medical Practitioners for Cardioprotection. Phytother. Res. 15: 519-523.

22. Chaudhari NB, Chittan KP, Patil VR (2009) Hepatoprotective Activity of C. *fistula* Seeds Against Paracetamol-Induced Hepatic Injury in rats. Arch Pharm Sci & Res Vol 1, No. 2 218-221.
23. Chopra RN, Nayar SL, Chopra IC (2006). Glossary of Indian Medicinal plants: National Inst. Of Science Communication and Information Resources Page No.-54.
24. Chowdhury SA, Mustafa Kamal AKM, Alam MN, Gafur MA, Ray BK, Ahmed K, Faruq O (1996). Sennoside B Rich Active Concentrate from *Cassia fistula*. Bangladesh J. Sci. Res. XXXI 31: 91-97.
25. Das S, Sarkar PK, Sengupta A, Chattopadhyay AA (2008). Clinical Study of Aragvadha (*Cassia fistula* Linn.) on Vicharchika (Eczema). J. Res. Educ. Indian Med. 27-32.
26. Das S, Sarma G, Barman S (2008). Heptoprotective Activity of Aqueous Extract of Fruit Pulp of *Cassia fistula* (AFCF) Induced Liver Damage in Albino Rats. J. Clin. Diagn. Res. 2: 1133-1138.
27. Dhar ML, Dhar MM, Dhawan BN, Mehrotra Ray C (1968). Screening of Indian Plant for Biological Activity: Ind. J. of Exp. Bio. 1: 232-247.
28. Duraipandiyan V, Ignacimuthu S (2007). Antibacterial and Antifungal Activity of *Cassia fistula* L.: An Ethnomedicinal Plant J. Ethnopharm. 11: 590-594.
29. EI Saadany SS, EI-massry RA, Labib SM, Sitohy MZ (1991). The Biochemical Role and Hypocholesterolaemic Potential of the Legume *Cassia fistula* in Hypercholesterolaemic Rats. Die Nahrung. 35: 807-815.
30. Esposito AM, Diaz A, De-Gracia I, De-Tello R, Gupta MP (1991). Evaluation of Traditional Medicine: Effects of *Cajanus cajan* and *Cassia fistula* L on Carbohydrates Metabolism in Mice, Rev. Med. Panama, 16: 39-45.
31. Gobianand K, Vivekanandan K, Pradeep K, Mohan CVR, Karthikeyan S (2010). Antiinflamatory and Antipyretic Activities of Indian Medicinal Plant C.*fistula*.L. in Wistar albino rats. Int. J pharmacol 1811-7775.
32. Govindrajan M. (2009) Bioefficacy of C. *fistula* L. (Leguminosae) Leaf Extract Against Chikungunya Vector, *Aedes aegypti* (Diptera : Culicidae). 13: 99-103.
33. Growther L and Janardhanan J (2010), Antibacterial Actvity of Traditional Medicinal Plants Against Methicillin Resistance *Staph. aureus* and Methicillin Sensitive *Staph aureus* The IUP J. Biotech. Vol. IV (I), 7-12.
34. Gupta M, Maziumder UK, Rath N, Mukhopadhyay DK (2000). Antitumour Activity of Methanolic Extract of *Cassia fistula* L. Seed Against Ehrilich Ascites Carcinoma. J. Ethnophrmacol. 72: 151-156.
35. Gupta UC and Jain GC (2009). Study on Hypolipidemic Activity of *Cassia fistula* Legume in Rats Asian J. Exp. Sci. 23(1): 241-248.
36. Gupta V, Agrawal A, singh J and Tiwari HPC (1989). Isolation and Characterization of Two Flavoral & a xanthone glycoside from the Stem Bark of C. *fistula* Linn. Indian J. of Chem 28B: 282-284.
37. Gurib-Fakim A, Gueho J, Sewraj MD, Dulloo E (1994). Plantes Medicinales de I'lle Maurice, Editions de L'Ocean Indian, Maritius, p. 580.
38. Hanif AM, Nadeem R, Bhatt: HN, Ahmad NR Ansari TM (2006). J. Hazardous matter 10: 139 (2): 345-355.

39. Hernandez CLC and Leonido FMG (2011) Weight-lowering Effects of *Caesalpinia pidcerrima, C. fistula* and *Senna alata* Leaf Extracts. J. of Mediwal Plants Research Vol. 5 (3) 452-455.
40. Jahangir A, Nagi AH, Shahzad and Zia A (2010). The Helpato-protective Effect of *C. fistula* Leaves in Isoniazid and Rifampicin Induced Hepatotoxicity in Rodents. Biomedica Vol. 26: 25-29.
41. Jawahar L, Gupta PC (1972) Galactomannan from the Seed of *C. fstula*. Planta Media. 21: 70-77.
42. Kaji NN, Khorana ML, Sanghvi MM (1968). Studies on *Cassia fistula* Linn. Indian J. Pharm. 30: 8-11.
43. Kalantri H and Zsuga J (2011) Protective Effect of *C. fistula* Fruit Extract on Bromobenzene -induced Nephrotoxcity in mice. Human exp.Toxicol. 30 (4).
44. Kannampali P, Chandrasekaran VRM, Kuppannan GA, Sivanesan K (2005). Effect of Pretreatment of *Cassia fistula* Linn Leaf Extract Against Subacute CCl_4 Induced Hepatotoxicity in Rats, Indian J. Exp. Biol. 43: 526-530.
45. Kannampali P, Chandrasekaran VRM, Kuppannan GA, Sivanesan K (2007). Effect of *Cassia fistula* Linn Leaf Extract on Diethylnitrosamine Induced Hepatic Injury in Rats. Chemico-Biological interaction. 167: 12-18.
46. Kapadia GJ, Khorana ML (1966). Studies of Active Constituents of *Cassia fistula* pulp. I. Colorimetric Estimation of Free rhein and Combined sennidin-like Compounds. Lloydia. 25: 55-58.
47. Karthikeyan S Gobianand K (2010) Antiulcer Activity of Ethanol Leaf Extract of *C. fistula*. Pharm Bio. Aug; 48 (8): 869-77.
48. Kashiwada Y, Toshika K, Chen R, Nanaka G, Nishioka I (1990). Tannin and Related Compounds. XCIII. Occurrence of Enantiomeri Pranthocyanidins in the Leg. Plant, *C. fistula, C. javanica,* L. Chem. Pharm. Bull. 38: 888-893.
49. Khanna RK, Chandra S (1996). Forest/Domestic Waste as a Source of Natural Dyes. J. Econ. Bot. 20: 497-500.
50. Khatib NA, Wadulkar RD, Joshi RK, Majagi SI (2010). Evaluation of Methanolic Extract of *C. fistula* Bark for Cardioprotective Activity. Int. J. Res. In Ayurveda & Pharmacy, 1 (2), 565-571.
51. Kirtikar KR, Basu BD (1975). In: B. Singh and M. Pal Singh (Eds), Indian Medicinal Plants, Dehradun. 2: 858.
52. Kumar A, Pande CS, Kaul RK (1966). Chemical Examination of *Cassia fistula* Flowers. Indian J. Chem. 4: 460.
53. Kumar VP, Chauhan NS, Padhi H, Rajani M (2006). Search for Antibacterial and Antifungal Agents from Selected Indian Medicinal Plants. J Ethnopharmacol; 67: 241-45.
54. Kuo YH, Lee PH, Wein YS (2002). Four New Compounds from the Seeds of *Cassia fistula*. J. Nat. Prod. 65: 1165-1167.
55. Lal J, Gupta PC (1976). Partial Hydrolysis and the Structure of the Galatomannan from *Cassia fistula* Seeds. Plants med. 30: 378-383.
56. Lohar DR, Chawan DD, Garg SP (1975). Phytochemical Studies on *Cassia* Species of Indian Arid Zone. Curr. Sci. 44: 67.

57. Luximon-Ramma A, Bahorun T, Soobrattee MA, Aruoma Ol (2002). Antioxidant Activities of Phenolic, Proanthocyanidins, and Flavonoid Components in Extracts of *Cassia fistula*, J Agric. Food Chem. 50: 5042-5047.

58. Mahesh VK, Sharma R, Singh RS (1984). Antraquinonnes and Kaempferol from *Cassia fistula* species. J Nat. Prod. 47: 733-751.

59. Malpani SN, Manjunath KP, Hasanpasha S, Savadi RV, Akki Kusum S and Darade SS (2010). Antidiabetic Activity of *Cassia fistula* linn. bark in Alloxan Induced Diabetic rats. Int. J. of Pharm. Sciences. 02: 382-385.

60. Mazumdar UK, Gupta M, Rath N (1998). CNS activities of *Cassia fistula* in mice, Phytother. Res. 12: 520-522.

61. Mehdi SH, Qamar A, Khan I and Tayyaba PI (2011). Studies on Larvicidal and IGR Properties of Leaf Extract of *C. fistula* and *Saraca indica*. J. of Herbal Med. and Toxicology 5(1): 79-86.

62. Misra TN, Singh RS, Pandev HS Pandev RP (1996). Chemical Constituents of Hexane Fraction of *Cassia fistula* pods. Fitoterapia LXVII (57): 173-174.

63. Modi FK, Khorana ML (1952). A Study of *Cassia fistula* Pulp. Indian J. Pharm. 4: 61-63.

64. Mondal AK, Parul S, Mandal S (1998). Biochemical Analysis of Four Species of *Cassia* L. Pollen. Aerobiologia 14: 45-50.

65. Morimoto S, Nonaka G, Chen R (1988). Tannin and Related Compounds. LXI. Isolation and Structures of Novel bi-and Triflavonoids from the Leaves of *Cassia fistula* L; Chem. Pharm. Bull. 36: 39-47.

66. Muthusamy SK, Ramasamy S, Harinarayan VR, Praveen KS (2006). Wound Healing Potential of *Cassia fistula* on Infected albino rat model. J. Surgical Res. 131: 283-289.

67. Narayanan V, Seshadri TR (1972). Proanthocyanidins of *Cassia fistula*. Indian J. Chem. 10: 379-381.

68. Narong C, Teerapol S, Wilairat C, Worawidh W (2007). In *vitro* Study of Disease Virus. Kasetsari J. (Nat. Sci.). 41: 97-103.

69. Niranjan GS, Katiyar SK (1979). Chemical Analysis of Some Wild Leguminous Seeds. J. Indian Chem. Soc. LVI (56): 722-725.

70. Nirmala A, Eliza J, Rajalakshmi M, Edel P, Daisy P (2008). Effect of Hexane Extract of *C. fistula* Bark on Blood Glucose and Lipid Profile in Streptozotocin Diabetic Rats. Int. J. Pharmacol 2008; 4: 292-296.

71. Padmanabha Rao TV, Venkateshwarlu V (1965). "Fistucacidin" from the Bark and Heartwood of *Cassia fistula* Linn. Bull. Nat. Ins. Sci. 31: 28-33.

72. Panda SK, Brahma S and Dutta SK (2010). Selective Antifungal Action of Crude Extracts of *C. fistula* L.: A Preliminary Study on *Candida & Aspergillus* Species. Mal. J. Microbiol. Vol 6 (1), 62-68.

73. Panda SK, Padhi LP, Mahanty G (2011). Antibacterial Activities and Phytochemical Analysis of *C. fistula* leaf J. Adv. Pharm Tech Res; 2: 62-67.

74. Patel D, Karbhari D, Gulati D, Gokhale D (1965). Antipyretic and Analgesic Activities of *A. sapticatum* and *C. fistula*. Pharmaceutical Biology, 157, 22-27.

75. Patel N, Gautam JK, Shaoo P, Gupta A, Manish G (2010). Antipyretic Potential of Different Extracts of *C. fistula* L. Bark. Inter J of Res. In Ayurveda and Pharmacy 1(2), Nov-Dec. 634-636.

76. Patel RP, Patel KC, (1956). Antibacterial Activity of *Cassia fistula*. Indian J. Pharm. 18(4): 107-110.
77. Patwardhan S, Vandal P, Singhani AK, Somani R (2009) Studied Hepatoprotective Activity of Ethanolic Extract of *C. fistula* Bark Against CCl_4 Induce Hepatic Damage in Rat. Pharmacologyonline 2: 50-63.
78. Perumal R, Samy S, lggnacimuthu S., Sen A (1998). Screening of 34 Medicinal Plants Antibacterial Properties. J. Ethnopharm. 62: 173-182.
79. Phongpaichit S, Pujenjob N, Rukachaisirkul V, Ongsakul M (2004). Antifungal Activity from Leaf Extracts of *Cassia alata* L., *Cassia fistula* L. and *Cassia tora* L. Songklanakarin. J Sci. and Tech. 26: 741-748.
80. Priya S, Afsar Z, Khanam S, Bhuvaneshwari (2010) Studies on Antifungal Activity of Different Extracts of *C. fistula* and Bioactivity Guided Isolation and Identification of Antifungal Agent. Internat J. of Pharma Word Res. Vol. 1 (2).
81. Rajan S, Baburaj DS, Sethuraman M and Parmimal S (2001) Stem and Stem Bark Used Medicinally by the Tribal Irulas and Paniyas of Nilgiri District, Tamilnadu. Ethnobotany 6, 19-24.
82. Rajeshwari R, Thejomoorthy P, Mathuram LN, Narayan Raju KVS (2006). Anti-inflammatory Activity of *Cassia fistula* linn. Bark Extracts in Sub-acute Models of Inflammation in Rats. Tamilnadu J. Vet. Anim Sci. 2(5): 193-199.
83. Raju I, Moni M, Subramanian V (2005). Anti-inflammatory and Antioxidant Activities of *Cassia fistula* Linn Bark Extracts. Afr. J. Trad. CAM. 2(1): 70-85.
84. Ramesh C, Dharmendra KBK, Sinstien JW, Saleum BS, Girish K (2010) Anti Urolihiatic Activity of Used Bark Extracts of *C. fistula* in Rats. JPBMS, 2(12).
85. Rani M, Kalidhar SB (1998). A New Anthraquinone Derivative from *Cassia fistula* Linn. Pods. Indian J. Chem. 37B: 1314-1315.
86. Rastogi RP and Mehrotra BN(2004) Compendium of Indian Medicinal Plants, Central Drug Research Institute, Lucknow and Nat. Institute of Science Communication and Information Resources, New Delhi (4) 155-156.
87. Sakulpanich A and Gritsanapan W (2009). Extraction Method for High Content of Anthraquinones of *Cassia fistula* pods. J. Health Res. 4: 167-172.
88. Sakulpanich A, Gritsanapan W (2009). Determination of Anthraquinone Glycoside Content in *C. fistula* Leaf Extract for Alternative Source of Laxative Drug. Int. J Biomedical & Pharmaceutical Sci-3(1), 42-45.
89. Sangetha SN, Zuraini Z, Sasidharan S, Suryani S (2008). Antimicrobial Activities of Cassia Suranttensis and Cassia fistula. J. Mol. Biol. Biotech. 1: 1-4.
90. Sartorelli P , Camila Salomone C, Juliana Quero R, Mrcelo Jose P Ferreira and Andre G Tempone (2009). Antiparasitic Activity of Biochanin A, an Isolated Isoflavone from Fruits of *Cassia fistula* (Leguminosae). Journal of Parasitology Research. 104: 311-314.
91. Sartorelli P, Samanta P, Andrade, Marcia SC, Melhem Frederico O, Prado Andre G Tempone (2007). Isolation of Antileishmanial Sterol from the Fruits of *Cassia fistula* using Bioguided Fractionation. Journal of Phytotherapy Research. 21: 644-647.
92. Satyavati GV, Sharma M (1989). In Medicinal Plant in India. ICMR, New Delhi.

93. Sen AB, Shukla YN (1968). Chemical Examination of *Cassia fistula*. J. Indian Chem. Soc. 45: 744.
94. Senthil Kumar M, Sripriya R, Raghavan VH, Sehgal P (2006) Wound Healing Potential of *C. fistula* on Infected Albino Rat model. J. Surg Res 131: 283-289.
95. Sharma A, Laxmi V, Goel A, Sharma V and Bhatia AK (2010) Anti Viral Activity of *C. fistula* Against IBR virus. J. immunol. Immunopath. 2010. 12(2): 114-119.
96. Sheikh NW, Patel RD, Upwar NI, Mahobia NK, Seth MV, Panchal UR (2010). *Analgesic* Study of Methyl Alcohol Extract of *C. fistula* Pod. J. of pharmacy Res. 3(9) 2218-2219.
97. Siddhuraju P, Mohan PS, Becker K (2002). Studies on the Antioxidant Activity of Indian Laburnum (*Cassia fistula* L): A Preliminary Assessment of Crude Extracts from Stern Bark, Leaves, Flowers and Fruit Pulp. J Agric. Food Chem. 79: 61-67.
98. Singh KN and Bardwaj UR (1975). Hypoglycaemic Activity of *Albizzia stipulata, Albizzia moluccana* and *Cassia fistula* Leguminous Seed Diets on Normal Young Rats. Ind. Journal of Pharmacology. 7: 47-50.
99. Singh P and Karnwal P (2006) Ind. J. of Microbiology 46(2):169-1.
100. Singh RP and Jain DA (2011). Evaluation of Antimicrobial Activity of alc. and aq. Extract of Five Plants Used in Traditional Medicine in North India. Int. J. of pharm Tec. Res. Vol. 3, (1) 376-380.
101. Sunil Kumar KC, Muller K (1998). Inhibition of leukotriene Biosynthesis and Lipid Peroxidation in Biological Models by the Extract of *Cassia fistula*. Phytotherapy Res. 12: 526-528.
102. Suresh KP, Sucehta 1 S, Sudarshana DV, Selvamani P, Latha S (2008). Antioxidant Activity in some Selected Indian Medicinal Plants Afr. J. Biotech. 7 (12): 1826-1828.
103. Trease GE, Evans WC (1985). Pharmacognosy, 12th Ed; English Language Books Society, Bailliere Tindall. P. 394.
104. Vaishanav MM, Gupta KR (1996). Rhamneilin 3-O-gentiobioside from *Cassia fistula* Roots. Fitoterapia. LXVII: 78-79.
105. Vaishanav MM, Tripathi AK, Gupta KR, (1993) Fitoterapia 64 (1): 93.
106. Van OFHL (1976). Some Aspects of the Pharmacology of Anthraquinone Drugs. Pharmacology (supl). 14(1): 18-29.
107. Vasi IG, Kalintha VP (1980). Chemical Examination of the Fruit Pulp of *Cassia fistula* Linn, J. Inst. Chemist. 22: 85-86.
108. Vasudevan DT, Dinesh LR, Gopalkrishnan S, Sreekanth SK, Shekhar S (2009). The Potential of aq. and Isolated Fraction from Leaves of *C. fistula* L. as Antibacterial Agent Int. J. Chem. Sci.: 7(4) 2363-2367.
109. Venkatesan D, Karrunakaran CM (2010). Antimicrobial Activity of Selected Indian Medicinal Plants J. Phytol 2 (2): 44-48.
110. Vimalraj TR, Kumar SS, Vadivel S, Ramesh S and Thejomoorthy (2009). Antibacterial effect of *C. fistula* Extract on Pathogenic Bacteria of Veterinary Importance. Tamil Nadu J. Veter & Animal Science 5 (3) 109-113.
111. Wasu SJ and Mulay (2009). Hepatoprotective Effect of *C. fistula* Linn. Ethnobotanical Leaflets 13: 910-916.

112. Yadav R and Jain GC (1999). Antifertility Effect of Aqueous Extract of Seeds of *C. fistula* in Female Rats. Adv. Contra caption. 15: 293-301.

113. Yadav R, Jain GC (2009). Effect of Aqueous Extract of Seed of *C. fistula* on the Uterine Biochemical mileu of Female Albino rats. Pharmacology 1: 859-867.

114. Yogesh M, Mohan JSS (2006). Screening of Indian Plant Extracts for Antibacterial Activity. Pharmaceutical Bio. 44(8): 627-631.

115. Ziyaurrahman AR, Pathan DN, Shakeel M, Maruf M (2011). Evaluation of Effect of Hydroalcoholic Extract of *C. fistula* Linn Against Neurophathic Pain. Int. J. of Res. Pharmacy 2 (1): 195-201.

5

Drying
An Important Post Harvest Processing Step for Medicinal Plants

Vasudha Agnihotri

INTRODUCTION

Medicinal plants (MPs) are more appreciable and in great demand due to their unique curative properties. Medicinal plants are the oldest known health care products in traditional medicine, which existed before the arrival of modern medicine, and are used as such in many countries. The records of the herbal medicines are available since 5000 years (Kirtikar & Basu, 1933, Chopra et al, 1992). As per the traditional medicine programme of the World Health Organisation (WHO), nearly 80% of the world population particularly rural communities rely on plant based natural products (Dubey et al., 2004). Traditional medicine, for example, which is related to traditional Chinese medicine (TCM), Indian ayurveda and Arabic unani medicine and to various forms of indigenous medicine, as well as the complementary or alternative medicine utilized in industrialized countries, is achieving growing credibility in many parts of the world. The percentage of people using traditional medicines increases in developed countries: 40-50 percent in Germany, 42 percent in the USA, 48 percent in Australia and 49 percent in France (Titz A. 2004). The last three decades have seen substantial growth in herb and herbal product markets across the world. Rapidly rising exports of medicinal plants during the past decade attests to worldwide interest in these products as well as in traditional health systems. According to the Secretariat of the

G. B. Pant of Institute of Himalayan Environment and Development, Kosi- Katarmal, Almora, Uttarakhand, India.

Convention on Biological Diversity, global sales of herbal products totalled an estimated US$60 000 million in 2002 (WHO. 2003).

MPs are valuable raw crops for manufacturing different kinds of industrial products (Fig. 5.1). These are used as:

- Fresh material;
- Dried conserved material;
- Thermo- chemically processed material; and
- Industrially finalized material.

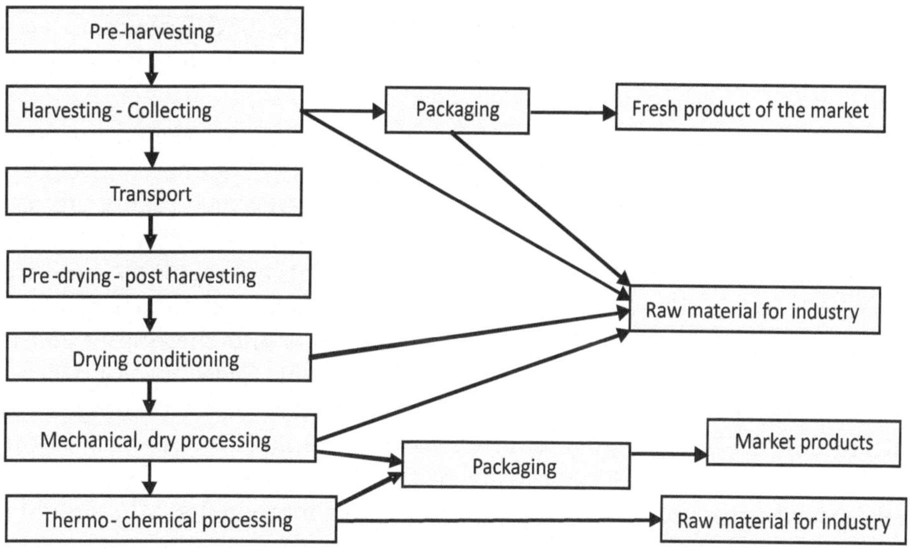

Fig. 5.1: Flow Chart of MPs Products (Öztekin & Martinov, 2007)

Modern pharmacopoeia still contains at least 25% drugs derived from plants and many others which are synthetic analogues built on prototype compounds isolated from plants. Demand for medicinal plant is increasing in both developing and developed countries due to growing recognition of natural products for health products, pharmaceuticals, food supplement, cosmetics etc as these are non-narcotic, having no side-effects, easily available at affordable prices and sometime the only source of health care available to the poor (Kalia, A.N., 2005). According to an all India ethnobiological survey carried out by the Ministry of Environment & Forests, Government of India, there are over 8000 species of plants being used by the people of India (Report of the Task Force on Conservation & Sustainable use of Medicinal Plants, Planning commission, Govt. of India, 2000)

Medicinal plant sector has traditionally occupied an important position in the socio cultural, spiritual and medicinal arena of rural and tribal lives of India. Now these are also famous in urban areas in the form of health related applications from a common cold to memory improvement and treatment of poisonous snake bites to a cure for muscular distrophy and the enhancement of body's general immunity in the form of antioxidant supplements. In the oral traditions local communities in every ecosystem from the trans Himalayas down to the coastal plains have discovered the medical uses of thousands of plants found locally in their ecosystem. India has one of the richest plant medical cultures in the world. It is a culture that is of tremendous contemporary relevance because it can on one hand ensure health security to millions of people and on the other hand it can provide new and safe herbal drugs to the entire world. There are estimated to be around 25000 effective plant based formulations used in folk medicine and known to rural communities all over India and around 10000 designed formulations are available in the indigenous medical texts.

Although many plants are used traditionally for medicinal purposes, most of them are not registered. Worldwide, out of an estimated 2,50,000 to 5,00,000 higher plant species identified so far, about 35000 plants are used for medicinal purposes (Kuipers, 1995; Lambert et al, 1997; Heywood, 1999; Nickel and Sennhauser, 2001). Only about 100 plants are regularly cultivated whereas remaining is collected in their natural habitat. Medicinal plants are mainly produced to extract the active ingredients and these are used for pharmaceutical purposes. Without active ingredients, MPs are not different from forages. The concentration of active ingredients in the plants are very low, usually within the range of 0.1- 2% of dry matter. The properties of the active ingredients are influenced by processing procedures. To control the influence of agro- ecological conditions on active ingredients, MPs should be cultivated.

Many producers prefer wild collections because of natural availability of the material and relatively low labor costs. Wild collected medicinal plants cannot meet the parameters with regards to unknown contaminations, falsifications or site specific differences. Wild collection also affects the survival of many species in their natural habitat, due to which these species come under threat. The quality and quantity of wild materials cannot meet the requirements of the market that is getting stringent in enforcing related standards. This situation creates ample opportunities for countries with ecologically suitable conditions to derive economic benefits from MPs cultivation.

MPs form a numerically large group of economically important plants which provide basic raw materials for medicines, perfumes, flavours and cosmetics. These plants and their products not only serve as valuable source of income for small land holders, farmers and entrepreneurs but also earn valuable foreign exchange by way of export. The WHO has estimated present demand of medicinal plants is approximately US $14 billion per year and is expected to increase more than US $5 trillion in 2050 (Uttaranchal State Level Project Planning Committee, 2003). In India, the MPs related trade is estimated to be approximately $1 billion per year (Joshi et al., 2004) and the demand of Ayurvedic products produced in India is increasing drastically.

Due to minimum side effects, people are more tilted towards herbal medicines. In case of herbals, their purity and uniformity of the constituents is very important, so their physico-chemical, pharmacological and pharmacognostic properties are studied along with quantitative characteristics. The assessment of any herb as medicine is estimated only on the basis of their therapeutic constituents, which can provide a clue for new drug discovery. These active constituents works more effectively in synergism with other constituents present in the herbal drug as these constituents increases the bioavailability of the active constituents effective for the particular disease. So it is safe and better to use herbal drugs rather than pure/synthesized active ingredient.

Crude drugs are usually the dried parts of medicinal plants (roots, stem wood, bark, leaves, flowers seeds, fruits, and whole plants etc.) that form the essential raw materials for the production of traditional remedies of Ayurveda, Siddha, Unani, Homeopathy, Tibetan and other systems of medicine including the folk, ethno or tribal medicines. The crude drugs are also used to obtain therapeutically active chemical constituents by specialized methods of extraction, isolation, fractionation and purification and are used as phytochemicals for the production of modern allopathic medicines or herbal/phytomedicines.

As mentioned in Charak Samhita, every step during raw herb collection, drying, storage, pre-processing, processing, storage and packing etc is important to decide the quality. It is estimated that as high as 30% of the raw material reaching the manufacturers is of low quality and is, therefore, rejected. Quality problems in finished products can be due to use of the wrong species, lack of organ specificity, harvesting at a non-optimum stage of growth, non-optimum cultivation parameters such as soil, light, water, temperature and nutrients, contamination by microbial and chemical agents, non-optimum drying and storage, non-optimum extraction strategy and long-term finished product storage.

Therefore, value addition is required to increase profitability and to reduce losses (Med herb green pages, 2009). Systematic cultivation of many medicinal plants needs specific cultural practices and agronomical requirements. These are species-specific and are dependent on soil, water and climatic conditions. Hence research and development work has to be done to formulate good agricultural practices which will include appropriate selection and identification, propagation methods, cultivation techniques, harvesting, stepwise quality control of raw material up to processing stage, post-harvest treatment, storage and safety. These aspects have to be incorporated into protocols for the cultivation of medicinal plants.

For having good quality materials, agricultural practices, harvesting and post harvesting practices, work on high yielding varieties, propagation methods, efficient harvesting techniques, quality control procedures, control on energy losses, manufacturing practices, R & D on product and process development, marketing strategy, availability of local market for processed materials, availability of latest technologies and proper training for these technologies etc. play an important role. The genetic make up and physic-chemical properties of MPs of various cultivars also affect the post harvest losses. Due to ongoing demands of medicinal plants, there is need to work on good harvesting and storage practices (Kala et al., 2006) in order to increase the quality of existing plant materials.

POST HARVEST PROCESSING

The post harvest loss phenomenon is highly complex and governed by various natural and man made factors. Post harvest loss reduction technology encompasses the usage of optimum harvest factors, reduction of losses in handling, packaging, transportation and storage with modern infrastructure machinery, processing into a wide variety of products, home scale preservation with low cost technology. Use of thermal processing, low temperature, drying, chemical and biological reactions coupled with other preservation techniques are applied to enhance the storability. Importance of Post-harvest technology lies in the fact that it has the capability to meet requirement of growing population by eliminating losses making more nutritive items from raw commodities by proper processing and fortification. This step is important for all types of crops including vegetables, fruits, grains as well as medicinal plants.

As a general approach, the following practices can help you maintain quality:

1. Harvest during the coolest time of day to maintain low product respiration.
2. Avoid unnecessary wounding, bruising, crushing, or damage from humans, equipment, or harvest containers.
3. Shade the harvested product in the field to keep it cool. By covering harvest bins or totes with a reflective pad, you greatly reduce heat gain from the sun, water loss, and premature senescence.
4. If possible, move the harvested product into a cold storage facility or postharvest cooling treatment as soon as possible. For some commodities, such as berries, tender greens, and leafy herbs, one hour in the sun is too long.
5. Do not compromise high quality product by mingling it with damaged, decayed, or decay-prone product in a bulk or packed unit.

6. Only use cleaned and, as necessary, sanitized packing or transport containers.

There are various guidelines available for post harvest processing of plant materials, given by World Health Organisation (WHO) as well as National medicinal Plant Board, Govt. of India. These includes Inspection and sorting of plant materials, primary processing, drying specific processing as require by some plants as well as about the processing facilities. There are number of factors, which are responsible for the post harvest loses, such as system of harvesting, processing, storage, handling and marketing.

Harvesting

Some of the important points, which need to be taken care of while harvesting various categories, are given below. (DOC: NMPB-GFCP-01):

Underground part

- In case of annual plants, well developed and mature roots should be collected.
- Roots of biennial should be collected in either the fall of the first year or spring of the second year.
- In case of perennial plants, roots should be harvested late in the fall or early in the spring.
- The root material that is rich in essential oils should be handled carefully to prevent bruising of the epidermis, where the oils typically reside, which could result in loss of essential oil or its degradation.
- Underground parts like roots and rhizomes should be collected only after the seed shedding. It also facilitates regeneration of species.
- Where taproot is the desired produce and needs to be uprooted, harm to other plant species in the vicinity should be minimized. Underground parts should be collected with minimum possible digging by using appropriate tools.
- When roots of species that are propagated vegetative in nature are collected, enough underground part should be left at site to allow regeneration.

Annual herbs/Whole plants

- Harvesting should be done at flowering stage but prior to any visual decline in any of the plant parts.
- Whole population in a given area should never be harvested. Adequate population should be left in nature for regeneration to facilitate future collections.

- Use of mathematical procedures including computer software to estimate collection of individuals from a population may be resorted when target area is large to ensure even harvesting throughout the habitat.

Stem Bark

- Stem bark should not be harvested when the tree is under new growth (like spring season)
- The bark should be collected from mature branches of the trees leaving the main trunk intact. Bark from entire branch or trunk should not be taken at one time.
- Bark should be stripped longitudinally (partially along the length of the stem) to allow smooth conduction of water and nutrients.
- It should not be collected again from same tree unless adequate time has been allowed for it to be reformed completely.
- The rhytidome (outer dead bark) should be removed except where it is the usable part of the produce.

Stem or Wood

- Only select mature branches of a tree or shrub should be harvested at a time. The branches from the same plant should not be harvested every year. Where the trunk is used as medicinal produce, the main axis should be harvested.

Leaves

- The leaves of herbaceous plants should be collected before their flowering, unless otherwise specified. As far as possible, leaves should be collected from mature trees. Where bio-active contents in the leaves do not fluctuate with age, the collection could be extended to later stage also.
- The source plant should not be ripped off the leaves completely. Certain percentage of leaves should be left to ensure normal physiological processes of the plant.
- Tender leaves should not be harvested unless they constitute the officially recognized produce. Leaves turned pale, those infected, deficient and unhealthy should be discarded.
- The leaves should be harvested during the season when growth and leaf production is the highest.
- If the leaf size is decreasing the rate of harvest should be lowered as it indicates stressful condition.
- If the plant size in a population appears to be decreasing, even if vegetative sprouting is increasing (i.e. the population is becoming dense), the rate of harvest should be lowered.

- The rate of harvest should be decreased if there is heavy pressure from grazing, fire or other incidents that may negatively affect the plants.
- When environmental conditions are stressful for the plants leaf harvesting should be postponed or should be harvested in less quantity.

Flower and Floral Parts

- Flowers must be harvested (or if specified, flowering tops) when they have just opened or shortly afterwards to capture its aroma.
- The flower buds must be collected before the buds open and in early morning hours. In this case the departure of insects must be encouraged by shaking the materials.
- All the flowers from perennials like shrubs, trees and climbers should not be harvested completely. Similarly, flowers from a complete population of annual plants should not be collected at a time. Enough flowers must be left over the plants to allow the natural process of pollination, fertilization, fruit/seed formation and dispersal.
- Floral parts like stigma, anthers, petals etc should be collected at appropriate time of their maturity to ensure the availability of desired active substance.

Fruits and Seeds

- Fruits and seeds should be collected only on maturity unless immature ones constitute the medicinal produce (e.g. Emblica officinalis, Aegle marmelos) except the fruit of family Apiaceae that dehisce on drying should also be collected before maturation.
- In case of shrubs and trees, all the fruits from individual plant should not be collected at a time leaving behind a few healthy ones for further multiplication of the species. Similarly, the whole population of annuals should not be ripped off all the fruits and seeds at a time.
- Trees, shrubs or their branches should not be cut for ease of collection of fruits and seeds.
- Immature, infected and deformed fruits should be separated and discarded appropriately.
- If the medicinal plant produce consists of fresh fruits (e.g. Phyllanthus emblica) the same should be transported to cold storage or pulping units immediately after harvesting.
- Wherever required, seeds should be removed completely from the fruit rind before they are traded.

Gums and Resins

- Collectors/collection managers should ensure minimum harm to the mother plant while collecting the exudates. Only a few small longitudinal incisions should be made to collect the exudates and the exposed parts should be treated appropriately to avoid any fungal or bacterial infestation after the exudates has been collected.
- Incisions, too close to the ground, easily approachable by the cattle and wild animals, should be avoided. The collection container should be designed in a way to prevent rain, bird droppings and any other such possible contaminations.
- Where there is a likelihood of some foreign matter being mixed with the collect gums and resins, it should be carefully removed.
- Source tree or shrub should be allowed appropriate recovery period before collecting the exudates again from them.
- Flow of gum is more in hot weather. Therefore, tapping in such species, should be done between June-October.
- No fire should be ignited near the base of the tree to increase gum/resin flow.
- Younger trees should not be tapped. The girth of the trees has to be decided below which tapping of gum/resin will not be allowed.
- Long sharp cut blazes are best as they give pure resin/gum and the bark heals faster. Irregular cuts add impurities to the resin. Long cuts are better as they provide more area for exudation and heal faster. Square and round cuts take longer time to heal as the distance between the two walls is more.
- Sharp knives or chisels can be used to make blazes.
- Instead of letting the gum or resin solidify on the bark, it is better to fix a collection trough e.g. coconut shell, hollow bamboo etc.
- On the same tree more than one blaze is made, these should be staggered for optimum exudation. After 3 years of tapping, sufficient rest should be given to the tree to rejuvenate from the injury.

Others (Galls, Lac etc.)

- Galls should be collected only from stipulated species
- Collectors must ensure that no live insects are present inside the galls

Inspection and Sorting (WHO. 2003)

Raw medicinal plant materials should be inspected and sorted prior to primary processing. The inspection may include:

- visual inspection for cross-contamination by untargeted medicinal plants and/or plant parts;
- visual inspection for foreign matter;
- Organoleptic evaluation, such as: appearance, damage, size, colour, odour, and possibly taste.

Primary Processing

Primary processing varies from material to material. This process should be carried out based on the national of regional quality standards, regulations and norms of both the producer and purchaser countries/areas. Standard operating procedures (SOPs) should try to be followed. If modifications are made in any step, they should be justified by adequate test data demonstrating that the quality of the medicinal plant material is not diminished. Peoper care should be taken unpackning of harvested or collected raw MP materials. Prior to processing, the medicinal plant materials should be protected from rain, moisture and any other conditions that might cause deterioration. Medicinal plant materials should be exposed to direct sunlight only where there is a specific need for this mode of drying. Medicinal plant materials that are to be used in the fresh state should be harvested/collected and delivered as quickly as possible to the processing facility in order to prevent microbial fermentation and thermal degradation. The materials may be stored under refrigeration, in jars, in sandboxes, or using enzymatic and other appropriate conservation measures immediately following harvest/collection and during transit to the end-user. The use of preservatives should be avoided. If used, they should conform to national and/or regional regulations for growers/collectors and end-users.

All medicinal plant materials should be inspected during the primary-processing stages of production, and any substandard products or foreign matter should be eliminated mechanically or by hand. For example, dried medicinal plant materials should be inspected, sieved or winnowed to remove discolored, mouldy or damaged materials, as well as soil, stones and other foreign matter. Mechanical devices such as sieves should be regularly cleaned and maintained. All processed medicinal plant materials should be protected from contamination and decomposition as well as from insects, rodents, birds and other pests, and from livestock and domestic animals.

Drying

Drying is defined as the decreasing of crop moisture content, aimed at preventing enzymatic and microbial activity, and consequently preserving the product for extended shelf life (Martinov, 2007). It is the most common and fundamental method for post-harvest preservation of medicinal plants because it allows for the quick conservation of the medicinal qualities of the plant material in an uncomplicated manner (Muller and Heidnl, 2006). Factors such as scale of production, availability of new technologies and pharmaceutical quality standards must be considered for medicinal plant drying in modern times. Drying represents 30 to 50% of the total costs in medicinal plant production (Qaas and Schiele 2001) and, therefore, it is crucial that factors determining the high costs should be identified. Currently, energy demand of drying represents a significant cost factor, especially with the increased price of fossil fuels. Thus, energy requirements of drying are considerable and represent a major expense in the drying procedure, which is already the greatest cost in the processing of medicinal plants. As safety and quality demands for medicinal plants are increasing worldwide, importance of proper drying has increased a lot. Drying performance takes authoritative influence on the quality of the product and, therefore, on its value (Garg, 2001).

Drying time, temperature and water activity influence the quality of the final product. Low temperatures generally have a positive influence on the quality of biological materials, but require longer processing times, which may have a detrimental effect and a higher cost. Low water activity retards or eliminates the growth of microorganisms, but results in higher lipid oxidation (Okos *et al* ., 1992). Fresh medicinal plants normally contain a high level of moisture, due to that there is the big risk of microbiological activity. The moisture in the plants has similar properties as pure water. It can serve as medium for chemical, enzymatic and microbial reactions, many of which lead to ultimate loss of quality and nutritional value. So, in the fresh state of plants, deterioration and spoilage occur under ambient conditions. At lower moisture values, the water is more bound to the material, and cannot take part in the deteriorative reactions. Consequently, it is not so much the water content, but its state, nature or availability in the plants, expressed by the moisture that plays a role in the deteriorative processes. Changing the availability of water, by reducing the moisture, can result in an effective prevention of plants from spoilage (Quirijins, 2006). Therefore, the immediate and adequate drying is the most important operation in post harvest processing to avoid quality losses. It increases the shelf life of material.

For every medicinal plant there is specific value of final moisture content at which the quality of material is utmost. For reaching this stage controlled drying is must. During drying process, water present deep inside the plant/ parts must move to the surface by internal diffusion. The applied external heat evaporates the surface moisture, while the internal moisture can be forced to the surface and then evaporated or it can be evaporated internally and then transported to the surface. The transfer of heat depends on the air temperature, air humidity, air flow rate, pressure, surface area, the physical nature of the material as well as its composition and the process by which the heat is transferred to the material be it by conduction, convection or by radiation. To speed up the heat and mass transfer, the material is often cut into small pieces or thin layers. A large plant surface area combined with the air movement during drying favors quick evaporation of water from the plant's surface. The larger the temperature gradient between the heating medium and the food, the greater the rate of heat transfer into the food, which provides the driving force for moisture removal. The hotter the air, the more moisture it will be able to carry away from the drying product. The rate at which the water is evaporated from surface of the plant must be balanced with the rate at which water is removed from inside. Unbalanced evaporation rates can result in deterioration of the final product (Tanko et al., 2003).

During drying of medicinal plants, many changes occur simultaneously resulting in a modified overall quality. In general, drying leads to reduction of visual, organoleptic and functional characteristics that affect significantly the final quality. Reactions lead to well-known changes in the fresh biological products during drying: Change of color, loss of aroma, textural changes, reduction of essential oil content, cracking and altering of shape. These reactions are caused by both the increase in product temperature and the removal of moisture. For these reasons, it is necessary to purpose adequate drying strategies and to known the optimal values of the process parameters in order to obtain the required quality characteristics and the decrease of the energy consumption.

Medicinal plants can be dried in a number of ways: in the open air (shaded from direct sunlight); placed in thin layers on drying frames, wire-screened rooms or buildings; by direct sunlight, if appropriate; in drying ovens/rooms and solar dryers; by indirect fire; baking; lyophilization; microwave; or infrared devices. When possible, temperature and humidity should be controlled to avoid damage to the active chemical constituents. The method used for drying may have a considerable impact on the quality of the resulting medicinal plant materials. For example, shade drying is preferred to maintain or minimize loss of colour of leaves and flowers; and lower temperatures should be employed in the case of medicinal plant materials containing volatile substances. The drying conditions should be recorded. In the case of natural drying in the open air, medicinal plant materials should be spread out in thin layers on drying frames and stirred or turned frequently. In order to secure adequate air circulation, the drying frames should be located at a sufficient height above the ground. Efforts should be made to achieve uniform drying of medicinal plant materials and so avoid mould formation.

Due to risks that occur by natural drying many buyers accept only technically dried products. In developing countries, the use of batch dryers presents a compromise between investments and effects. The control of drying process is very poor in conventional batch driers, resulting in lower quality and higher input of energy. New development of control equipment enables control in batch dryers, which is not only satisfactory but is almost comparable to that in big band driers. An improvement in the quality of the product to be dried and at the same time a decrease in the drying cost and time are achieved through the utilization of a controlled conventional drying method, which should be based on utilization of renewable energy sources. It is an important process in the production chain in order to add value to the medicinal plants. As consequence of drying, there is a reduction of the weight and volume that has a positive effect for transport and storage as well as for the preparation for other industrial processes (distillation, extraction, etc).

Optimizing this process will result in lower production cost and increased product quality. In order to optimize practices for thermal processing and drying of biological materials, extensive research has been carried around the world on various drying methods such as fluidized-bed drying, spouted-bed drying, particulate medium conduction drying, flash drying, freeze drying, spray drying, drum drying, tunnel convective drying, tray drying, microwave drying, radio frequency drying, infrared drying, electric field drying, superheated steam, osmotic dehydration, conveyor drying, impingement drying, solar drying, rotary drying, etc. (Mujumdar, 1995). All drying methods have been developed to optimize the drying of target materials, where not all drying processes are suitable for all types of biological materials (Sadykov *et al.*, 1997). The quality of biological materials is so specific that drying of each product should be studied on an individual basis. In the case of biomaterials, their phytochemical content and quality must be maintained during drying, as research has demonstrated their ability to provide health benefits (Dillard and German, 2000).

Phytochemicals are very reactive and their content varies depending on plant cultivar, ripeness at harvest, storage conditions, and level of processing. Production of vegetal ingredients must ensure the preservation of their inherent quality attributes. In general, the concentration of bioactive compounds will steadily decrease during processing. The development of processing methods to minimize the loss of bioactive components is imperative

The methods available for drying can be grouped into natural and mechanical drying on the heat source or energy utilization (Cai et al, 2004). In natural drying, exposure to the sun and/ or the desiccating effect of air currents promotes the removal of water from the material. Downs and Compton (1955) mentioned that natural drying is easy to control and seldom damages the crop and also reported that it also depends on the weather conditions. This method is good for those medicinal plants, for which the harvesting is followed by dry season and their phytochemicals are not photosensitive. Mechanical drying includes solar drying, batch or continuous (kiln, tower and cabinet dryers, tunnel, belt, belt-trough, fluidized bed, explosion-puff, foam-mat, spray, drum and microwave) drying and vacuum shelf/belt/drum/ freeze drying (Raghavan and Orsat, 2007) which have been used for drying of biomaterials as such or in the form of liquid extracts. Some of the drying methods used for medicinal plant's processing are as follows:

Sun and Solar Drying

In direct solar drying called "sun drying" the product is heated directly by the sun's rays and moisture is removed by natural circulation of air due to density differences. In countries where harvesting time occurs at the beginning of the dry season, the most popular method of drying is exposure to the sun. Crops are often left to dry in the field before harvesting. In some countries, various crops are dried on scaffolds or inverted latticework cones. At the village level, probably the most common practice is to spread the harvested product on the ground on a specially prepared area (e.g. matting, sacking, or concrete) exposed to the sun. With solar energy, like any other drying processes, the temperature and duration of exposure to light have to be monitored to retain the functional properties specific to the products being dried. Various types of solar dryers have been reported.

Solar heat is trapped with a solar collector constructed from an aluminum sheet painted black (Sharma *et al.*, 1995). The collector may be fixed to the drying bin in such a way that an air space exists between it and the bin wall. Energy absorbed by the collector heats the ventilating air by a few degrees as it is forced through the air space. Various solar energy dryers have been designed around the world. Abdel-Rehim and Fahmy (1998) developed a photovoltaic dryer with dual packed beds for drying medicinal herbs. Their dryer is equipped with electrical heaters powered by a photovoltaic system. Flat type solar collector dryers have been designed in Poland with corrugated absorbers equipped with a backup coal-fired air heater. The solar dryer is equipped with variable speed fans to modulate the airflow according to transient changes in solar irradiance and heat output (Wisniewski, 1997). A special construction is presented of a solar greenhouse dryer into which a flat-bed dryer was integrated with a cost-effective construction cover of greenhouse foil (Müller et al. 1989) (Fig. 5.3). The roof surface serves as a solar collector during the summer months when the fossil-fuel requirement can be substituted completely. A tunnel solar dryer was investigated for solar drying of various commodities with great success (Kulanthaisami *et al.*, 2005). The dryer (Fig. 5.2) consists of a concrete slab, painted black, and a transparent cover material made of polythene film over a framed tunnel in which air is passed by natural convection with an exhaust fan. The plastic cover has the property to transfer short wave radiations which are converted into long wave thermal radiation inside the tunnel, which raises the temperature 15-20 °C above ambient. This drying method ensures a better quality product when compared to open sun drying while ensuring the control of the drying environment at minimal equipment cost.

Fig. 5.2: Tunnel Solar Dryer (Kulanthaisami *et al.*, 2005).

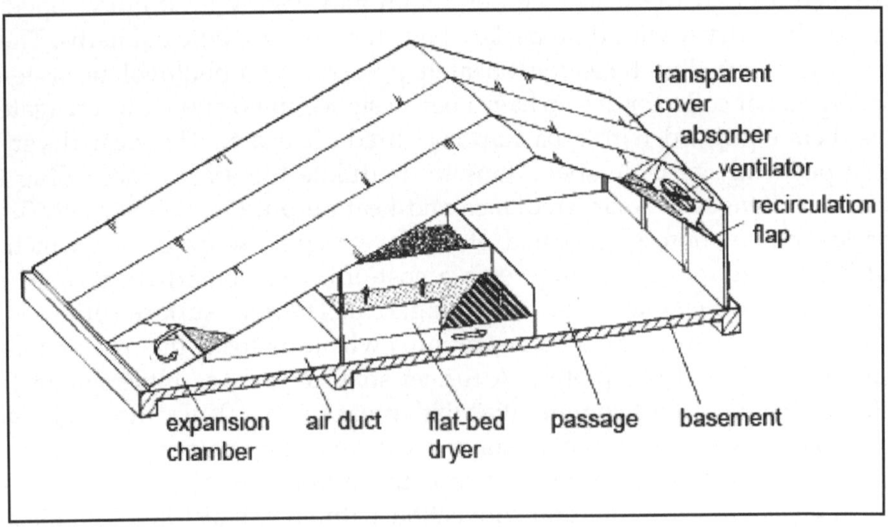

Fig. 5.3: Flat-bed Dryer Integrated in a Solar Greenhouse Dryer (Muller and Heidnl, 2006)

Drum Drying

In drum drying, heat is transferred to the material by conduction with heated revolving drums. The dried product is flaked off the drum with a scraper. Drum dryers have high drying rates and high energy efficiency. The technique is used mainly for viscous or pureed foods but some work on medicinal plants (eg. *Ginkgo biloba*) have also been reported (Schmid & Balz, 2005)

Microwave Drying

Apart from the popular conventional procedures based on conduction, convenction, or infrared radiation, heat drying utilizing microwave energy is an attractive solution to many problems in process technology. In microwave drying, heat is generated by directly transforming the electromagnetic energy into kinetic molecular energy, thus the heat is generated deep within the material to be dried. Medicinal plants are dried by applying microwave power to plant materials in a chamber under reduced pressure to reduce the moisture content of the plant materials without significantly reducing (oxidizing) the concentration of active medicinal component in the dried plant materials and thereby produce a dried medicinal plant product which more closely approaches the medicinal properties of the fresh plant than those of dried products produced by conventional air drying processes. Retention of polyphenols in conventional dried herbs is very low. Microwave drying contributes to reduction of active compounds losses, e.g. in mint (Arslan et al., 2010) and oregano (Jaloszyñski et al., 2008). Durance T.D. et al, 2000 have found that vacuum microwave dehydration process significantly increases the retention of key active components (hypericin and alkamides) of medicinal plants such as St. John's wort and Echinacea respectively when compared to air-drying. The present invention provides a new process for drying medicinal plants by maintaining their potency and economic value, which was found greater than the same products when air dried and drying time was also greatly reduced.

Infrared Drying

In this type of drying the materials absorb the rays and transform them to the heating power, and finally the water among the materials is evaporated. The heating power released by the infrared ray are mostly distributed on the surface of the materials, so the infrared ray drier is also used to dry the filmily-formed materials which only need drying on the surface. Besides the material temperature, the way in which the heat is supplied and the moisture is taken away from the drying chamber deûnitely plays a role in the quality of the dried herbs. When infrared drying is combined with vibro-ûuidized bed, Fig. 5.4 the drying rate as well as the quality of the dried pro duct is improved signiûcantly (Chu, Z.D., 1998).

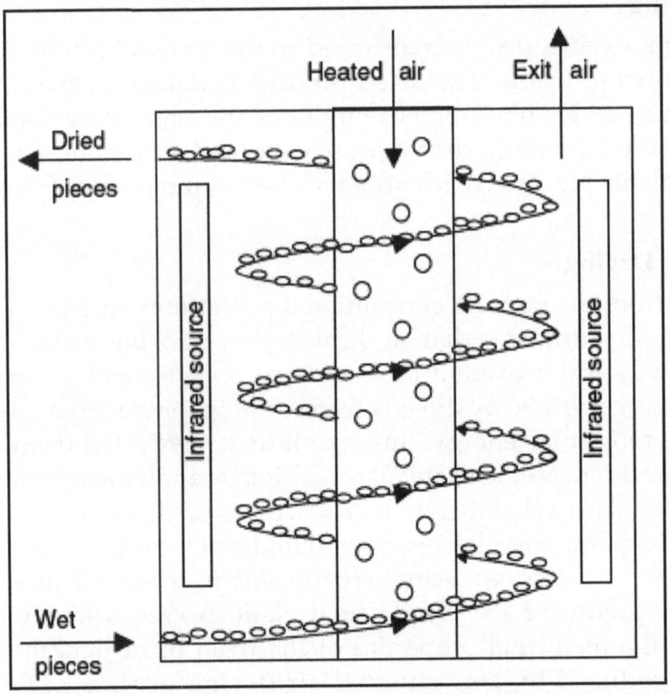

Fig. 5.4: Vibrio- fluidized Bed Dryer with IR Heating (Chu, Z.D., 1998)

Vacuum Drying

Vacuum drying is another process, in which moist materials dried under sub-atmospheric pressures. The lower pressures allow drying temperature to be reduced and higher quality to be obtained than with classical processes (Jaya & Das, 2003). Drying of grape by products under vacuum (500 mm Hg, <50°C temperature) 95% of nutritious ingredients, vitamins, ferments and other biologically active components were preserved (Kutovoy et al, 2005).

Freeze Drying

Freeze drying operates at low temperatures and low pressures which can help to reduce quality degradation (Abascal et al., 2005). The frozen water changes directly into vapour under vacuum, this process is called sublimation, yielding particular dried product characteristics. The food pieces are frozen, and vacuum is applied in the airtight drying chamber. In freeze drying, the plant materials remain at low temperature, yielding high retention of nutrients. It is an ideal preservation method, but is very expensive and lends itself only to the drying of high value products. (Tanko et al, 2005). A freeze drying study of medicinal herbs demonstrated that the quality of the freeze-dried product was slightly lower than fresh material, but the quality remained considerably higher than for oven dried samples at 35-40°C (Tambunan et al., 2001).

There are many other drying techniques available for dehydration of medicinal plants. As active ingredients of different medicinal plants are concentrated in certain parts eg. leaf, flower, fruits, bark or root and therefore drying method for these parts will usually be specific. Any given process can be detrimental to a certain product, with a significant reduction in the retention of its bioactive ingredients or their activity level. On the other hand, exactly same process can be suited to yield higher levels of health promoting bioactive compounds during the processing.

Specific Processing

Some medicinal plant materials require specific processing to improve the purity of the plant part being employed; reduce drying time; prevent damage from mould, other microorganisms and insects; detoxify indigenous toxic ingredients; and enhance therapeutic efficacy. Common specific processing practices include pre-selection, peeling the skins of roots and rhizomes, boiling in water, steaming, soaking, pickling, distillation, fumigation, roasting, natural fermentation, treatment with lime and chopping. Processing procedures involving the formation of certain shapes, bundling and special drying may also have an impact on the quality of the medicinal plant materials.

Antimicrobial treatments of medicinal plant materials (raw or processed) by various methods, including irradiation, must be declared and the materials must be labeled as required. Only suitably trained staff using approved equipment should carry out such applications, and they should be conducted in accordance with standard operating procedures and national and/or regional regulations in both the grower/collector country and the end-user country. Maximum residue limits, as stipulated by national and/or regional authorities, should be respected.

Precautions to be taken during Drying

1. Drying medicinal plant material directly on bare ground should be avoided. If a concrete or cement surface is used, medicinal plant materials should be laid on a tarpaulin or other appropriate cloth or sheeting. Insects, rodents, birds and other pests, and livestock and domestic animals should be kept away from drying sites.
2. For indoor drying, the duration of drying, drying temperature, humidity and other conditions should be determined on the basis of the plant part concerned (root, leaf, stem, bark, flower, etc.) and any volatile natural constituents, such as essential oils. Different parts of the plant should be treated differently during drying.

3. The underground parts (root, rhizomes) should be thoroughly washed and thereafter dried to reduce the moisture content before packing the produce.
4. Annuals, especially small herbs, creepers, grasses are more prone to contamination as well as cross-contamination. It is easier to sort the annuals immediately after the collection rather than after drying.
5. The bark should be split in pieces of appropriate size to ensure complete drying. Unless otherwise required in specific cases, barks should be dried in direct sunlight
6. Stem or wood should be cut in smaller pieces to facilitate faster drying. Material can be made into small chips or shavings to facilitate drying and packaging. Unless otherwise required in specific cases, stems and woods should be dried in direct sunlight.
7. Generally leaves should not be dried in direct sunlight, unless they have external moisture, in which case they may initially be dried in direct sunlight for some time and be shifted to shade or indirect sunlight as soon as the external moisture is wiped dry. The produce should be turned periodically while drying to facilitate faster and even drying.
8. The delicate flowers and floral parts should not be dried in direct sun light. Flowers that are fleshy may be initially dried in sun to get rid of surface moisture and shifted to shade or indirect sunlight afterward
9. As per the need of the produce, fruits may be split or cut into small pieces to facilitate drying and packaging. Complete drying of fruits should be ensured before they are packed. Randomly selected individuals fruits should be dissected to ensure that there is no inherent moisture left.
10. If possible, the source of heat for direct drying (fire) should be limited to butane, propane or natural gas, and temperatures should be kept below 60 °C (Youngken, 1948) If other sources of fire are used, contact between those materials, smoke and medicinal plant material should be avoided

Storage

After drying next important step is storage, which is well connected with the drying. Before storage, the material should be properly dried. Storage condition like, temperature, duration and humidity conditions play an important role for maintaining quality of MP material in terms of active ingredient content. So the main objective of storage is to reduce metabolic activity, rendering the medicinal plant less susceptible to deterioration. The effect of temperature (Smith and Burford, 1992), light (Heptinstall et al, 1992) and storage period on parthenolide concentration of feverfew leaves (Tanko et al, 2003) have shown the importance of storage conditions on plants quality.

CONCLUSION

For getting good quality medicinal plant materials, both the preprocessing and post processing steps are important before extraction of desired compounds or preparation of other products. For getting a high quality product, the appropriate part of medicinal plants must be harvested at optimum stage of development, should be dried using suitable technology available, and stored at optimum conditions that should not decrease the phytochemical concentrations present in the respective plant materials. By following all these procedures, high quality product can be achieved.

REFERENCES

Abascal K., Ganora L. and Yarnell E. (2005). The Effect of Freeze Drying and its Implications for Botanical Medicine: A Review. Phytotherapy Research, 19, 655-660.

Abdel-Rehim ZS, Fahmy FH. Photovoltaic Dryer with Dual Packed Beds for Drying Medical Herb. *Drying Technol.* 1998; 16(3): 799-811.

Arslan, D., Özcan, M.M. & Okyay Menges, H. (2010). Evaluation of Drying Methods with Respect to Drying Parameters, Some Nutritional and Colour Characteristics of Peppermint (Mentha x piperita L.). Energy Conversion and Management, 51, 2769-2775.

CaiT, Chen, F. and Qi J (2004). Dehydrated Oriental Mushrooms, Leafy Vegetables, and Food Preparation Herbs and Condiments. In: Hui Y.H., Ghazala S., Graham, D.H., Murrel K.D. and Nip, W.K. (eds.) Handbook of Vegetable Preservation and Processing. New York: Marcel Dekker, 373-393.

Chopra, R.N., Nayer, S.L., Chopra, I.C., (1992). Glossary of Indian Medicinal Plants, 3rd edn. Council of Scientific and Industrial Research, New Delhi, 7-246.

Chu, Z.D., (1998). Drying of Small Pieces of Chinese Medicine, in Modern Drying Technology , Eds. Y.K. Pan and X.Z. Wang, Chemical Industry Press, Beijing, pp. 810-841.

Dubey, N.K., Kumar, R., Tripathy, P., (2004). Global Promotion of Herbal Medicine: India's Opportunity. Current Science, 86: 37-41.

Dillard C.J., German J.B., (2000). Phytochemicals: Nutraceuticals and Human Health. J. Sci. Food Agric.; 80 (12): 1744-1756.

Downs S. and Compton E., (1955). Crop Drying with Heated Air. Agricultural Engineering 36: 90-92.

Draft Standard for Good Field Collection Practices of Medicinal Plants, DOC: NMPB-GFCP-01(CD), pp. 30-34.

Garg, R., P.and Kumar (2001). Developments in Solar Drying. In: Proceedings of the Second Asian-Oceania Drying Conference (ADC 2001) (pp. 297{319). Batu Feringhi, Pulau Pinang, Malaysia.

Heptinsatll S, Awang D, Cowson B, Kindack D., Knight D, and May J. (1992). Parthenolide Content and Bioactivity of Feverfew (*Tanacetum parthenium*) (L.) Schultz- bip)). Estimation of Commercial and Authenticated Feverfew Products. Journal of Pharmacy and Pharmacology 44: 391-0395.

Heywood, V.H., (1999), Conservation and Sustainable Use of Wild Species as Sources of New Ornamentals. *Acta Horticulturae*, 500, 21-9.

Jaloszyñski, K., Figiel, A. & Wojdylo, A. (2008). Drying Kinetics and Antioxidant Activity of Oregano. Acta Agrophysica, 11(1), 81-90.

Jaya S., Das H. (2003). A Vacuum Drying Model for Mango Pulp, Drying technology, 21(7), p. 1215.

Joshi K., Chavan P., Warude D., Patwardhan B., (2004). Molecular Markers in Herbal Drug Technology. Current Science, 87: 159-165.

Kala C.P. Dhyani P.P., and Sajwan B.S. (2006). Developing the Medicinal Plants Sector in Northern India: Challenges and Opportunities. J Ethnobiol Ethnomed., 2: 32.

Kalia, A.N., (2005). Text Book of Industrial Pharmacognosy. Oscar Publication.

Kirtikar K.R. & Basu B.D. (1933). Indian Medicinal Plants, Second Edn.Vol. II 908-910.

Kuipers, Sopphie Emma. (1995), "Trade in Medicinal Plants", in NWFPs-ll, "Medicinal Plants for Forest Conservation and Health Care" FAO, Rome.

Kulanthaisami S, Mahendran R, Subramanian P, Venkatachalam P, Raghavan GSV, Sampathrajan A. (2005). Industrial Application of a Solar Tunnel Dryer. In *Paper presented at the Asia Pacific Drying Conference*, Science City, Kolkota, Dec. 12-15, 2005.Proceedings of ADC 2005, Vol. 2, 998-1009.

Kutovoy VA, Muminov MI, Karimov M, Sandalov VN. (2005). Intensification of Vacuum Drying of Bioproducts. In Proceedings of the 3rd Inter-American Drying Conference, IADC, Orsat V, Raghavan GSV, Kudra T (eds). Published by McGill University: Montreal, Canada, 2005; Paper II-1.

Lambert, John; Shrivastava, Jithendra and Vietmeyer, Noel. (1997), Medicinal Plants, Rescuing a Global Heritage, World Bank Technical Paper No. 355.

Martinov, M., Oztekin, S., & MÄuller, J. (2007). Ä Drying in Medicinal and Aromatic Crops; Harvesting, Drying and Processing. Haworth Food and Agricultural Product Press.

Müller, J., Reisinger, G., Kisgeci, J., et al., (1989). Development of a Greenhouse-type Solar Dryer for Medicinal Plants and Herbs. Solar and Wind Technology, 523-530.

Muller Joachim and Heidnl Albert, (2006). Drying of Medicinal Plants. In: Bogers R.J., L.E. Craker and D. Lange (eds.), Medicinal and Aromatic Plants, © *Springer*, 237-252.

Mujumdar AS. *Handbook of Industrial Drying* Vol. 2, (2nd edn). Marcel Dekker, Inc: New York, 1995.

Nickel, W. and Sennhauser, E. (2001). Medicinal Plants: Local Heritage with Global Importance.

Optimization of Research and Development Sector. in Medherb Green Pages-India and Indonesia 2009, 77-78.

Okos MR, Narsimhan G, Singh RK, Weitnauer AC. (1992). Food Dehydration. In Handbook of Food Engineering, Heldman DR, Lund DB (eds). Marcel Dekker, Inc: New York, USA, 437-562.

Qaas, F. and Schiele, E., (2001). Einfluss der Energiekosten auf die Rentabilität im Trocknungsbetrieb. *Zeitschrift für Arznei- und Gewürzpflanzen*, 6 (3), 144-145.

Oztekin S, Martinov M (2007). Medicinal and Aromatic Crops: Harvesting, Drying and Processing. Haworth Food Agricultural Products Press, New York, p. 320.

Quirijins, E. (2006). Modelling and Dynamic Optimization of Quality Indicator Profiles during Drying. Wageningen, The Netherlands: Ph.D. Thesis Wageningen University.

Raghavan G.S.V. * and Orsat V., (2007). Recent Advances in Drying of Biomaterials for Superior Quality Bioproducts. Asia-Pac. J. Chem. Eng., 2: 20-29.

Schmid W., Balz J. P. (2005). Cultivation of ginkgo biloba l. on Three Continents. ISHS: III WOCMAP Congress on Medicinal and Aromatic Plants - Volume 2: Conservation, Cultivation and Sustainable Use of Medicinal and Aromatic Plants. Acta Horticulturae 676.

Sadykov RA, Pobedimsky DG, Bakhtiyarov FR. (1997). Drying of bioactive products: inactivation kinetics. Drying Technol.; 15(10): 2401-2420.

Sharma VK, Colangelo A, Spagna G. (1995). Experimental Investigation of Difference Solar Dryers Suitable for Fruit and Vegetable Drying. Renew. Energy; 6(4): 413-424.

Smith R and Burford M (1992). Supercritical Fluid Extraction and Gas Chromatographic Determination of the Sesquiterpene lactone parthenolide in the medicinal herb, feverfew (*Tanacetum parthenium*). Journal of Chromatography 627: 255-261.

Tambunan AH, Yudistra, Kisdiyani, Hernani, (2001). Freeze Drying Characteristics of Medicinal Herbs. Drying Technol.; 19(2): 325-331.

Tanko, H.M., Carrier D.J., Sokhansanj S. and Crowe T.G. (2003). Effects of Drying Temperature and Storage on Parthenolide Concentration of Feverfew (*Tanacetum parthenium* L.) Leaves. Journal of Nutraceuticals, Functional and Medicinal Foods 4: 27-37.

Tanko, H.M., Carrier D.J., Duan L., Clausen Ed (2005). Pre- and Post-harvest Processing of Medicinal Plants. Plant Genetic Resources, 3 (2); 304-313.

Titz A. (2004). Medicinal Herbs and Plants – Scope for Diversified and Sustainable Extraction. 22-26 July 2004, Bangalore.

WHO. (2003). WHO Guidelines on Good Agricultural and Collection Practices (GACP) for Medicinal Plants Geneva.

Wisniewski G. (1997). Drying of Medicinal Plants with Solar Energy Utilization. Drying Technol.; 15(6-8): 2015-2024.

Youngken Heber W., (1948). *Textbook of Pharmacognosy*, Blakiston; 6th Edition.

6

Ecological and Economic Impacts of Shifts in Property Rights on Commons in Indian Himalayas

Hemant K Gupta* and **Pankaj Sharma**

ABSTRACT

The policies, legal systems and institutions set-up by government impact the management of natural resources by communities. The land use change due to shift in tenure property rights have caused ecological and socio-economic impacts on common resources (CRs) in the mountainous Indian state of Himachal Pradesh. The village commons are prominent sources of meeting various livelihood needs as the communities use them for grazing, collection of timber, fuel wood, NTFPs, recreation etc. and are prime targets of overuse, encroachments and spread of invasive species. The land, forest including alpine pastures and water are used jointly by the government as public property and by communities as CRs. Water used as CRs by the government for generation of hydroelectric power, irrigation and drinking purposes as public property. Estimation of the availability of CRs by de jure and de facto approaches shows significant differences in the Himalayan region. The effect of land reforms and land tenure, the state policy of reverting common lands to individuals and diverting to uses such as housing, roads, rail, water supply & communication, mining, industry, hydro-projects & vast network of transmission lines have been analyzed. The state promulgated acts bifurcating village common lands into categories to be managed by Forest and Revenue Departments and later reverted back to owners in apportionment to their share of land revenue leading to creation of individual property rights. Thus en masse

State Council for Science, Technology & Environment, 34, SDA Complex, Kasumpti, Shimla-9, Himachal Pradesh, India.

change in property rights have led to ecological impacts due to construction of roads and buildings effecting hydrological cycle, watershed functions and livelihoods of the people. The ecological impacts and processes in four agro-ecological zones in Himachal Pradesh on common resources i.e. land, water & pastures are discussed as well as shrinking of commons, its biophysical degradation and loss of management systems have been elaborated and analysed.

Keywords: Common Resources (CRs), Land use change, Village common land, Tenure, Ecological impacts, Livelihoods, Himachal Himalayas

INTRODUCTION

Ever since the publication of Hardin's articles "The Tragedy of Commons" there has been a growing debate on common pool resources, property rights, and resource degradation. The concept has been used to explain over exploitation of forests and fisheries, overgrazing, air and water pollution, abuse of public lands, population problems, extinction of species and other problem of un-enforced i.e. when there is open access; no individual bears the full cost of resource degradation. The result is "free riding' and over exploitation, what Hardin termed as "tragedy of commons" (Hardin 1968). The term "common pool resources" is used to refer to the physical qualities of resource systems and not to social institutions that human beings have attached to them. "Common property" or "common property regimes" is used to refer to a property rights arrangements in which a group of resource user share rights and duties towards a resource. Property terms refer to social institutions and not to any inherent any natural and physical qualities of the resource. The often used terms "common property resources" is avoided because it risks confusing property (a social institution) with resources (a part from physical and biological world).

Hardin's (1968) classic essay on the tragedy of the commons points out the hazards of open access, without stating clearly that the problem was lack of property rights or management regimes (the openness of access), not the sharing of use (common use). However, Hardin (1994) rectified the concept by distinguishing between the unmanaged (not owned) commons subject to tragedy and the managed (owned) commons where property rights may be able to prevent misuse of the resources. Thus, common property regimes are such institutional arrangements, which govern the access of people to renewable resources, and they constitute a most important middle ground between extremes of open access and private property. Common property resources (CPRs) are alternatively, referred to as common pool resources Communal forests, grazing areas and natural and constructed water resources are managed collectively and individual access is regulated by group rules (Ostrom, 1990).

The Context of Property Rights

Resources are generally classified by their physical characteristics, ownership patterns and use patterns. Going by physical characteristics, they represent natural occurrence or man-made creation. Examples are water, minerals, forests, crops land, manmade capital, human capital and so on. A variety of ownership patterns or property rights of such resources are also distinguishable. Examples are private ownership, state ownerships common and community ownership, open access and several other variants. Property is the result of 'secure claim to a resource or the services that the resource provides. The ownership rights and regimes define or delineate the management systems. Alternative forms of property rights are private, public, state, common property and open access (Ciriacy- Wantrup and Bishop, 1975; Hardin, 1968).

A distinction must be made between property rights and tenure. Using the given definition, property rights bring in some kind of management status to the ownership of property. Tenure on the other hand, refers to an act of pure ownerships with no reference to management (Singh, 1994). In India several land tenurial systems exists in all States. They are not associated with any specific or precise management system, except that the society is free to enjoy the resource under such rights.

CPRs of land, water, forest, fisheries, wildlife, and agriculture constitute towards the people's livelihood despite the decline in their area and physical productivity both cultivated and uncultivated lands and resources are an integral part of Indian agrarian systems. All resources, including CPRs are capable of being nationalized privatized or managed collectively and all are equally capable of being unspecified and unmanaged. This is because a particular resource may be controlled under any single regime or more than one regime (Gibbs and Bromley 1989). Common Property Land Resources (CPLRs) provide livelihood support to the rural poor apart from performing several useful ecological functions. Quick and significant reduction in the extent of CPLRs, largely due to the breaking down of institutional arrangements, has brought down the ratio of uncultivated land to cultivated land (Jodha,1995).

It has indicated that while population has been the biggest contributor towards the pressure on CPRs land, the process of encroachment has also reduced the size and status of CPRs land, fragmented land holdings, land holdings in the vicinity of a forest, tiny farm sizes and acquisition of grazing lands by developmental agencies and increased pressure by outsider grazer on the grazing lands were the important factor in the process of encroachment and shrinking common pool land resources (Negi, 2000).The encroachment of CPRs are more in developed villages whereas the extent of area under CPRs was higher in the background villages. The exogenous development with outside commercial interests, process of commercialization of collective resources, public policies and market forces resulted in the decline of CPRs. The importance of multiple social and institutional arrangements is manifestation of "social capital" and erosion or collapse of these arrangements leading to a decline of CPRs. In other words once "social capital" depletes, CPRs become open access resources and its process of depletion begins. Local customs/social groups have played an important role in designing informal institutional arrangement for collective tasks for managing CPRs in different parts of country. For example, culture of religious rules both formal and informal, have worked very effectively for management of irrigation channels (*Kuhls*) in Himachal Pradesh. However, these informal binders are seen to lose their effectiveness over the years, and as a result voluntary participation in resource management is declining. Also due to elected village councils (*Panchayats*) and non-recognition of traditional arrangements or customary arrangements which embodied social capital, the community lost collective stake and control over CPRs culture of group action got replaced by individualistic tendencies, disintegration of village community started and social capital got depleted subsequently. Land, water and forests are the three most important natural resources in mountains and the case study of Himachal Pradesh in India highlights the ecological and economic impacts of shifts in property rights on commons in this paper.

THE PROBLEMS OF COMMONS

Communities all over India have access to several types of commons, by tradition and in some cases by convention. With the breaking up of such traditional rights and the coming of land reforms all over country, the nature of holdings has changed. Common property land resource refers to land identified with specific types of property rights whereas wastelands are a class of land reflecting specific ecological characteristics (without regard to property rights). The Wasteland refers to a quality of land resources based on productivity and ecology- linked definition or concept of quality whereas, CPRs are based purely on ownerships and property right system; hence the two differ in concept as well as magnitude (Kadekodi 2004). It is important to recognize that at the time of implementing a land regeneration programme, the issue of property rights cannot be ignored. This is all the more relevant in creating a common pool of lands for regeneration and for designing proper benefit sharing rules and self governing design principles (Ostrom 1990)

The situation of common in India give the impression that whatever strong community hold persisted, the commons continued to serve the purpose of meeting everybody's requirements. The decline of commons in India in the past was not necessarily due to population pressure, internalization or over exploitation of the resources. It took place mainly because of the withdrawal of customary rights and rules, imposition of revenue motivation and even privatization in the management of such resources and the emergence of state control.

The land is used either as a private property (*individual ownership*) or managed as public property (*government property*). The land as private property is used for agriculture, horticulture and for residential purposes. The land as public property is further used either as a Common Property Resource or as a Common Pool Resource. Village common lands, *Panchayat** lands, Public wastelands are used as a common pool resource for grazing of cattle, construction of village ponds, water harvesting structures, public buildings and establishing community woodlots etc.

Forests are also used jointly both by the Government as public property and by communities as a Common Property Resource. The policies, legal systems set-up and institutions set-up by government for the management of the public lands used by the communities' impact the management of these natural resources by communities. Land in alpine pastures is primarily used as a common pool resource for grazing and collection of medicinal herbs etc. Fallow lands are also sometimes used as a common property resource for grazing.

The Water is primarily used as a Common Property Resource by the Government for generation of hydroelectric power, supply of water for irrigation and drinking purposes and by community as a Common Pool Resource for drinking and washing. Similarly by the Government for conservation of environment and production of forestry goods uses forests as a Common Property Resource for the State. And as a Common Pool Resource by communities for grazing of cattle, collection of timber, fuel wood, fodder, fruits, leaves, seeds non-timber forest products (medicinal herbs etc. bamboos, grass) recreation etc.

The rural economy of Himachal Pradesh is mainly dependent on common property resources (CPRs) and their use, availability and sustainability is the prime concern of the people living in the state. The economic well being of the farmers is directly or indirectly related to the management and productivity of these resources. CPRs are the resources, which are collectively used by a group of people. CPRs in turn contribute to the production and consumption needs of rural masses in terms of availability of fodder, fuelwood, small timber, fruits and medicinal herbs. CPRs also contribute to the people's income and employment generation. The overuse and exploitation of these resources have reduced the CPRs over years and have undergone considerable changes (GoHP 2000).

Encroachment, privatization and government appropriation has been the main processes taking resources out of communal control and use. The present case study discusses the processes in relation to the above processes and assesses the status of a representative CPRs i.e. land, forests and pastures and their management patterns in Himachal Pradesh.

STUDY AREA

The Western Himalayan Region and Himachal Pradesh

Himachal Pradesh is located in the western Himalayan region. The State lies between 32° 22′ to 33° 12′ N and 75° 47′ to 79° 04′ E and referred to as the Land of gods, Himachal is also known as the Himachal Himalayas. The word Himachal translates to "unshakable Snowy Mountain" (Ahluwalia 1988). 12 districts of the state cover 55,673 km^2, approximately 1.7 per cent of the total land area of India and around ten per cent of the total area of the Himalayas. The elevation varies from 350 meters in the foothills to 6975 meters in the high hills. The human population of the state is 6.08 million, of which 90.2% is rural and 9.8% is urban. the Ravi, the Beas, the Sutlej, the Chenab and the Yamuna river flow through this mountainous state. It has a relatively thin population density of 109 persons per km^2. The scheduled caste & scheduled tribes constitute 24.4% and 4.2% of the state population. The livestock population is 5.11 million (1.1% of country's livestock population).

Topography and Agro-climatic Regions

Himachal Pradesh has high geographic and topographic variation ranging from the *Shiwalik* hills in the south to the Himalayan ranges in the North. The physical characteristics often change within very small distances and have a bearing on the climatic conditions that range from sub-tropical to temperate, and sub-alpine to alpine. These climatic and ecological possibilities have implications for land use in different parts of the State (Gupta 1999). On the basis of agro-ecological variations, the State is divided into four major agro-climatic zones, viz. *(i)* low hill zone, *(ii)* mid hill zone, *(iii)* high hill zone and *(iv)* alpine zone.

The low hill zone comprises the areas adjoining the States of Punjab and Haryana and has some agro-ecological similarities with these plains. The elevation of the zone ranges up to 1,000 m above msl. The zones occupy about 35 per cent of the geographical area and have 33 per cent of the cultivated area and have highest population density. Climatic conditions of the zone make it relatively more suitable for agriculture; hence, irrigation is important from farming perspective. Pasture and forests cover for about 40 per cent of the geographical area is covered by the mid-hill zone ranges up to 2,000 m above mean-sea-level, and has about 22 per cent of the geographical area of the State. The zone accounts for about 53 per cent of the total cropped area and 45 per cent of the irrigated area of the State. A major portion of the uncultivated area is in pastures. Pastures and forests cover about 29 and 40 per cent of the geographical area of the zone. The forests are limited to the north and north-eastern slopes. Forests, common pasture lands, small gravity irrigation channels (*kuhls*) are the important CPRs in this zone.

The altitude of the high hill zone ranges from 2,000 to 3,000 m above msl. About 25 per cent of the geographical area of the State falls in this zone. A high proportion of this area is under natural pastures and forests. It has about 18 per cent of the cultivated area of the State. The topography of the high hills and the alpine zone put constraints on harnessing of the natural streams for irrigation. The small gravity irrigation channels (*kuhls*) and small rainwater storage tanks are the major source of irrigation. In fact, after forests and community lands, the *kuhls* are the major CPRs of this region as well.

The alpine zone or the high hills temperate dry zone comprises the high mountain regions and accounts for more than 8 per cent of the geographical area of the State. Rainfall is scanty and occurs in summers with an average of 20 cm per annum. The winters are severe and receive precipitation in the form of snow. Mostly tribal communities of the State inhibit the region. Since opportunities for cultivation of crops are limited, people are also engaged in sheep and goat rearing and related cottage works.

Table 6.1: Agro-climatic Zones of Himachal Pradesh

Zone	Name	Elevation (m)	TGA (%)	Agriculture Area
Zone I	Shivalik hill	350-650	17	40
Zone II	Mid hill	651-1800	17	37
Zone III	High hill	1801-2200	27	21
Zone IV	Cold dry	>2200	39	2

(TGA: Total Geographical Area)

RESULTS AND DISCUSSION

The Commons in Himalayas: A Historical Perspective

Chakaravarty-Kaul (1996) documents a number of cases from former British Punjab (about three fourth of modern Himachal Pradesh) where ancient system of managing the commons as *shamlat* and *mauzas* land protected the wastelands. The most important characteristics that defines 'commons' is limitation to entry and a well define group to manage rights in these area. Prior to the British rule, Punjab had a mix of arable farming and pastoral activities plus municipal and collective activities based on common lands. The common lands (*Banjar kadim*) were held collectively by the village custodian body (*malikan-deb*). There was also sub-section of the village called *patties*, which were held in common. Thus, with the village common (*shamlat-deh*), there was wasteland called *shamlat-patti*. The detailed account of changes in all such commons, for examples, due to legislation, canal irrigation system, population growth, and market factors. Historically, these changes occurred over time. Reductions of commons, shifting from long fallows to short fallows, conversion to private lands and other such factors has reduced the commons in Punjab to some extent. Some of the changes may be attributed to the revenue objectives of the British government. The analysis of the land tenure system in Punjab suggests that the type of partition of the commons as used by the British, partly for the revenue objective and partly to develop records to individual rights that led to private motives among the villagers; and land resources began to be treated as 'marketable'. This process ultimately led to the transfer of land to outsiders and moneylenders who had no incentives to maintain the integrity of the villagers. The commons of Punjab survived till 1947, but disappeared with the land reforms, which created open access to the commons; or rather bought about the 'tragedy of commons' in Punjab.

Hoskin and Stamps (1967) give an account of decline of common due to population pressure and open access to grazing land in medieval England. Unlike the open field system in England, several parts of former Punjab have a different pattern of sharing common fallow lands. In England the common was a compact field for grazing. In Punjab, different methods of scattering the commons among the villagers were practised. In one method (*khet bat*) such lands were classified by their soil type, moisture condition and vegetation into hars. This was the first step in the division of village fields-these were than rotated between civilizations and grazing and then distributed among village shareholders by some methods of lottery (*kura or dheri*). Thus, ultimately if a village was a *malikan-deh* and a *skin deh* the never lost his right to the decision making process.

Common Property Resources in Himachal Himalayas

Communities regard water channels, springs, village common lands, and temple groves as common property resources (CPR), and in most cases this is officially sanctioned, the locals also regard some state forest to be a CPR. Temple sacred groves are considered to be the property of the deity (*deota*). A village committee often does the management of the groves. The communities have very strict rules for the conservation of temple groves. Infringement of rules often leads to imposition of fines and may even lead to social, economic and religious boycott of the culprit families from the village community (Gulati, 2000, Gupta 2006).

The framework of law established the rights of people in forest and structured the use of resources through various land and forest settlements in late 19th and early 20th century. Even though these rights were initially defined as individual rights, they were in fact practised as communal rights following the Indian and *Pahari* tradition. The resting of forest rights to individuals rather than the village made it difficult to regulate the activities of their members. The village was given a portion of the state forest, within which each landholder of the village could exercise recorded forest rights, but management, regulation and enforcement were to be carried out by the Forest Department (Gupta, 1999).

In most parts of the state, local people tend to follow by common consensus, management practices for land and forest that are traditional and customary in nature. Such management practices often have a social religious or economic origin and can have a significant impact on the health and sustainability of forest. Effectively, they are treating the areas as CPR. The use of forests as a CPR by communities is however, subject to the classification forest as Reserved Demarcated Protected (Class I and II), or Undemarcated Protected (Class III), Forest. The Reserved Forests cannot be considered CPRs as people have practically no rights of privileges in them.

In addition to formalization of forestlands as CPRs, forest settlements also delineated a buffer zone between forest lands and villages. These buffer zones were the village common lands, or *shamlat* and common grazing lands. These village common lands were also CPRs but the ownership was vested in the village communities. Creation of Class III Undemarcated Protected Forests and recognition of village common lands created a balance between the use of forestry resources or national and other needs and meeting the bona-fide domestic requirements of the local population.

Estimation of Availability of Common Property Resources

As in any management process, so too in CPRs management, an assessment of the magnitude and health of the resource base is thus important. Such information provides a platform to the resource managers for setting management targets and enabling them to plan for the attainment of the same. Himachal Pradesh has had a rich heritage of maintaining common property resources, as well as institutions related to the use of these resources (Berkes et al. 1997). The present management crisis therefore can at best be termed paradoxical. Therefore, historical and current management strategy or efforts need to be analyzed and related economic and ecological impacts of tenure on property rights.

In a study by Chopra *et al.* (1990), an attempt was made to quantify the magnitude of common property land resources in the 1970's at the all India level. Another set of data on common property land resources was generated by the National Sample Survey (NSS), 54th Round, in the year 1998. Based on all these information, several alternative estimates of common property land and forests resources for recent periods in India have been presented and analyzed.

Right to CPRs may either be ownership, user rights or both. Legal approach (*de jure*) as adopted by the NSSO for estimating the area of "village common land". NSSO definition is "Accessible resources that are appropriated, possessed and/or managed jointly by a socially identifiable group and over which no single individual has exclusive right". Accessibility of resources is established by law. A major drawback of this approach is that only those resources lying within administrative limits of the village (revenue village), controlled by village institutions (Panchayat) have been taken into consideration i.e. village *panchayat* grazing and pasture lands, Village forest and wood lots not under forest/revenue department and Van *panchayat*, Village sites and threshing floors (*Bon, 2002*). The *de facto* approach used by Chopra and Gulati (2001), estimate based on nine fold classification of land use by All India Land Use Survey (AISLUS) estimation or under estimation from one item to another.

Table 6.2: Estimation of the Availability of Common Property Resources in India

Particulars	De jure Approach	De facto Approach
CPRs (ha)	4,20,220 ha	7,00,420 ha
CPRs (%) of the total geographical area:		
Forest land	15%	23%
Non-Forest Land	16%	36%
Non-agricultural land	23%	64%
	61%	–
CPRs per HHds (ha) out of which:	0.31 ha	0.41 ha
Forest Land	0.05 ha	0.16 ha
Non-Forest land	0.07 ha	0.28 ha
CPRs per capita (ha) out of which:	0.06 ha	0.08 ha
Forest Land	0.01 ha	0.03 ha
Non-Forest land	0.01 ha	0.05 ha

Source: NSSO (1999) and Gulati & Chopra (2001).

However legal and *de facto* approaches are not contradictory and complementary help to evaluate the importance of forest and non-forest land resource actually appropriated by rural households and agricultural farmers (*de facto approach*) and those for which rural households and agricultural farmers have user rights which are legally sanctioned and recognised by law (legal approach).The difference between these two approach thus help to measure the importance of land resources for which rights are not well specified or which are disputed (except cultivated land used as seasonal commons). According to estimate, on the whole, besides the 142 million hectares of cultivated land, rural households and farmers currently appropriate 70 million hectares of uncultivated land as common property i.e. about half a hectare of cultivated land (Bon, 2002).

Forest land in India represents 76.52 million ha, (23.3% of the total area). Forest land is 95.8%, State land (23.8% of total land area). From the juridical point of view, land based ownership prevails over resource based ownership (timber and non-timber resources).Indian forest laws present the paradox of guaranteeing a large number rights and privileges to the local population and equally important powers to Forest Department to restrict these rights and privileges in a highly discretionary manner (Singh 2000). The identified CPR's based on classification of land is given in Table 6.3.

Table 6.3: Identification of CPR's

Classification Land	Current Property Rights	Can it be Accounted as a CPR?	Included in Source of Sanction of for Access (as Assumed in the Estimation
Net sown area	Private	No	On uncultivated owned land: limited user rights
Current fallow	Private	No	On uncultivated owned land: limited user rights
Fallow other than current fallow	Private	Yes	User rights by convention
Cultivable waste	Revenue Dept.	Yes	Partial user rights by convention
Pastures and other grazing land	Panchayat	Yes	User rights by law
Barren and uncultivated land	Revenue Dept.	May be	No access
Area put to non-agricultural use	Public	May be	No Access
Forest area	Forest Dept.		
Reserved		No	No access
Protected		Partial	Partial user rights
Unclassed		Yes	User rights by law

Land Use and CPR Lands in Himachal Pradesh

Among the major forms of land use, forests lands occupy about 30% of the total geographical area of the state (Gupta, 2007). Pastures and grazing lands form about another 35 per cent. Together, these two components along with the barren area and land put to settlement and other non-agricultural uses account for about 75 per cent of the total geographical area of the State. Only about 21 per cent of the area is available for cultivation (Table 6.1). These figures classify of a heavy dependence of the State on these land resources that are mostly considered as the common property resources. A part of these lands are also termed as the wastelands, mainly from the point of their suitability for agriculture. No firm estimates of the extent of so termed wastelands of the State are available. However, one estimate puts the figure at 35 per cent of the geographical area under various types of land uses in the region are linked to each other and there is a heavy dependence on common property resources. Out of the ten land uses identified in a study in Kullu district of Himachal Pradesh, seven were having elements of CPRs components (Davidsons-Hunt, 1997), because of the interplay of *de jure* and *de facto* property rights in these resources. The commons in the study area were noted to be quite complicated. However, this is not the only isolated case of the type because of mountain specificity such inter-linkages are common in this hilly region. Since forests are the major natural resource of the State and until recently were the major revenue earning resource for the State. Apart from the direct incomes from the sale of timber, forests also contribute to the State exchequer by way of extraction of fuelwood and fodder, grasses, resin and gums, and various valuable medicinal and aromatic plants; the invaluable services rendered for maintenance of general ecological environment. As pointed out earlier, the people in this hilly region have had an intimate socio-economic and ecological relationship with their forests. In fact, it was the realization and acceptance of this intimate relationship and proved of crucial importance in formalizing various user rights in the forest, when the forests were brought under formal management regimes by the government.

Land use pattern in the Himachal have been shifting over time. The indicative refrences in land use (Table 6.4) in Himachal Pradesh provides some insight into the directions in which the land use pattern has shifted among various categories. These indicative references on land use in the State provide some insight into the directions in which the land use pattern has been shifting overtime. The shifting in the forest area is because of the reclassification of the area, as a result of which the area under the legal control of the Forest Department has increased. Distribution of the Geographical Area under Major Land uses in Himachal Pradesh is given in Table 6.4.

District wise detail of Land Use Classification as per village paper (Cadastral Survey) is given in Table 6.5.

FOREST RESOURCES AS CPR

The centralized structures and arrangement to regulate the use of natural resources have failed to fulfil the needs of rural communities (Agrawal, 1997; Jodha, 1997). Several studies have concluded that forests and trees are of special significance in the subsistence economy of the mountainous regions (Jodha, 1997; Thakur, 1993, Gupta, 2006). Forests in Himachal Pradesh are supporting rural economy by way of providing fodder, fuelwood, timber, herbs and medicinal plants. The average dependency of people on forests, fulfil their requirements of fodder (50%), fuelwood (90%) and timber (85%) (Singh,1995).

Table 6.4: Distribution of the Geographical Area Under Major Land Uses in Himachal Pradesh

Particulars	Temporal References Points (Years)						
	1950-51	1960-61	1970-71	1980-81	1990-91	1992-93	2000-01
Forests	23.69	30.80	21.76	26.96	30.85	30.57	24.04
Barren and uncultivated	6.49	4.25	4.05	4.72	5.46	4.30	17.75
Land put to non-agri. uses	7.41	6.75	5.87	5.40	5.74	5.93	6.89
Culturable waste	9.11	7.03	5.72	7.94	3.72	3.55	2.73
Permanent pasture and otherGrass lands	21.30	27.40	40.51	33.93	33.72	35.43	33.62
Land under misc. tree cropsand groves	1.47	1.25	1.39	1.31	1.43	1.26	1.25
Current fallow	3.10	2.30	2.00	1.38	1.32	1.43	1.19
Other fallow lands	0.43	0.12	0.07	0.42	0.45	0.67	0.29
Net cropped area	27.00	20.10	18.63	19.12	17.31	16.86	20.8
Total geographical area (byVillage papers, 'oooha)	1941.07	2635.12	2932.50	2985.20	3367.60	3395.40	4547.3

Data source: Statistical Outline of Himachal Pradesh (various issues). (% of total geographical area)

Table 6.5: Details of Land Use Classification of Himachal Pradesh

Name of District	G.A.	VPA	FA	BUL	Land put Non to Agri.	PPGL	TA (5 to 8)	CF	OF	CW	LUMTC	TAA	TA	Net CNFA {15(-)9}
1	2	3	4	5	6	7	8	9	10	11	12	13	14	15
Bilaspur	1167	1118	133	49	144	407	773	11	12	62	1	299	1118	385
Chamba	6515	6924	2720	55	117	3526	6418	22	02	62	–	419	6923	505
Hamirpur	1118	1102	184	144	180	47	555	58	22	116	–	352	1103	548
Kangra	6739	5780	2316	172	774	879	4141	103	08	269	92	1166	5779	1638
Kinnaur	6553	6237	376	1309	1246	3177	6108	18	–	36	1	75	6238	130
Kullu	5503	501	–	11	61	–	72	34	–	28	4	363	501	429
Lahaul & Spiti	13693	9112	1354	4158	1357	2201	9070	4	–	06	1	31	9112	42
Mandi	3951	3978	1754	250	–	964	2968	104	02	45	3	857	3979	1001
Shimla	5131	5083	1287	119	150	2492	4048	108	57	124	68	677	5082	1034
Sirmaur	2826	2248	483	85	107	569	1244	42	25	157	372	408	2248	1004
Solan	1937	1809	203	142	108	555	1208	40	14	143	16	389	1810	602
Una	1540	1549	181	232	291	133	837	17	23	236	67	369	1549	712
Total	**55,673**	**45,441**	**10,991**	**6726**	**4535**	**15,150**	**37,402**	**561**	**165**	**1284**	**625**	**5405**	**45442**	**8040**

Source: Economics and Statistics Department (H.P.) 2005-2006

Definition: GA.=Geographical Area; **VPA**=By Village Paper Area**; BUL**=Barren & Un-Cultivated land; **F.A.** =Forest Area; **PPGL**= Permanent Pasture & Grazing land; **CF**=Current Area **OF**=Other Fallow**; CW**=Culturable Waste; **LUMTC**=Land under Misc. Tree & Crops; **TAA**=Total Area of Agriculture**; TA** =Total Area

Table 6.6: Common Property Land Resources of India and Himachal Pradesh, 1990-2001

(In thousand hectares)

	Non-forest Areas			Forest CPR**			Total CPR (6+7)
	PLCPR	PPG	CWL	OTHFL	TOTNFCPR	PROT+UNCL	
India	13,031	11,740	14,830	9,260	48,861	34,869	83,730
Himachal Pradesh	392	1136	125	15	1668	3351	5019

Source: CMIE and Land Utilization Statistics of Ministry of Agriculture

Definitions: *PLCPR* = *Private lands to which common access may exists;* ***CWL*** = *Culturable wasteland;* ***PPG*** = *Permanent pastures and grazing lands;* ***OTHFL*** = *Other than current fallow;* ***PROT+ UNCL****= Protected and unclassed forests lands;* ***TOTNFCPR = PLCPR+CWL+ PPG+OTHFL, OTNFCPR*** *= (Total non-forest common property land resources);* ***TOTCPR = TOTNFCPR + (PROT+UNCL; TOTCPR:*** *(Total common property resources (forest and non- forest together)*

The importance of forests lies not only in meeting various basic requirements but also sustaining agriculture production. The forests are regarded as 'support areas' for agriculture and have to be regarded as the dominant form of land use in the hilly areas. No sustainable agriculture is possible in the hills without proper conservation and development of forest and common lands.

The nature and degree of dependence varied depending upon purpose, agro-climatic conditions and income status. Studies have shown that average households are dependent on forest lands for more than 80 % of fuelwood requirements and about 15% of it is met from own sources (Gupta, 1999). On average 58% of fodder requirements is met from forests, the remainder from farm forestry, grasslands, pastures and crop residues. 98.6 % of bedding material, stakes branches and poles required by households are met from forests. Almost 100% of the timber requirement for the construction and repair of houses is met from 'Timber Distribution' grants by FD till recently. The open-access regime of use of forest has led to their over-exploitation and misuse resulting in degradation and continuous deterioration of forestlands. It has affected the availability of domestic fuel, fodder and food resulting into a scarcity of the products. This has been attributed to the absence of any institutional arrangement to deal with the situation (Thakur, 1993).

The policy response to the breakdown of customary institutions is typically to go for some combination of private property, state taxes or state regulation. However, a good case can be made for strengthening the capability of people at a local level to manage these pressures themselves and to devise local solutions to local problems.

The common property rights may exist for lands which are forests. Hence the break-up of total forest area on the basis of legal status and ownership can be still more controversial. According to the forest statistics of India, legal ownership of 95.8 per cent of the forest area is vested in the states. Only 2.5 per cent of the forest area is with corporate bodies defined as municipal and other corporate bodies and village *panchayats*, etc. Local communities however, have right of access to parts of the state owned forest. Though reserved forests have always been treated as inaccessible, protected and unclassed forests are partly accessible. The unclassed or public forest lands are those given over with even fewer restrictions for the use of the public. Unclassed forests, with very low productivity, are always open to use by local communities. Accordingly, both protected and unclassed forests are treated as forming a part of common property forests resources, however, this may yield an overestimate of land to which common access may exist. It is therefore, the subset of total forest area minus reserved forest to which common property rights are assumed to exist.

District-wise Forest area by legal classification in Himachal Pradesh which may have a element of CPR is given in Table 6.7.

Table 6.7: District-wise Forest Area by Legal Classification in for the Year 2002-03 (Area in km²)

District	Geographical Area	Reserved Forest	Demarcated Protected Forest	Un-demarcated	Un-classed Forests	Municipal Forests	Cantonment Forests	Other Forests	Total Forests
Bilaspur	1,167	0.90	185.56	241.85	–	–	–	–	428
Chamba	6,522	372.53	3,960.33	685.06	–	5.31	6.42	1.00	5,030
Hamirpur	1,118	–	99.06	57.36	27.13	–	–	35.00	219
Kangra	5,739	76.01	558.02	1,635.82	504.54	0.80	–	67.00	2,842
Kinnaur	6,401	–	304.46	4,788.15	–	–	–	–	5,093
Kullu	5,503	160.52	3,209.15	1,582.02	–	–	–	–	4,952
Lahul & Spiti	13,841	70.54	396.61	9,665.76	–	–	–	–	10,133
Mandi	3,950	–	1,575.57	37.72	246.73	–	–	–	1,860
Shimla	5,131	53.46	1,148.89	2,161.49	–	1 8.69	–	35.00	3,418
Sirmaur	2,825	1,064.70	56.66	–	32.40	4.26	–	685.00	1,843
Solan	1,936	53.55	287.92	214.13	165.77	–	6.98	–	728
Una	1,540	43.92	48.02	130.06	–	–	–	265.00	487
Total	55,673	1,896.13	11,830.25	21,199.42	976.57	29.06	13.40	1,08.00	37,033
% age of Total Forest Area		**5.12**	**31.95**	**57.25**	**2.63**	**0.08**	**0.04**	**3.00**	**100.00**

Source: Forest Department, Himachal Pradesh

*Other Forests include roads & railway strips, area under section 38 I.F.A & LPA & HP Pvt. Forest

WASTELAND RESOURCES

From the point of view of ecological development, it is important to understand the extent and magnitude of wastelands. While CPRs are defined and identified within the property right regimes, wasteland is to be understood with in framework of ecological configuration and characteristics, beyond the property right regime. Therefore, a wasteland situation is quite distinct from a common property situation. As part of policies on revival of land form degradation in India, a large number of programmes have been developed by the concerned departments such as agriculture, rural development, wastelands departments, soil conservation, and eco-regeneration and so on. Therefore estimates of wasteland in India have been made as per their ecological characteristics and institutions which manage them is given in table 6.8.

Table 6.8: Estimates of Wasteland in India and Himachal Pradesh (Lakh hectare)

Area	Non-Forest Degraded Area	Non-Forest Forest Area	Reported Degraded Area	Forest Degraded Area	Total Geographical Area	Total
India	2103.07	936.85	753	358.89	1295.74	2856.07
Himachal Pradesh	20.34	14.24	35.33	5.34	19.58	55.67

Source: NWDC (1989), Indian Council of Forestry Research and Education, Lakh= 0.1 million

The non-forest land which has been affected by ecological problem such as salinity, wind and water erosion is been given in Table 6.9.

Table 6.9: Details of Non-forest Wastelands by Ecological Problems

	Saline/alkaline Land	Wind Eroded Area	Water Eroded Area	Total
India	71.65	736	129.26	936.91
Himachal Pradesh	–	14.24	14.24	–

Source: NWDC (1989)

Dependence on Forests and CPR lands

CPR's in the mid to high Himalayas are a main source of the high inputs of green manure required to sustain upland agricultural production, and of grazing and collected animal fodder to sustain the livestock which play a major role in the agricultural economy. They are also the source of the considerable amounts of wood needed for cooking, heating and house construction (Agarwal, 1997, Arnold, 1998). Over the last century Forest Department control over forestland and products from those lands has expanded considerably, to include nearly all-steep uncultivable lands. If all forestland not under intensive management is included, CPRs comprise 60 to 80% of wet forest regions in the Himalayas, *Shivaliks*.The natural forests, community forests, common grazing lands, are the major common property resources that are under tremendous pressures in the Himachal Himalayas. Although the *de jure* control of some of these resources may rest with the government or an agency, yet *de facto,* many of these resources, in many cases, are used as common properties. Sustainability of these resources is now crucial, not only for the economic well being of the people in this hilly region but also from the point of view of the larger economic and ecological implications for the country as a whole. Their structure and reliability influence the use pattern and sustainability aspects of various common property resources in a region (Baker 1998; Negi, 2002).

Forests are the major natural resources of the State and until recently were the major revenue earning resources for the State. Apart from the direct incomes from the sale of timber, forest also contribute to the State ex-chequer by the way of extraction of fuel wood and fodder, grasses, resin and gums, and various valuable medicinal and aromatic plants; not to mention the invaluable services rendered for maintenance of general ecological environment. The people of this hilly region have had an intimate socio-economic and ecological relationship with their forests. Thus the people were aware of maintaining the economic and ecological sanctity of forests while drawing various direct benefits from their forests. Hence, the hill people looked upon the forests with reverence. In fact, it was the realization and acceptance of this intimate relationship that proved of crucial importance in formalizing various user rights in the forests, when the forests were brought under formal management regimes by the government (Singh, 1995, Berkes et al, 1998, Gupta 1999). Forests in the vicinity of villages are mostly used as common property resources, because of traditional user rights in these forests in some cases and further because of the general lack of proper management and checks in other cases.

During the time of princely States, forests in the Himachal Pradesh were not managed under a planned management regime. However, because of the low population pressure and also because of the few opportunities for trade in timber, the forest utilization strategies did not seriously consider the forest degradation scenario. In fact, there are no definite records of specific efforts made in the field of forest management during the period of *Rajas/ Ranas* in the State. These rulers of small principalities used the forests as their personal properties, mainly as game reserves. Later on under the British rule forest management was formalized.

As, for example, in Kangra district, the forests were placed under the control of the Deputy Commissioner, who managed the forests as per the guidelines of Barnes' Regular Forests Settlements. The Forest Department started the formulation and documentation of the regular forest management plans for different forests by preparing forest Working Plans. Subsequently, people's participation was also sought in forest management to ensure protection of forests from fires and also from the acts of illicit felling of trees. In this regard, some local people's organisations were also encouraged. Negi et al. 1997 had estimated sources and proportions such as market, CPR's and private lands for meeting various forest-based timber,fuelwood and fodder requirements in Himachal Pradesh as given in Table 6.10.

Table 6.10: Prominent Sources of Meeting Various Forest-based Timber, Fuelwood and Fodder Requirements in Himachal Pradesh (*% of total use in an average household*)

Particulars	Sources and Proportion		
	Market	CPRs	Owned Lands
Timber	92.45	7.52	Negligible
Fodder (grasses)	10.90	61.66	27.44
Tree fodder	–	57.81	42.19
Agri. by-product	24.38	–	75.6
Fuel wood	17.90	50.21	31.89

Source: Negi et al. 1997.

NSSO 1999 has estimated CPR Land (ha) per household by type of land percentages of CPR land to total geographical area in Himachal Pradesh as per population size class, common village land (ha) per household by population and reduction in common village land diminished during 5 years size-class of villages possession of livestock and (ii) collection of fodder from CPR by availability as is given in tables 6.11 to 6.13.

Table 6.11: Common Village Land (ha) per Household by Population Size-class of Villages

Less than 100	101-200	201-600	601-1200	1201-2000	2001-5000	More Than 5000	All
1.70	0.23	0.19	0.26	0.04	0.39	0.07	0.33

Source: NSSO (1999).

Table 6.12: Number (per 1000) of Households Reporting (i) Possession of Livestock and (ii) Collection of Fodder from CPR by Availability of CPR Land and Forest in Himachal Pradesh

Estimates	Forest Within	No. Forest with Reach but with CPR land per hh (ha)				Estd. (00)	Samples
		Less than 0.1	Less than 0.1	0.1-0.4	0.4 or more	Any	
P	820	753	1122	722	807	8251	1542

Source: NSSO (1999).

Table 6.13: Reduction in Common Village Land Diminished during 5 Years per 1000 ha of Common Village Land 5 Years Ago by Size-class of Village in Himachal Pradesh (NSSO, 1999).

Less than 100	101-200	201-600	601-1200	1201-2000	2001-5000	More than 5000	All	Reduction in CPR land (00 ha.)
–	181	291	23	18	486	–	1000	0

Source: NSSO (1999).

Population Pressure on Common Land Resources

There are some common lands in and around the forests, the use of which is not governed by any formal rules and hence the situation is equally alarming in the use of these CPRs components of forests and non-forest areas. Some field-level estimates show this situation more clearly by using micro-level information gathered through surveys as given in Table 6.14. It is evident from these figures that irrespective of the agro-climatic regions, the pressures on CPR lands have been increasing significantly over time (Jodha, 1997). The pressure is relatively high in the mid-hill region, where the population per ha of CPR lands has increased by more than 300 per cent in 1991 as compared to 1961. Similarly the increase in the other two regions is very high; more than 200 per cent against the same benchmark of 1961.

Table 6.14: Population Pressure on CPR Lands in Different Zones of Himachal Pradesh

Years	Population/ ha of CPR Lands		
	Low Hills	Mid Hills	High Hills
1961	0.69	2.73	1.00
1971	0.95	3.28	1.64
1981	1.32	5.20	1.96
1991	1.83	9.13	2.31

Source: Singh, 1995.

While population has been the biggest contributor towards the pressure on CPR lands, the increasing commercial farming and agriculture, shift in government policies have contributed to the encroachment pressure on CPRs. It is observed that a higher proportion of marginal and small farmers were involved in the process of encroachment up to 5 per cent of their land holding size, while a higher proportion of medium and large farmers were engaged in the higher level of encroachment (Negi, 2002).

Land Tenure, Land Reforms and its effects on Commons

Land Tenure

Land tenure affects the accessibility to various lands including forests, which in turn influence the use and utilisation pattern of these resources.

The hill *Rajas* held personal control of all lands and bequeathed it to individual farming families. Thus, the paramount right of property was vested in the Raja as landlord, and the right of cultivation was derived by grant from the Raja and vested in the cultivators. The first right extended to the whole of the principality, the second primarily extended only to the plot specified in the grant, but carried with it further rights of common in adjacent waste. Rights for use of forest and pasture, where the resources were abundant and use very light, were dispensed by the *Rajas* to courtiers, military supporters, or others. The *Rajas* ordinarily granted small fields and limited local rights but kept the vast remaining areas of largely unutilised mountain land, including forest, for their own use as hunting grounds. However prior to British rule, the hill Rajas made no attempt to regulate access by farmers to forests and common lands for the purpose of forest resource utilisation. Since forest and grazing lands were vast in relation to the limited rural population of people and livestock, it seems likely that villagers themselves had little need for collective regulation of the common lands including forests (Tucker, 1982; 1983). So, in all probability, access to forests was unregulated, whether by Rajas or village communities. However, the land tenure systems, which evolved in the Rajas' domains, set traditions that decisively shaped resource use in the colonial century and later. As the British argued after taking control of the hill areas that they were merely translating the tradition of their predecessors, the hill Rajas, that the government held ultimate title to all land and might give usage rights to the people as it chose (Tucker, 1982, 1984).

Agrarian relations were characterized by sharecropping and other forms of tenancy and by the exaction of services known as *Beggar "Forced Labour"*. Although the agrarian structure in hill areas was generally characterized by a lesser degree of inequality than in the plains, it was not an equitable system. Beggar was formally abolished in 1948; subsequently the government introduced liberal land polices and enacted major land reforms. The most important were the:

- 1953 Himachal Pradesh Abolition of Big Landed Estates Land Reform Act;
- 1972 Himachal Pradesh Tenancy and Land Reform Act;
- 1972 Himachal Pradesh ceilings on Land Holdings Act; and
- 1974 Himachal Pradesh Village Common Land Vesting and Utilisation Act.

The government divested large landowners of their estates, the land ceiling being set at 24 bigha's (2 ha) for irrigated land, 36 *bigha* (three ha) for Un-irrigated land, and 72 *bigha* (6 ha) for orchards. The reform of 1974 vested Village Common Lands (*"shamlat"*) in the State. Much of the nationalized land was redistributed to landless of near landless households, with a target provision of five *bigha* (0.4 ha) per household. Similarly, under the law of

'*Nautor*', a landless farmer was allowed to cultivate government land, including (UPF) Undemarcated Proctected Forest Class III land, and expected to be granted secure title in due course.

The Himachal Pradesh Village Common Lands Vesting and Utilization Act, 1974

The Punjab Village Common Lands (Regulation) Act, 1961

In 1974, Himachal Pradesh Village Common Land Vestment and Utilization Act enacted to enable the Government, to give *shamlat* (common) lands to the landless people. Under this act the government took control of all common lands, and common grazing lands to supplement the pool of land available for distribution to those with little or no land. Rules and utilisation scheme for lands acquired under this act were prepared in 1975. A part of the land was to be kept aside for common purposes like grazing to be managed under the Punjab Village Common lands (Regulation) Act 1961. The acquired *shamlat* lands were divided into two categories: allotable and non-allotable. The non-allotable was to be transferred to the Himachal Pradesh Forest Department (HPFD). These non-allotable *shamlat* lands, once "*de jure*" community lands available for the exercise of rights, became "*de facto*" common lands, as the Revenue Department did not transfer the lands to the HPFD. Moreover, no action could be taken to demarcate and classify these lands as forests under the provisions of the Indian Forest Act 1927 as it was viewed as a mechanism for converting community lands into government lands and restricting the right of access by communities.

However, under these agrarian reforms about 87,000 occupancy tenants became owners of their tenancy lands, while some 80,000 landless people got about 0.4 hectare 5 bighas (Unit of land measurement in Himachal Pradesh of land). The majority of these persons belonged to Scheduled Castes and Tribes. Out of about 0.5 million agricultural families about 0.45 million families became landowners (Mittoo, 1978).

These reforms have been effective in reducing the level on inequality in the agrarian structure in state. Absolute landlessness became rare at the district level, although at that time wholly owned and self-operated holdings constitute only 68.4 per cent of the total and part-owned and part leased holdings a further 19.7 per cent. However majority of households still only have access to very small landholdings. Further beneficiaries under the land reforms mostly received only marginal lands. The average landholding size is 1.2 ha (GoHP, 2000).

While this liberal land policy has helped reduce landlessness and rural inequalities it has been largely unplanned and undirected with adverse implication for the rational utilisation of land in some areas and in particular creating problems for the Forest Department over the management of Class III/UPF land.

Nautor Rights '*Nautor*' is the name given to the breaking up of government wasteland and Class III land for cultivation and construction of houses, cattle sheds, and water mills. The forest settlement rules define it as a grant on payment of a *nazrana* (premium) of an interest in the land in un-demarcated waste owned by the government. Until 1896, the village headman of *negi* had the power to assign *Nautor Patta*, after the forest settlements began; the right was given to the Assistant Commissioner. These rules were superseded in 1946.

The problems of awarding *Nautor* became apparent quite early. The original concern of the British Government in defining Class III (Undemarcated Protected) forestland was not to claim the land but to ensure forest conservation. The people had a right to extend cultivation as long as it did not lead to soil erosion and forest destruction. But the settlement report noted that *Nautor* grants had already been given an all-available land. The Forest Department was perpetually complaining of the depletion of forests. As a result of the limited fights in Class I and II forests, all the pressure was on Class III forest.

In 1968, realizing the problems resulting from the ad hoc allotment of 'Nautor Land Rules' that hese stated that *Nautor* grants were only to be given on government land other than Reserved and Demarcated forests, i.e., in Undemarcated Forests. The State Government could grant *Nautor* in Demarcated Forests and in exceptional and special circumstances in Reserved Forests, but these were to be subject to the Forest Act. Nautor could be given for agriculture, horticulture threshing floors, and construction of houses of public buildings. Priority was given to landless people, marginal landholders, scheduled castes and tribes, families of people who had died in military service, ex-servicemen and others. The *Nautor* Rules provided detailed procedures for receiving objection and clearance from the gram panchayat. It also contained a provision for an assessment by the Forest Department of the tree resources on the plot. There were some ecological restraints, for example *Nautor* could not be given for agriculture on steep slopes, but the main purpose of the forest Department assessment was to know the value of the trees which must be felled and charged to the grantee. The main thrust was to allot land to the target groups. In the course of allotting *Nautor*, the revenue official prepared a map indicating the location of the patch and record of rights in favour of the grantee. Thus by the *Nautor* grants the patch and record of rights in favour of the grantee. Thus by the *Nautor* grants were made, particularly in the seventies.

With the shrinking of the land available for agriculture and other purposes, grants of *Nautor* became more restrained and more focused on the poorer and weaker sections of the community. In the eighties the approach changed radically. The forest (conservation) Act 1980 clearly prohibited the state government from diverting forestland for non-forest purposes without prior approval from central government. Although the practice of granting *Nautor* continued for sometime, it became clear that since Class III forest were protected forest, prior clearance from the centre was actually necessary. The amendment in 1987 further stipulated that forestland could not be granted to an agencies other than the government without prior permission. Thus by the mid eighties grants of *Nautor* to ordinary people had almost ceased, and proposals for approval for development work in *Nautor* land, like making roads and school, were submitted to central government.

Nautor has now come to an end, but only after granting land wherever feasible for agriculture. The Forest Department always objected to the grant of *Nautor*, but the Revenue Department always saw allotment of *Nautor* as a state welfare programme. The main cause of disagreement between the Forest and Revenue Departments was the problem of Undemarcated Protected or Class III Forests. The Revenue Department considered these lands not to be forests, because the revenue records don't contain entries for such lands as forests. They considered Class III Forest to be a bank of lands which could be used to make allotments to the landless and poor as per the policy of the government. Even demarcated forest which revenue records did not exist was considered to be revenue lands from which they could allot *Nautors*. At least 26 classification has been issued in the form of executive instruction since 1968. Although, *Nautor* grants have been suspended, no new land policy has been announced (Gulati, 2002).

Interplay of Private V/s Public Property through Policies

The Government policy to hand over common lands to the individuals Communication of new roads to hamlets making possible, In Sirmaur district common lands of both sides of roads has been sold to settlers from outside., Nomadic grazing effected as CPRs vanished, Pressure shifted to forest lands causing their degradation, invasive species caused declined in productivity. The CPRs are affected by diverting land to other uses, housing, roads, rail, water supply & communication, Mining, Industry, hydel projects-Reservoirs & vast network of HT transmission lines etc.

In case study of Sirmaur District in Himachal Pradesh change in common land acquired under the Himachal Pradesh Village Common lands Vesting and Utilisation, Act 1974, the common land was vested from 707 villages community land in Sirmaur District was vested with government. However this community land was given back to individual as per amendment in the Act in 2001 (Table 6.15). However, land from the nine villages was with the government and were given as mining purposes on lease. In a recent judgement of Himachal Pradesh High Court on dated 22.11.2007, CPW No. 1077 of 2006 has decided that the Himachal Pradesh Village Common lands Vesting and Utilisation, Act 1974 is an agrarian piece of legislation that development activities which are akin to the agricultural pursuits read with the expression 'common purposes' defined in the Act and not the mining activities which has been declared as development activity and is held unconstitutional and directed that the land should be given back to the individuals.

Table 6.15: Change in Common Lands in District Sirmour, Himachal Pradesh

Community Lands Vested to Government in 1974		Community Land as per Amendment in 2001 Given to Individual		Still with Government		Decision to be made	
Total Villages	Area (ha)	Total Villages	Area (ha)	Total Villages	Area (ha)	Total Villages	Area (ha)
707	6,08,331.3	692	43,746.64	9	29.3	6	184.97

Source: Deputy-commissioner, Sirmaur.

Forest Land Tenure

In law, the forest Department is responsible for management & administration of Reserved Forest, Demarcated Protected forest, DPF) (Class I and III), (UPF) Un- demarcated Protected Forest (Class III), and for trees on government grazing land. The Forest Department under the Himachal Pradesh Land Preservation Act of 1978 regulates utilization of tree on private land.

Throughout Himachal Pradesh, common land was vested in the state under the Village Common Land Vesting and Utilisation Act of 1974 except for some land along rivers, roads, and paths and common sacred groves near temples. However, government wasteland, grazing land and Class III forestlands are widely treated as open access resources. UPF/Class III land is regarded very differently by the Forest Department. The Revenue Department and various groups of local people, the forest Department view UPF/Class-III land as part of the forest estate, to be protected from encroachment and where possible, planted (typically with chir pine) and brought under settlement as DPF. In contrast, the Revenue Department views UPF/ Class-III land as bank of land on which to draw to meet the needs of *Nautors* and others for land to cultivate. The most villagers find this the more congenial view and, legally or not, continue to break such land for cultivation or for planting as orchards. However, both the extension of cultivation and the increased area planted under trees and declared DPF, reduce the land available for grazing livestock thus placing pastures under increased pressure. In the area under DPF has been shown increased by 2933 hectare in the year 2002. This affects both local flocks and flocks belonging to transhumance grazers. All of these activities reflect an unplanned, undirected and frequently irrational approach to land management and affecting or degradation of village commons.

Grass Lands and Pasture Lands

Pastures or common grazing lands are another important common property lands, particularly in the alpine region. Utilization of these land resources in most cases is on the basis of socio-cultural norms of a particular area. At most times, there are accepted norms that have been traditionally set up by the society or the local public agencies. The local democratic institutions like *panchayats* are also engaged in the setting up, modification and/or enforcing these norms. Different types of users use these different types of grazing lands: who are: *(i)* local people; *(ii)* settled animal grazers; and *(iii)* nomadic grazers. The grazing is, it is mostly the nomadic and settled grazers that become the reference points. Local people or farmers graze their animals in the near vicinity of their dwellings on a day-to-day basis. The other two categories of animal keepers move out of the village or dwelling places for longer duration, often months, to graze their animals. Sheep and goats are the major animals that are routinely taken to highland pastures for grazing. The nomadic *graziers, gujjars,* being the most prominent members of this group, mostly keep buffaloes and roam along their set routes for grazing their herds (Chakravarty, 1997, Tucker, 1986.

Grazing areas or pastures lands in the vicinity of the village have traditionally been so managed that grazing is restricted to the periods when it does not effect growth of grasses. Animal rearing in the hills is dependent on natural grasslands, which are the major contributor (Table 4) towards the total fodder requirements of a household for its livestock (Thakur, 1996, Negi *et al.*1997). In the recent past, these lands used to be open and boundaries only demarcated notionally among different users. Over time, however, some permanent boundary markers are being put to use. At times; it is possible to notice stonewalls and wooden or even iron poles demarcating the boundary among *ghasni* users at a particular location. This is quite a deviation from the practice where the lands were informally so demarcated that each user family knew the boundaries of the village pasture lands under its control. The growing emphasis on the fixed or prominent boundary markers seems to be the reflection of the growing tendency to privatize these common lands, through the process of first gaining operational control and later claiming title to these lands. This also implies the growing population pressure on the farmlands and hence the tendency to hedge against the acute land pressures in the times to come.

There are two distinct types of grazing pattern depending on the altitude and climate. In the lower and middle hills the predominant livestock are cattle, whereas in the pastures of the higher hills and alpine areas most of the grazing animals are sheep and goats.

Effect of Land Reforms

Extension of agricultural land is partly due to a land policy of *"laissez-faire"* and *"fait accompli"*, it is exacerbated by political system to influence the electorates for votes, illegal encroachments, public & common by various categories, expansion of cultivable lands and the official regularization of encroachments. The pressure of high human and animal populations on uncultivated lands and the small size of farmlands (1.57 ha) pose a constant challenge to the conservation of ecosystems, as well as to the subsistence of rural populations, engaged in the agricultural sector. The expansion of cultivation on marginal land is due to population pressure on land, seen in the smaller number and shortening of agricultural fallow. The reduction and impoverishment of cultivable waste, forest and pastures, resulted in a gradual privatization of crop residues and in a decline of seasonal grazing on private lands. The reduction in pastures and increasing livestock gradually resulted in overgrazing and degradation of pastures. The fall in natural regeneration and intensified pruning of branches, gradual opening of the canopy and increase of invasive species *Lantana camara and Ageratum* spp. are major ecological impacts. Demand for fuel wood has also contributed to the intensive pruning of branches. Scarcity of fuel wood was compensated by using combustibles of lower quality: dried dung, crop residues and dry leaves at the expense of the fertilization of cultivated land. Over the long run, degradation of pastures and forest ecosystems have resulted in soil erosion by rains, more degraded land (agriculture, pastoral and forest) and disturbed water cycles.

Decline of CPRs

Jodha (1994) suggests several other micro-level indicators which can be broadly grouped into physical degradation indicators and CPR management indicators. The physical degradation indicators are: number of CPR products collected by the communities; trees and shrubs per hectare; number of ponds; number of CPR plots where biodiversity has declined; and CPR area where grazing capacity has declined. Common property resources management indicators include protection of CPR area; regulation of CPR usages; and investment in development of CPRs. Jodha (1985) also describe the declining state of commons in Rajasthan due to population pressure and commercialization. Decline in community based tank irrigation has taken place due to the change of property rights regime, from commons to the state.

The decline is visible in shrinking of their areas, bio-physical degradation, and some indicators of physical degradation are CPR-products collected, per hectare number of trees and shrubs, number of watering points (ponds) in grazing CPRs, number of CPR plots where rich vegetation, indicated by their nomenclature, is no more available, and loss of management systems. CPRs are generally neglected and are declining rapidly in different areas. The decline is visible in *(i)* shrinkage of their areas; *(ii)* bio-physical degradation; and *(iii)* loss of management systems.

The Process of CPR Decline is due to increased population pressure, regressive land distribution polices, occupational change, degree of commercialization, factionalism, group dynamics, socioeconomic differentiation, dependence on state patronage, population growth, group action (Social capital), introduction of land reforms, introduction of village *panchayats,* market forces, side effects of other developments.

The above changes in community arrangements attributed to the replacement of the customary arrangements by formal administrative, legal and political arrangements were accentuated by the penetration of market forces (Jodha, 1997). But in the past, market driven devices did not extend to CPRs, however, with the replacement of local community arrangements by formal top- down interventions, individualizations of people's approach to CPRs, emergence of circumstances favouring conversion of CPR land into private property, " the land – scarcity-land price" links became operative in CPR context.

CONCLUSION

Ecological and Economic Impacts on Commons

The village common lands are primary targets of overuse, encroachment in higher hills. The village pastures overused (under control of forest department), to variable extents, biodiversity and Water resources are tapped for hydroelectric projects, traditional mills, small and higher mega project. Change in cultural economics values, Diversion of water resources, Communities not translating to common are deprived influential people production here, liquefiers are drying and springs are scarce, Availability of water is not irrigation area, and Village common lands are given to *nautors,* grazing lands presently is diversified to forest area effecting ground flora and regeneration are scanty.

Ecological connotation is key weather cycle, less, snowfall water scarcity, biodiversity, vegetation change, scrub growth has due to invading species, weeds, and impacting productivity of forest lands but also of marginal lands (Gupta, 2006).

Major resources, encroachment, Government policy to hand over common lands to the individuals, The construction of new roads to hamlets making accessibility possible, Sirmour common lands of both sides of road has sold to self hers other than local village community and no grazing lands hence forest and invading species, *Lantana* has increased. Examples: Land policy impacts, Sirmour land has been common lands to growers such as individuals. The construction of concrete structures is causing stress and strain on ecology of area.

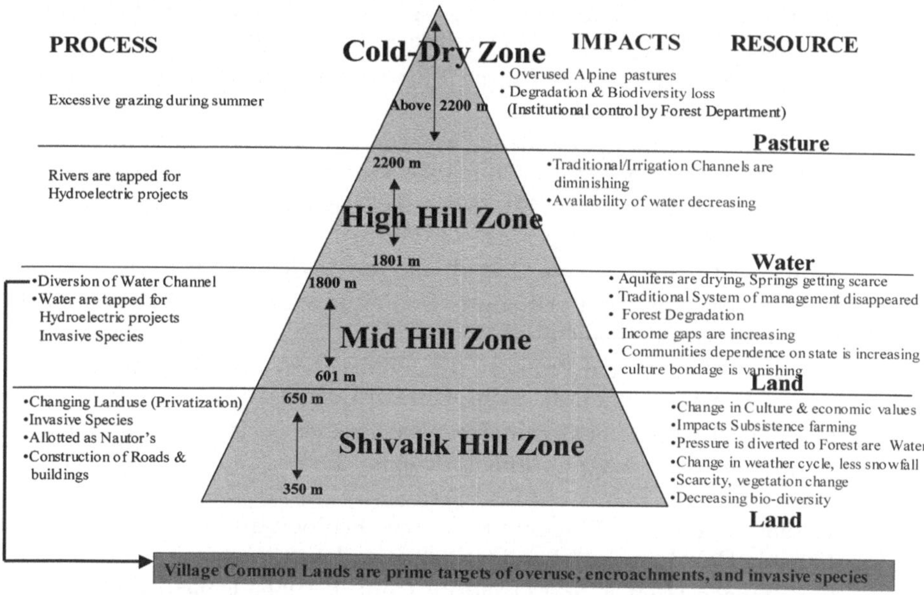

Ecological Impacts in Four Agro-ecological Zones of Himachal Himalayas

Davidson-Hunt (1997) concludes that the conflict between migratory graziers and settled agriculturists has been due to the change to horticulture leading to changed social relationships. In the past many households developed a working relationship with transhumant graziers which enabled them to rest in agriculture fields and in return obtain manure. This is not required for land under horticulture. Further, many households also indicated that they have reduced or eliminated sheep and goats. A village that no longer contained a significant pastoral component is no longer willing to allow pastoralists to graze sheep in their village grazing areas. For example, in Dashar; where establishing forest plantation could be done by excluding sheep, goats and pastoralists from grazing areas. These opinions are predominant in villages where households have shifted to horticulture and fall into the migratory route of graziers (Gupta, 1999).

REFERENCES

Agarwal Arun and Gibson C. Clark, 1999. Environment and Disenchantment: The Role of Community in Natural Resource Conservation. Ed. Jones Samantha and Carswell Grace. In the Earthscan Reader in environment, Development and Rural Livelihoods. pp. 629-649.

Agrarwal, Arun 1997. Forest Management under Common Property Regimes in the Kumaon Himalaya. In Ed. Shiva Koti, Ganesh, Varughese George,Ostrom Elinor, Shukla Ashutosh, Thapa Ganesh People and Participation in Sustainable development Undertaking the dynamics of Natural Resource Systems. pp. 64-74.

Agrawal and Ashwini 2006. Explaining Success on the Commons: Forest Governance in the Indian Himalayas. *World Development* 34 (1): 149-166.

Ahluwalia, M.S. 1988. History of Himachal Pradesh. Delhi: Intellectual Publishing House.

Arnold, J.E.M. 1993. Management of Forest Resources as Common Property. *Commonwealth Forestry Review* 72(3): 157-161.

Arnold, J.E.M. and Stewart, W. C. 1991. Common Property Resource Management in India. *Tropical Forestry Paper no. 24*. Oxford: Oxford Forestry Institute, Department of Plant Sciences, Oxford University. vii + 52 pp.

Baker Mark, J. 2005. The Kuhl of Kangra. Community-Managed Irrigation in the Western Himalya. Premanent Black. pp. 1-271.

Baker Mark, J. 1997. Common Property Resource Theory and the Khul Irrigation System of Himachal Pradesh, India. Human Organisation, pp. 199-208.

Baker, J.M. 1998. The Effect of Community Structure on Social Forestry Outcomes: Insights from Chota Nagpur, India. *Mountain Research and Development* 18(1): 51-62.

Berkes, F. 1989. "Common Property Resources-Ecology and Community Based Sustainable Development" London: Belhaven Press.

Berkes, F., Davidson-Hunt, I. and Davidson-Hunt, K. 1998. Diversity of Common Property Resource Use and Diversity of Social Interests in the Western Indian Himalayan. *Mountain Research and Development* 18(1): 19-33.

Berkes, F., Gardner, J. S. and Sinclair, J. 1997. Mountain Ecosystems and Sustainability: Conclusions and Policy Implications. Eds. F. Berkes and J.S. Gardner in Sustainability of Mountain Environments in India and Canada, Natural Resources Institute, University of Manitoba Winnipeg, Canada. pp. 377-403.

Berreman, G. D. 1970. Pahari Culture: Diversity and Change in the Lower Himalayas. Ed. K. Ishwran in *Change and Continuity in India's villages*. Columbia University Press, New York. pp. 73-104.

Bhati, J.P. and Singh R. and Sharma, L.R. 1992. Diversity of Mountain Farming Systems In Himachal Pradesh, India. Oxford & IBH Publishing Co. Pvt. Ltd. New Delhi, India.

Bon, Emmanuel, 2002.Common Property Resources at the Interface of Agriculture and Forestry Policies: Before and After 1988.In Traditional Ecological Knowledge, Conservation Of Biodiversity and Sustainable Development. ed. Depommier Denis, Ramakrishnan P.S.Institut Francais De Pondichery. pp. 190-209.

Bromley, W.D. 1992.The Common Property and Common-Property Regimes. In Making the Commons Work. Institute of Contemporary Studies, California. pp. 3-16.

Bromley, D.W. and M.M. Cernea 1989. The Management of Common Property Resources: Some Conceptual and Operational Fallacies, Discussion Paper (57), The World Bank, Washington, D.C.

Chakravarty-Kaul, M. 1998. Transhumance and Customary Pastoral Rights in Himachal Pradesh: Claiming the High Pastures for Gaddis. *Mountain Research and Development* 18(1): 5-17.

Chakravarty-Kaul, M., 1996. Common Land and Customary Law: Institutional Changes in North India Over the Past Two Centuries. Oxford University Press.

Demographic Patterns and Natural Resources Dynamics in the Punjab, 1881-1991". In: Ganesh Shivakoti, George Varughese, Elinor Ostrom, Ashutosh Shukla, and Ganesh Thapa's (ed.) People and Participation in Sustainable Development, Understanding the Dynamics of Natural Resource Systems. pp. 100-113.

Chopra, K and Gulati, S.C., 2001. Migration, *Common Property Resources and Environmental Degradation*, Sage Publications.

Chopra, K., Gopal K. Kadekodi, and Murty, M.N. 1990. Participatory Development: *People and Common Property Resources*, Saga Publication, New Delhi.

Davidson-Hunt, K. 1997. Gender, Class and the Common in the Indian Himalayas. Eds. F. Berkes and J.S. Gardner in *Sustainability of Mountain Environments in India and Canada*, Natural Resources Institute, University of Manitoba, Winnipeg, Canada. pp. 143-183.

David, F., Fikret Berkes, Bonnie MaCay, J. And James Acheson, M. 1990. The Tregdy of the Commons: Twenty-Two Years Later, Human Ecology. pp. 1-19.

FSI 2005. State of Forest Report, Government of India, Ministry of Environment and Forests, Dehradun, India. pp. 58-60.

Gadgil, M. 1985. Social Restraints on Resource Utilization: The Indian Experience'. In J.A. McNeely and D. Pitt, eds., Culture and Conservation: The Human Dimension in Environmental Planning, Croom Helm, Dublin.

Gadgil, M. 1990. India's Deforestation: Pattern and Processes. Society and Natural Resources. pp. 131-143.

Ghabru, S.K. 2006. Need for Sustainable Land Use Planning in Himachal Pradesh. In Sustainable Land Resources Management In: Himalayan Region. Ed. Raina JN, Sharma IP, Bawa R., Tripathi D. Bishen Singh, Mahendra pal Singh, Dehradun. pp. 23-43.

Ghate, R., 2004. Uncommons in the Commons. Community Initiated Forest Resource Management. pp. 1-206.

Gibbs, J.N. and Bromley, D.W. 1989 Institutional Arrangements for Management of Rural Resources: Common Property Regimes. In F. Berkes (ed.) Common Property Resources: Ecology and Community- Based Sustainable Development. Belhaven press, 25 Floor Street, London.

GoHP 2000. Common Property Resources in Rural Areas. In: State of the Environment Report-Himachal Pradesh by State Council for Science Technology and Environment, Shimla. pp. 10-13.

Gulati, A.K. 2000. Status of Participatory Forest Management: Implications for Policy and Human Resources' Development in Himachal Pradesh, India. In Aupam Bhatia's (ed.): Participatory Forest Management: Implications for Policy and Human Resources' Development ijn the Hindu Kush-Himalayas. pp. 27-38.

Gupta, H.K. 2006. Adapting to Climate Change in Himalayan Forest Based Landuse Systems. In Sustainable Land Resources Management In: Himalayan Region. Ed. Raina JN, Sharma IP, Bawa R., Tripathi D. Bishen Singh, Mahendra Pal Singh, Dehradun. pp. 107-123.

Gupta, H. K. 2007. Deforestation and forest Cover Changes in the Himachal Himalaya, India. International Journal of Ecology and Environment Sciences, 33 (2-3): 207-218.

Gupta, H.K. 1999. A Study of Factors Influencing Participation in Joint Forest Management in the Northwest Himalayas, India, Unpublished Thesis University of Aberdeen, Scotland UK.

Gupta, H.K. 2005. An Analysis of Policy, Legal and Institutional Framework of Common Property Management in the Himachal Himalayas, India: A Case Study in Securing Common Property Regimes in a Globalizing World.

Gupta, H.K. 2005. Forest Resource Management Through Traditionally in Vogue Participatory Approaches in Himachal Himalaya, "Quality of the Life in the Himalaya Region". (ed.) L.R.Sharma, Indus Publishing Company.

Gupta, H.K. 2006. Joint Forest Management: Policy, Participation and Practices in India. International Book Distributors, Dehradun, India. pp. 400.

Gupta, H.K. 2007. Local Institutions and Indigenous Forest Management Practices in the Indian Himalayas: A Case for Linking Traditions with Technology. In S. Feary (Ed.) Occasional Paper Forestry for Indigenous Peoples: Learning with Experiences with Forest Industries http://fennerschool.anu.edu.au pp. 32-40.

Gupta, P.N.1982. The Effects of Government Policy in Forest Management in the Himalayan and Siwalik Region of Uttar Pradesh, India. In Socio-economic Effects and Constraints in Tropical Forest Management. Ed. Hallsworth E.G. John Wiley & Sons. pp. 65-72.

Ham, Laurie. 1995. Livelihood Security in Mountain Ecosystems: Coping and Adapting in Two Himalayan Villages, India". Technical Report No.5. Winnipeg: Natural Resources Institute, University of Manitoba.

Hardin, G. 1968. The Tragedy of commons. Science, 162: 1243-1248.

Hardin, G. 1994. The Tragedy of the Unmanaged Commons Trends Ecol. Evol., 9: 199.

Hardin, G. 1994. The Tragedy of the Unmanaged Commons: Population and the Disguises of Providence pp. 162-185.

Hoskin, W.G. and Dudley Stamp 1967. The Common Lands of England and Wales, Collins Press, London.

Iyengar, S and Shukla, N. 2002. Common Property Land Resources in India: Some Issues in Regeneration and Management. Edited by Dinesh k. Marothia: Institutionalizing Common Pool Resources. Concept Publishing Company New Delhi. pp. 301-333.

Jodha, N.S. 2002. Decline of Rural Commons Role of Population Growth and Public Policies.In Institutionalizing Common Pool Resources. ed Marothia K. Dinesh.Concept Publishing Company, New Delhi. pp. 34-52.

Jodha, N.S. 1995. Common Property Resources and the Dynamics of Rural Poverty in India's Dry Regions. Unasylva, 180 (46): 25-29.

Jodha, N.S. 1986. "Common Property Resources and the Rural Poor in Dry Regions of India". Economic and Political Weekly. 21, (27): 1169-1181.

Jodha, N.S. 1998. Reviving the social system links in the Himalayas. In Linking Social and Ecological Systems: Management Practices and Social Mechanisms infor Building Resilience Ed. F. Berkes, C. Folke and John Colding Cambridge University Press. pp. 285-310.

Kadekodi, K. Gopal, 2004. Common Property Resource Management. Reflection on Theory and the Indian Experience. Oxford University Press. pp. 279.

McKean, M. 1992. Success on the Commons: A Comparative Examination of Institutions for Common Property Resource Management. *Journal of Theoretical Politics*, 4(3): 247-281 (1992).

Mckean, M. and Ostrom, E. 1995. Common Property Regimes in the Forests: Just a Relic from the Past? *Unasylva*, 180 (46): 3-15.

Mittoo, H.K. 1978. India-The Land and the People, Himachal Pradesh by National Book Trust, India, A-5 Green Park, New Delhi-110016.

Murty, M.N. 1994. Mangement of Common Property Resources Limits to Voluntary Collective Action. Environment and Resource Economics 4: 581-594, 1994.

Nadkarni M.V. 2002. Commons, Development and the Poor. In Institutionalizing Common Pool Resources. ed Marothia K. Dinesh. Concept Publishing Company, New Delhi. pp. 79-91.

National Sample Survey, 1999. Common Property resources in India, NSSO 54th Round, Ministry of Statistics and Programme Implementation, GOI.

Negi Y.S. 2002. Common Property Resource Management in Himachal Himalayas. In Institutionalizing Common Pool Resources. ed Marothia K. Dinesh. Concept Publishing Company, New Delhi. pp. 53-78.

Negi, Y.S., Tiwari, S.C., Sharma, L.R. and Gupta, M. 1997. Estimation of Consumption Pattern and Supply of Forest Products in Himachal Pradesh. Nauni-Solan: Department, of Social Sciences, Dr. Y.S.Parmar University of Horticulture and Forestry.

Oakerson J. Ronald, 1992. Analyzing the Commons: A Framework. In Making the Commons Work. ed Bromley. W. Daniel. Institute of Contemporary Studies, California. pp. 41-62.

Ostrom Elinor, 1994. International Food Policy Research Institute. Neither Market nor State: Governance of Common- Pool Resources In The Twenty- First Century.

Ostrom Elinor, 1997 Neither Market Nor State: Governence of Common-Pool Resources in the Twenty-first Century. British Library Document Supply Centre, pp. 1-65.

Pirta R. S., 2007. Nature and Society in Himachal Pradesh "Ecology and Human Well –Being". Published by Institute of integral Himalayan Studies, Shimla.

Prakash, S. 1998. Social Institutions and Common Property Resources in the Mountains. Mountain Research and Development, 18(1-3).

Rao, V.M., 1992. Land Reform Experiences: Perspectives for Strategy and Programmes, Economics & Political Weekly, 27: 50-64.

Romm, Jeff, 1986. Forestry Policy and Development Policy. Journal of World Forest Resource Management, Vol (2), pp. 85-103.

Rasul Golam and Madhav Karki, 2006. Political Ecology of Degradation of Forest Commons in the Himalayas: with Special References of Chitgaon Hill Tracts of Bangladesh. pp. 1-20.

Sabarwal Vasant, K. 2001. Edited by Arun Agarwal and K. Shivaramakrishan Social Nature. Resources, Representation and Rules in India. Environmental Alarm and Institutionalized Conservation in Himachal Pradesh, 1865-1994. pp. 68-85.

Sanwal Mukul,1989. What we know about Mountain Development: Common property, Investment Priorities and Institutional Arrangements, Mountain Research and Development. pp. 3-14.

Sharma, IP 2006.Land Degradation in Himalayan Region: Causes and Control. In Sustainable Land Resources Management In: Himalayan Region. Ed. Raina JN, Sharma IP, Bawa R., Tripathi D. Bishen Singh Mahendra Pal Singh, Dehradun. pp. 73-77.

Shukla Nimisha, and Iyengar 2002. Common property Land Resources in India:Some Issues in Regeneration and Management. In Institutionalizing Common Pool Resources. Eds: Marothia K. Dinesh. Concept Publishing Company, New Delhi. pp. 301-333.

Singh, K. 2002.Integrating Common Pool Resources Management with Rural Development Programmes. In Institutionalizing Common Pool Resources. ed Marothia K. Dinesh.Concept Publishing Company, New Delhi. pp. 92-111.

Singh, Kartar 1994. Property Rights and Tenures in Natural Resources in Kerr John M., Dinesh ,K. Marotia, Kartar Singh, C. Ramasamy and William R. Bentley (eds) *Natural Resource Economics*, Oxford and IBH Publishing Co., New Delhi, pp. 131-59.

Singh, Kartar, N. Singh and R.P. Singh, 1996. Utilisation and Development of Common Property Resources: A Field Study in Punjab', Indian Journal of Agriculture Economics, Vol. 51 (1-2), pp. 249-59.

Singh, C., 2000. India's Forest Policy and Forest Laws, Natraj Publisher, Dehra Dun. pp. 1-338.

Singh, D. V. 1995. Role of Forests in Rural Economy of Himachal Pradesh. *Indian Forester* 121(3):207-213.

Singh, D. 1995. Changing Size and Status of Common Property Resources and Ecological Stress in Himachal Pradesh. In: Proceedings of the International Seminar, Natural Resources: Management and their Linkages with Farming Systems. Nauni-Solan: Department of Social Sciences, Dr. Y.S. Parmar University of Horticulture and Forestry.

Somnathan, E. 1991 Deforestation, Property Rights and Incentive in Central Himalya. Economic and Political Weekly. pp. 37-47.

Thakur, D.R. 1993. Balancing the Ecology and Development of Forests in Himachal Pradesh. *Indian Journal of Regional Science* 25(2): 61-71.

Thomson T.J. Feeny D. and Oakerson J. R.1992.Institutional Dynamics: The Evolution and Dissolution of Common-Property Resource Management. In Making the Commons Work. ed Bromley. W. Daniel. Institute of Contemporary Studies, California. pp. 129-160.

Tucker R.P. 1987. Dimensions of Deforestation In: The Himalayas: The Historical Setting. Mountain Research and Development, Vol 7(3):328-331.

Tucker, R.P. 1982. The Forests of the Western Himalayas: The legacy of British colonial administration. Journal of Forest History, 26(3): 112-123.

Tucker, R.P. 1986. The evolution of transhumant grazing in the Punjab Himalayas. Mountain Research and Development, 6 (1): 17-28.

Vasan, S. 2003.Occasional Paper, Institute of Economic Growth Occasional Papers in Sociology. Exploring the Policy- Implementation Interface: Timber Rights in Himachal Pradesh, India. pp. 1-37.

Vasan, S. 2002. Community Forest Management: Historical Legacy of Himachal Pradesh in where Mortals and Mountain Gods Met; Society and Culture in Himachal Pradesh. Ed. L. Thakur. IIAS, Shimla. pp. 30-48.

Vasan, S. 2006. Living with Diversity: Forestry Institutions in the Western Himalayas. Indigenous Community Forestry: Transformation, Adaption And Potential. Indian Institute of Advance Study, Shimla. pp. 155-182.

Wade, Robert 1992. Common Property Resource Management in South Indian Villages. In Making the Commons Work. ed Bromley. W. Daniel. Institute of Contemporary Studies, California. pp. 207-228.

7

Sacred Plants in India Sacred Trees of the Hindus – Mythological and Social Linkages

Nidhi Bhakuni

INTRODUCTION

Plants have played an important role in many of the world's religions, and have been given deep and sacred meanings throughout the ages. Plant worship has its roots in ancient times and continues to be an element of modern Indian traditions. Tree cults, in which a single or groves of trees have been worshipped, have flourished in India throughout history. Our mission is to protect herbal medicine as the medicine of the people. We teach our community about plants as foods, medicines and allies in our evolutionary process. We believe in the integrity and intelligence of whole plant foods as vs. extracting bits and pieces, beauty and wholeness. It is mentioned of the Kalpavriksha in the ancient scriptures indicating that the worship of the tree is indeed an ancient Indian practice. The Ancient Aryans worshiped nature. Plants, Trees and the other elements were always revered and several rituals were connected to them. Tree worship continues to be an element of modern Indian traditions. There are many trees which are considered Sacred.

Trees being nature's major processors of solar energy which is vital for our existence, and yielding flowers, fruit, wood or medicine, have been worshipped by the Hindus as a matter of gratitude. Manu believed that they were conscious like humans and felt pleasure and pain. Indian sages and seers eulogized asvattha or peepal (*Ficus religiosa*), gular (Ficus *glomerata*),

Ph.D. Scholar Dept. of Botany, D.S.B. Campus, Kumaun University Nainital, Uttarakhand, India.

neem (*Azadirachta indica*), bel (*Aegle marmelos*), bargad or banyan (*Ficus bengalensis*), Asoka (*Sereca indica*), amala (*Phyllanthus emblica*), Arjuna (*Terminalia arjuna*) and many other trees which acquired social and religious sanctity with the passage of time. Bel, rudraksa (seeds of *Elaeccarpus*) and ber (*Zizyphus jujuba*) are considered dear to Lord Siva, sal (*Shorea robusta*) and pipal to Lord Visnu; kadamba (*Anthocephalus cadamba*) to Lord Krishna; mango (*Mangifera indica*) to Lord Hanuman, ashoka to Kamadeva; silk cotton (*Bombax malabaricum*) to the goddess Laksmi; and coconut or sriphala (*Cocos nucifera*) to Varuna or the lord of waters, and to many other gods and goddesses.

The five trees (pancha-vrksa) which adorn Lord Indra's garden (Nandana) in his paradise (Svarga) are:

1. mandara (*Erythrina stricta*) with scarlet flowers in horizontal clusters at the ends of branches; its shade relieves one of physical ailments and mental stress;
2. parijata (*Nyctanthes arbor-tristis*) with bark of gold, leaves of copper color, and fragrant, rejuvenate fruit; it arose out of the ocean of milk and was taken away by Indra to his paradise from where it was brought to Dvaraka by Lord Krsna at the instance of his wife Satyabhama. After the passing away of the Lord and the submerging of Dvaraka in the ocean, it was taken back to heaven;
3. samtanaka, a tree of wonder having leaves which promote fertility in men; its identification remains obscure;
4. haricandana or sandalwood (*Santalum album*) well known for its fragrance and cooling effect, it keeps evil spirits at bay; and
5. kalpa vrksa or kalpa taru, the tree of eternity which emerged as a result of the churning of the ocean of milk; it was lifted to Svarga by Indra, and is frequently mentioned in Sanskrit literature for its wish-fulfilling quality.

The Pauranic lore has it that Brahma metamorphosed into a palasa, Visnu into a pipal and Rudra into a bargad after being cursed by Parvati, the wife of Lord Siva. Neem is customarily believed to be the abode of the goddess Sitala; pipal of the goddess Laksmi (on Sundays), amala of both lord Visnu and Lord Siva, and Sami (*Ficus benjamina*) of Lord Hanuman, the son of the wind-god. Deodar (*Cedrus deodara*) is believed to be the adopted child of Lord Siva. Pipal is said to form a link between earth and heaven. The flowers of five trees-asoka, mango, navamal lika (*Ixora parviflora*), pink lotus (*Nelumbe nucifera*) and blue lotus (*Nymphae stel-lata*) –adorn the tip of the bow of Kama, the god of love. Kadamba reminds one of Lord Krishna's flute and bargad of Lord Siva's matted hair which reflect in the tangled roots of the tree.

Some trees are considered sacred due to their association with prophets and holy men. The barged, for example, is sacred to Hindus because the sage Markandeya took shelter on its branches during the deluge; Lord Rama lived in a grove under five banyan trees near Nasik when he was in exile; and lord Krishna played around it during his childhood. Sala is sacred to Buddhists because Lord Buddha took birth and passed away under it; so are pipal and bargad, as the Lord meditated under them for gaining supreme realization. The trees considered sacred in the Jaina tradition were associated in some way with the Tirthankaras: bargad with Rsabha Deva, sala with Sambhavanatha and Mahavira, bel with Sitalanatha, kadamba with Vasupujya, pipal with Ananta, Asoka with Mallinatha, and bakula with Neminatha. Ber (jujube) is viewed with reverence by the Sikhs because Guru Nanak Dev planted a sapling of it on the banks of the river being when he was at Sultanpur Lodhi. Guru Gobind Singh stayed under a jujube tree in a village of Seeloana in Ludhiana district. Both the sites have been converted into shrines. The ritha tree, under which Guru Nank Dev sat during his sojourn in the Himalayas, began to bear sweet fruit, and now a shrine has come up centered on it. The ber under which Baba Buddha (1506-1621) used to sit supervising the excavation of the sacred pool at the Amritsar Golden Temple has also become an object of worship for the devotees.

Specific directions for the plantation of sacred trees are mentioned in the Vrksa Ayur-veda: bargad should be planted in the eastern side of the house; bel and peepal in the west; mango and amala in the south; Asoka in the southeast and a wave-leafed fig tree, in the north. Auspicious stars for planting them all are Svati, Hasta, Rohini, Sravana and Mula. The day, time, month or occasion of worship of sacred trees has a mythical, astrological or utilitarian basis. Amala and pipal are worshipped especially in the month of Kartika (October-November), bel and gular in Sravana (July-August), kadamba in Asadha (June-July), Sami in Asvina (September-October), bargad in Jyestha (May-June), and so on. A number of festivals and vratas are also observed in their honour as per the table given at the end of this article.

Due to their ecological value and efficacious properties, trees continue to be used in the religious and social ceremonies of the Hindus. The trunk of banana is used to erect welcoming gates and its leaves to make the ceremonial pavilion. The five most sacred leaves of peepal, gular, pilkhan (*Ficus lacor*), bargad and mango-are ubiquitously employed in making prayers and offerings. On auspicious occasions, mango leaves are tied to a string and hung on doors; leaves of palasa and bargad make workable plates and bowls during community feasts. Leaves of some other trees are also customarily offered to deities of bel to lord Siva, of banana and arjuna to Lord Ganesa, and of amaltas (*Cassia fistula*) to all the gods and goddesses. The red flowers of the Indian coral tree are used in the worship of Lord Visnu and Lord Siva;

of kaner (*Nerium indicum*) in the worship of Lord Siva and the Sun-god; of ketaki (*Yucca gloriosa*) in the worship of Laksmi, and of panas or breadfruit (*Artocarpus integrifolia*) in the worship of Lord Vishnu.

The use of some flowers is prohibited in worship rites-of sirisa or parrot tree (*Albizzia lebbeck*) in the worship of Lord Ganesa and vijaya sala (*Pterocarpus marsupium*) in the worship of Lord Siva. Supari or areca nut which symbolizes Lord Ganesa is commonly used in various rites. Banana is offered to Lord Visnu and Laksmi on the eleventh day of the bright half of Pausa (December-January) and to the Sun god on the sixth day of the bright fortnight of Kartika (October-November). Mango and bel fruits are also included in the worship material-the former is offered to all gods, the latter especially to Lord Siva.

The wood of sacred trees like bel, bargad, sami, palasa and pipal is never used as fuel as it invites the wrath of gods. But it is employed, in other ways, in sacrificial rites and ceremonies. Sandalwood is turned into paste and applied to the forehead. The wooden seat used during the sacred thread ceremony is made of mango or palasa; the brahmacarin is also made to walk with a stick of palasa. During the sacred thread ceremony the brahmacarin has to perform sacrifice using pipal twigs called samit. After a person dies, twigs of bel are placed near the central pillar of the house and those of neem scattered near the corpse.

Sacred trees are invoked on special days for long life, for the expiration of sins, for averting mishaps, or for the fulfillment of a particular wish. Young girls are symbolically wedded to the pipal tree or bel fruit to avoid future widowhood. Tree trunks are tied with thread and circumambulated 108 times and adorned with vermilion and sandal-paste; earthen lamps are lighted under them-and the effect of all these is considered equal to a thousand sacrifices. The Saivites count prayers by using rosaries made of rudraksa berries. Kautilya laid down that those who cut even small branches or sprouts of trees yielding fruit and flowers, or providing shade in parks, places of pilgrimage, hermitages, and cremation or burial grounds should be sternly dealt with. In ancient India, people offered prayers and performed other rites to expiate themselves from the crime of harming or up-rooting a holy tree. To plant a pipal, banyan or some other sacred tree at a holy place or on the roadside continues to be regarded by the Hindus as an act of virtue. The Brhat Parasara Smrti (10.379) admonishes in this context: He who plants and nurtures the following trees will never see hell: one each of the holy fig (pipal), margosa (neem) and banyan (bargad), ten tamarind trees and three each of wood apple, the holy bel, myrobalan and five mango trees. The Hindu religious mind was thus keen on environmental stability.

Additionally, the sacred plants are used for healing purposes. True healing puts into order the body, mind and spirit with the past, present and future. Such integration is possible by various means, including by the ceremonial use of the sacred plants. Throughout history these plants have been employed to heal disorders of body, mind and spirit, and today a whole new emerging body of study is currently examining the healing properties of some of these plants. Many will balk at the notion of a spirit world, and will prefer to insist that the activity of the sacred plants is chemical, and that visions of the divine or spontaneous healings are purely acts of the individual mind. Sacred groves of India are forest fragments of varying sizes, which are communally protected, and which usually have a significant religious connotation for the protecting community. Hunting and logging are usually strictly prohibited within these patches. Other forms of forest usage like honey collection and deadwood collection are sometimes allowed on a sustainable basis. Sacred groves did not enjoy protection via federal legislation in India. Some NGOs work with local villagers to protect such groves. Traditionally, and in some cases even today, members of the community take turns to protect the grove. However, the introduction of the protected area category community reserves under the Wildlife (Protection) Amendment Act of 2002 has introduced legislation for providing government protection to community held lands, which could include sacred groves.

In many cases, human life ends with death and burial in the ground. Plants are just the opposite. They emerge from the earth and draw nourishment from it. For this reason many mythological traditions associate plants with birth and rebirth and with the eternal cycle of life springing forth from death. Various trees, shrubs, herbs, grains, flowers, and fruits appear in myths and legends as general symbols of rebirth, decay, and immortality. Human beings share the earth with innumerable varieties of plants, animals and other living organisms. Through their presence, human modify the land, working the earth to yield a continuing supply of resources. Increasing evidence pointing to the anthropomorphic face of nature deems it necessary to recognize and protect cultural landscapes. This entails not only the protection of biological diversity, but cultural diversity too.

PLANTS MYTHOLOGY

Plants have played an important role in many of the world's mythologies and religions, and have been given deep and sacred meanings throughout the ages. The most ancient cross-cultural symbolic representation of the universe's construction is the world tree. In Indian mythology number of plants have been given sacred value and worshipped by different cultures. Some important plants of sacred value have been discussed here.

Ashoka (*Sereca indica*)

The beautiful, perfumed flowers of the Ashoka tree are used in temple decoration. Prized for its beautiful foliage and flowers, the Asoka tree has much religious significance. This tree is revered by the *Hindus, Buddhists and*

Jains. It is said that Lord Buddha was born under this tree in Lumbini. Some says that *Lord Mahavira* renounced the world under the Ashoka tree in Vaishali. The Hindus worship this tree because it is dedicated to *"Kama Deva"* (God of Love). The Ashoka tree gets a mention in the epic *Ramayana* as the *"Ashoka Vatika"* (garden of Ashoka trees) where Hanuman first meets Sita. Literally meaning "the *"sorrowless tree"*, it is believed that drinking the water in which the flowers have been washed is widely considered a protection against grief among the Indians.

Banyan (*Ficus bengalensis*)

Banyan Tree symbolizes the Trimurti-Lord Vishnu, Lord Siva and Lord Brahma. The tree also symbolizes *life* and *fertility* in many Hindu cultures. That is the reason, banyan tree is worshiped by those who are childless and this tree should never be cut. The tree can grow into a giant tree covering several hectares. *The Great Banyan* in the Indian Botanic Garden, Howrah, is considered to be the largest tree in the world. *Lord Dakshinamurthy*, who is worshiped as the "ultimate guru", is usually depicted beneath a banyan tree. He symbolizes Lord Shiva and is seen as the destroyer of ignorance and embodiment of knowledge.

Bel (*Aegle marmelos*)

In India, Bel tree is considered to be very scared because it is associated with Lord Siva. It is said that Lord Shiva is pleased by offerings of leaves from the Bel Tree, also known as *bilva* tree. Thus, the Brahmanas worshiped Lord Siva by for a period of one fortnight by offering bel leaves and that way satisfied Lord Siva greatly. The fruit, flowers and leaves of the tree are all sacred to Siva. Planting these trees around home or temple is sanctifying and is equivalent to worshiping a *Linga* with bilva leaves and water. The trifoliate leaf or tripatra of the bel tree is believed to symbolize the three functions of the Lord-the *creation, preservation and destruction* as well as *his three eyes*. The offering of the leaves is a compulsory ritual while worshipping Lord Siva all over India. The Bel tree is also sacred to the Jains. It is said the 23rd Tirthankara, Bhagwan Parasnathji attained *"Nirvana"* enlightenment under a Bel tree. Besides religious significane, almost all parts of the tree have medicinal qualities Bel is an ingredient in many Ayurvedic and Siddha formulations.

Bamboo (*Bambusa vulgaris*)

The common names of Lord Krishna-Venugopal, Bansilal, Murali and Muralidhar reflect his association with *Bansuri* or *Venu*, his constant companion. *Bansuri* is actually a flute made of bamboo. That is the reason; bamboo is revered in India because it is associated with Lord Krishna.

Banana (*Musa paradisiaca*)

Though banana is not a tree but it is considered a tree because of its structure and size. It is a very sacred tree and all parts of the tree are used for some purpose or the other. For example, the trunk of banana is used to erect welcoming gates. The leaves are used to make the ceremonial pavilion. In some pooja, the leaves are used to serve *"prashad"*. Just as leaves of bel tree are customarily offered to Lord Siva, it is believed that offering of the leaves of banana pleases Lord Ganesa. Banana as a fruit is offered to Lord Vishnu and Laksmi. In fact, the eleventh day of the bright half of Pausa (December-January) is considered to be very auspicious to offer banana to Lord Vishnu and Goddess Laxmi and sixth day of the bright fortnight of Kartika (October-November) is considered auspicious to offer banana to the Sun god. In some regions, banana tree is worshipped while performing *Kadali Vrata* or fast. According to tradition, during Vaisakha, Magha or Kartika sukla caturdasi, a banana tree is planted and nurtured till it bears fruit. It is said that worshiping the tree with flowers, fruit, etc. will help in the welfare of one's family.

Bhang: Aconite (*Aconitum napellus*)

Its leaves and roots are extremely toxic and were used by the ancients as a poison. The Greek's called it *akoniton* (without dirt) because it grows on rocky ground and *lykoktonon* (wolf-slaying) because it was traditionally applied by their arrows when hunting wolves.

To all Hindus, the *Bhang Tree* is a very Holy Tree. There are many beliefs associated with the Bhang Tree. It is believed that a guardian lives in the Bhang leaf. To see in a dream the plant or water or leaves of Bhang is considered lucky as it brings wealth and prosperity into the dreamer's power. To meet someone carrying Bhang is a sure sign of success. Bhang is a popular drink made of the leaves and flowers of the Bhang tree and considered to be a *"prashad"*. It is must for every devotee to have bhang on *Mahashivratri*. It is also said that nothing good can come to the man who treads underfoot the holy Bhang leaf. A longing for Bhang is a sign of happiness. Since ancient times, Yogis take deep draughts of Bhang so that they can centre their thoughts on the Eternal without any disturbance because bhang has that intoxicating power in it. In fact, the students of ancient scriptures at Benares are given Bhang before they sit to study. Bhang has also many medicinal virtues. It is also believed that no god or man is as good as the religious drinker of Bhang. It is also said that to restrict the use of such a holy and gracious herb as the hemp or Bhang would cause widespread suffering and annoyance.

Coconut (*Cocos nucifera*)

In Sanskrit, the name for the coconut palm *"Kalpa vriksha"*, which means *"the tree which provides all the necessities of life"* or *"wish-fulfilling tree"*. The coconut tree is given a special place in most Hindu households and great care is taken to nature the tree. In the southern part of India, it is must for every household to plant coconut trees. There is a popular saying, *"Water the plant for five years, and reap coconuts for life"*. The coconut is used for all religious purposes. In fact, it represents the main *"sthapana"* of any pooja. The whole pot filled with water, mango leaves and coconut, also known as *"Purnakumbha"* is a symbol of Goddess Lakshmi or Fortune and the coconut represents divine consciousness. To break a coconut in the beginning of any event is considered to be very auspicious. Coconuts are offered in Temples to worship to various Gods and Goddesses. The fruit is also believed to represent Lord Siva and the three black marks on the coconut shell, symbolizes his eyes.

Lotus (*Nelumbe nucifera*)

The *Lotus* is always considered as an evocative symbol of beauty, purity and divinity and a highly revered flower by all Hindus. In Hinduism many of the deities are pictured sitting upon a lotus or holding a lotus flower. Rising up pure and unsullied from the depths of the muddy swamp, the lotus represents the manifestation of God. The pure white lotus flower is the only plant to fruit and flower simultaneously. The flower is *a* symbol of Goddess Lakshmi. One of the incarnations of the Mother-Goddess or Devi and wife of the Hindu god Vishnu, Lakshmi is the goddess of fortune and prosperity as well as the epitome of feminine beauty. According to Hindu mythology she was born radiant and fully grown from the churning of the sea. Lakshmi is always portrayed as sitting on a lotus flower which is her traditional symbol. That is why this flower held in high esteem. The Lotus flower has also symbolized spiritual enlightenment. It is said that the Lotus in Eastern Culture has a similar symbolism to the Rose in Christianity.

Mango (*Mangifera indica*)

The mango tree is another sacred tree of the Hindus. The significance of this finds mention in the Ramayana, Mahabharata and the Puranas. The mango as a fruit is a symbol of love and fertility. The leaf of the tree is used during most religious and social ceremonies of the Hindus. A *"Purnakumbha"* is a pot filled with water and topped with fresh mango leaves and a coconut and considered to be the *"staphna"* of the puja. The pot symbolizes Mother Earth, water is the life giver, coconut the divine consciousness and the mango leaves symbolizes life. The whole *"Purnakumbha"* is symbolizes Goddess Lakshmi and good fortune. On various auspicious occasions, mango leaves are used to adorn entrances at home to signify good fortune. Mango blossoms are used on Basant Panchami day in the worship of Goddess Saraswasti. The tree is also sacred to the Buddhists because it is believed that Lord Buddha performed during his lifetime the instantaneous creation of a large mango tree from the seed at a place called Shravasti.

Neem (*Azadirachta indica*)

It is said that on the first day of Chaitra, after Amavasya, it is very essential to worship the neem and eat its leaves, mixed with pepper and sugar, as a safeguard from fever. The neem tree besides having various medicinal benefits is a highly revered tree among the hindus because it is a manifestation of "Goddess Durga" or "Maa Kali". That is why the tree is sometimes referred to as Neemari Devi. The Tree is worshiped very intensely. Tamil Ladies, while worshiping Maa kali dress in red, carry branches of the Neem tree, and dance in public places swishing the branches as an act of exorcism and to purify the world. The multi-headed occult goddess Yellamma (a highly revered goddess in south India) sometimes assumes the appearance of a young neem tree. Young maidens worship this Goddess by cladding themselves all over in neem branches. In Bengal, neem is considered to be the tree which is the abode of *"Sitala"* (the great Pox-mother who can cause or cure disease). The customary treatment of pox is therefore to rub the body with neem leaves while making prayers to *Sitala*. It is also said that the smoke of burning neem protects both the living and the dead from evil spirits.

Peepal (*Ficus religiosa*)

The Peepal Tree also known as *"Ashvattha"* in Sanskrit is a very large tree and the first-known depicted tree in India. A seal discovered at Mohenjodaro, one of the cities of the Indus Valley Civilisation depicts the peepal being worshiped. According to the Brahma Purana and the Padma Purana, when the demons defeated the gods, Lord Vishnu hid himself in the Peepal Tree and that is why it is believed that the Peepal tree is a symbol of Vishnu and is worshiped since a long period of time. There is another belief that the tree represents the Trimurti-the roots being Brahma, the trunk Vishnu and the leaves Siva. Some says that Lord Krishna is believed to have died under this tree, after which the present Kali Yuga started. According to another belief, Goddess Lakshmi also inhabited the tree, especially on Saturday and hence it is considered auspicious to worship it. In fact women worship the tree to bless them with a son tying red thread or red cloth around its trunk or on its branches. According to the *Skanda Purana*, to cut down a peepal tree is considered a sin. Even Buddha is believed to have attained enlightenment under the peepal tree and the peepal is also sacred to Buddhist, hence it is also called the Bodhi tree or "tree of enlightenment".

Red Sandalwood Tree: (*Santalum album*)

According to Indian mythology, sandalwood tree is depicted as being entwined with serpents. Sandalwood remains cool and aromatic even when the poisonous serpent coils around it. This also has another meaning that the basic nature of an individual cannot change because of outer effects. Besides being used in fragrance industry, fine woodworking and aromatherapy, Sandalwood is commonly used for incense and religious ceremonies. The *Red Sandalwood Tree* is considered to be a very sacred tree and is like a sage among many people. It is said that all other trees are considered ordinary trees and are like ignorant men in front of a Red Sandal wood. Popularly known as *Chandan*, Sandalwood has an extraordinary fragrance. Sandalwood paste is used in all religious rituals. The paste is smeared on the foreheads of devotees of Vishnu and Siva and it is said that the sandalwood paste is meant to cool and protect the *"Agna chakra"* present between the eyebrows. In India, the death pyre is made using sandalwood branches for centuries. According to legend, Lord Ganesha was created by Goddess Parvati out of sandalwood paste that she used for her bath and breathed life into the figure.

Tulsi: (*Ocimum sanctum*)

According to Indian mythology, Tulsi plant is most loved by Lord Vishnu and Vrinda Devi, the Goddess ruling Tulsi is known as the personification of bhakti or devotion to the Supreme Being. Tulsi is considered to be associated with purity and a highly revered and used for all religious purposes among the Hindus. It is considered very auspicious to have a Tulsi plant in the front courtyard of many Hindu households. Tulsi is always associated with purity and a highly revered and used for all religious purposes among the Hindus. It is considered very auspicious to have a Tulsi plant in the front courtyard of many Hindu households. Tulsi beads can always be seen around the necks of serious yogis and mystics in India, worn to purifying the mind, emotions and body.

For conservation of biodiversity taboos seems to be beneficial as they restrict the use of plants and/or cutting these plants.

Tulsi is always associated with purity and a highly revered and used for all religious purposes among the Hindus. It is considered very auspicious to have a Tulsi plant in the front courtyard of many Hindu households. Tulsi beads can always be seen around the necks of serious yogis and mystics in India, worn to purifying the mind, emotions and body. Dispelling the unwanted influences of others, gross and subtle, is one of the many benefits bestowed by Tulsi plant and hence worshipped by all. Tulsi plants are also prized in Ayurveda, where they are considered an integral part of that sophisticated healing system. In practically every temple in India, no puja can be started without few Tulsi leaves. There is always a special place reserved for this sacred plant. The qualities and amazing powers of this plant are found throughout the oldest writings on Earth, the Sanskrit Vedas of ancient India, where it is stated that simply touching the wood is purifying at many levels.

Apple Tree (*Malus domestica*)

The apple-tree was an important orchard fruit of ancient Greece. It was associated with love and marriage. The apple-tree was an important orchard fruit of ancient Greece. It was associated with love and marriage.

1. Human/plant co existence can be seen through the examples of plant simile and metaphors. Some examples are given below:

- **Plant metaphors:** "We are the sprouts at your hands and feet. We are the branches at your trunk. We come in front of trees and stones. We are at your bark, at your fruit. We are your flowers. We are your tendrils. We are the ones who need your shade."
- **Plant simile:** Branches of tree are like the arms of a man and the grains of plant are like the face of a child.

2. Domestication has played an enormous part in the development of mankind and its material culture. It has resulted in the appearance of agriculture as a special form of animals and plant production. Tribes of different parts of world played an important role in domestication of plants as well as animals. These people came to know how to use the plants and what part should be used and what should not. Domestication of important crops and vegetables were done by different tribes of the world. Still they possess knowledge about the wild plants of economic use that are far beyond our reach. Useful plants are conserved and protected by the indigenous people and ethnic societies (tribals) and traditional people all over the world. In the last we can say that the ethno-botanical survey is important and very useful for mankind and for growth of society.

Rose (*Rosa domascena*)

The rose has many stories about it, Greek mythology tells of its beginnings. Chloris, Greek Goddess of Flowers, found a sad and weak nymph one day, and wishing to restore her to health asked The Graces to help. They granted the nymph the gifts of joy, brightness, and charm. Chloris wanted to do more for the dying nymph so appealed to the other gods and she was given nectar, beauty by Aphrodite, and Zephyr, the west wind, blew away the clouds so the sun could shine upon her. Chloris called this beautiful bloom Rose. It was believed that all roses were white in the beginning, and one of the many stories of how roses became coloured again comes from Greek mythology. It's told that the god Jupiter saw Venus bathing; she was so embarrassed that she blushed, and all the white roses surrounding her bath turned red in sympathy.

IMPORTANT FESTIVALS OR VRATAS RELATED TO TREES

Name of the Tree	Related Festival	Time of Celebration and Rituals
Amala	Amala, Ekadasi	11th day of Phalguna; bath with water soaked in amala fruit; eating it; worshipping it; and wor ship of Radha-Krishna
Amra or Mango	Amra-Puspa Bhaksana Vrata	1st day of Caitra Sukla; acting of Mango Blossoms and worship of Kamadeva
Asoka	Asoka pratipada	1st day of Caitra Sukla; only women worship the tree; they also observe fast seeking longevity

(Contd...)

Bakula	Bakula, Amavasya	Bakula flower are offered to the manes, seeking their blessing.
Vata or bargad	Vata savitri, vrata	Jyestha Purnima or amavasya day; having fast for three previous days, married woman worship the bargad tree by circumambulating, trying with the sacred protective thread (raksa sutra), and listening to the sacred Savitri-Satyavan story; some women stay awake during the night and complete the vow feeding a Brahmin; in western part of India, devout women observe this vow for five consecutive years after marriage.
Bilva or bel	Bilva tri- ratri Vrata	On a Tuesday of Jyestha Purnima when the constellation is Jyestha; worship of the bel tree for three consecutive nights as per Hemadri's injunction in the Skanda Purana; the vow comprises bath with water mixed with mustard seeds, partahking of sacred sattvic food (havisyanna), adorning the tree with two Pieces of cloth and placing the image of Uma- Mahesvara beneath it; homa is performed and 1,008 bilva leaves are offered; Brahmins are fed.
Bilva or bel	Sravana krsna, Ekadasi	Ceremonial offering of water to the bel tree
Bilva or bel	Bhadra sukla Caturthi	Offering of trifoliate leaves of be to lord Genesa
Bilva or Bel	Bilva Nimantrana	Asvina sukla sasthi; summoning the tree-goddess and worshipping the devi.
Bilva or Bel	Bilva Saptami	Asvina sukla Saptami; a twig of bel, bearing two fruits, is offered to Devi.
Bilva or Bel	Bilva Navami	Asvina Sukla Navami; bel leaves are offered to Shiva.
Karavira or Kaner or Oleander (Nerium Indicum)	Karavira Vrata	Jyestha Sukla prathama tithi; Kaner roots and branches are bathed and adorned with red cloth; offering of seven cereals (Sapta dhanya) and fruits are made followed by fasting; Savitri, Satyabhama, and other performed this when they were in trouble.
Kadali or Kela	Kadali Vrata	Vaisakha, Magha or Kartika sukla caturdasi; a banana tree is planted and nurtured till it bears fruit; wishing the welfare of one's family, a person should worship the tree with flowers, fruit, etc and circumambulate it.
Kadali or Kela	Yaksa-samantaka, Kadali Vrata	A golden banana tree is worshipped and offered to a brahmin on any auspicious day.
Kevada or Screw Pine (Panadanus odoratis-simus).	Kevada Teej	Bhadra sukla trtiya; soliciting unbroken married life, women offer Kevada leaves to Lord Siva.
Neem	Sitala Puja	Caitra navaratras; goddess Sitala who is said to reside in the neem tree is propitiated ritually; Pat Gosain festival in Bengal means neem tree worship; neem leaves are eaten on Vaisakha.

Sacred groves are scattered all over the country, and are referred to by different names in different parts of India. Sacred groves occur in a variety of places – from scrub forests in the Thar Desert of Rajasthan maintained by the Bishnois, to rain forests in the Western Ghats of Kerala. Himachal Pradesh in the north and Kerala in the south are specifically known for their large numbers of sacred groves. The Kodavas of Karnataka alone maintained over 1000 sacred groves in their region. Around 14,000 sacred groves have been reported from all over India, which act as reservoirs of rare fauna, and more often rare flora, amid rural and even urban settings. Experts believe that the total number of sacred groves could be as high as 100,000. It is estimated that around 1000 km² of unexploited land is inside sacred groves. Some of the more famous groves are the *kavus* of Kerala, which are located in the Western Ghats and have enormous biodiversity; and the *law kyntangs* of Meghalaya – sacred groves associated with every village (two large groves being in Mawphlang and Mausmai) to appease the forest spirit. Among the largest sacred groves of India are the ones in Hariyali, near Ganchar in Chamoli District of Uttarakhand, and the Deodar grove in Shipin near Simla in Himachal Pradesh. Kodagu, a small region of about 4000 km² in Karnataka, had over 1000 sacred groves. All numbers are quoted from the records of the *C.P.R. Environmental Education Centre* of the Government of India. Starred numbers are likely to increase.

State	No. of Groves	Local Name	References
Andhra Pradesh	750		B.R.P. Rao
Arunachal Pradesh	65	*Gumpa forests* (since attached to monasteries)	Dudley et al.
Assam	40	*Than, Madaico*	
Chhattisgarh	600*	*Sarna, Devlas, Mandar, Budhadev*	
Goa	NA*		SERBC document
Gujarat	29*		
Haryana	248		
Himachal Pradesh	5000	*Deo bhumi*	
Jharkhand	21*	*Sarna* more than 500 "Jaherthan" in Godda of Jharkhand	Marine Carrin
Karnataka	1424	*Devarakadu, Devkad*	Gadgil et al.
Kerala	2000	*Kavu, Sarpa Kavu*	M. Jayarajan
Madhya Pradesh	21*	*Devkot, Matikot, Devsthali, Budhadev*	
Maharashtra	1600	*Deorai/Devrai* (Pune, Ratnagiri, Raigarh, Kolhapur districts)	Waghchaure et al.

(Contd...)

Manipur	365	*Gamkhap, Mauhak* (sacred bamboo reserves)	Khumbongyam et al.
Meghalaya	79	*Law kyntang, Law lyngdhoh*	Upadhyay et al.
Orissa	322*	*Jahera, Thakuramma*	
Puducherry	108	*Kovil Kadu*	Ramanujam et al.
Rajasthan	9*	*Oran* (Jaiselmer, Jodhpur, Bikaner), *Kenkri* (Ajmer), *Vani* (Mewar), *Shamlat deh, Devbani* (Alwar), *Jogmaya*	
Sikkim	56	*Gumpa forests* (since attached to monasteries)	S.S. Dash Dudley et al.
Tamil Nadu	503	*Kovil Kadu*	M. Amrithalingam
Uttarakhand	18*	*Devbhumi, Bugyal* (sacred alpine meadows)	Anthwal et al.
West Bengal	670*	*Garamthan, Harithan, Jahera, Sabitrithan, Santalburithan*	R. K. Bhakat

WILD LIFE PROTECTION IN TRIBALS

"The tribal life of India has a long history. There are many laws for the Scheduled Tribes and at the same time they have their own customary or traditional code of conduct too. The legislative provisions are of two types, one for their welfare and the other that puts restrictions on their conduct. There are many laws to protect the environment. Some of them are; Wild Life (Protection) Act, 1972, Indian Forest Act, 1927, etc. These acts protect the wild life by declaring some areas as protected areas, reserved forests, protected forests, etc. These acts also affect the tribal laws, which are made for the welfare of the tribesmen. The regulations of many protected areas in the world strictly prohibit hunting, gathering of plant resources or other productive activities within park or reserve borders. This policy applies to all local people; even those who have traditionally had access to the area and possibly practiced sustainable ways of harvesting natural products from the wild lands. They are forced to continue their activities in buffer areas around the park, which may lack some resources and where they may face competition from enterprises which may be ecologically destructive, such as certain types of logging and agriculture. The Forest Rights Act, a law recognizing the rights of forest communities, has come into force, with the Union tribal affairs ministry issuing a formal notification to this effect on January 1, 2008.

The Scheduled Tribes and Other Traditional Forest-Dwellers (Recognition of Forest Rights) Act, 2006, was notified after more than a year of political interventions, bureaucratic twists and hectic lobbying by activists representing tribal and wildlife interest groups.

The main beneficiaries of the Act are scheduled tribes (STs) and other traditional forest-dwellers living in and depending on forests for their livelihood for three generations – 75 years prior to December 13, 2005. Essentially, the Act aims to provide a framework to record the rights of forest-dwellers, allowing them to cultivate forest land to the extent under occupation, subject to a ceiling of four hectares, the right to collect, use and dispose of minor forest produce, and rights inside forests that are traditional and customary, like grazing and maintaining homesteads. The act renders the Forest Conservation Act, 1980, the Wildlife Protection Act, 1972, and the Indian Forest Act, virtually invalid."

The Act also makes it mandatory for right holders to ensure sustainable use, conserve bio-diversity and maintain ecological balance, thereby strengthening the conservation regime of forests across the country.

REFERENCES

A. Anthwal, R. C. Sharma, and Archana Sharma, 2006. Sacred Groves: Traditional Way of Conserving Plant Diversity in Garhwal Himalaya, Uttaranchal , The Journal of American Science, 2(2), , Anthwal et al., Sacred Groves: Conserving Plant Diversity.

Alexander P. 2002. The Forest in Folklore and Mythology.

Bansi L.M. 2000. Trees in Indian Art, Mythology, and Folklore.

Baumann H., William T. S., Stearn E. R. 1993. The Greek Plant World in Myth, Art and Literature. Workman Pub Co.

Carrin M., Santal Autonomy as a Social Ecology , 16th European Conference on Modern South Asian Studies, Edinburgh, 2000.

Dudley N., L. Higgins-Zogib, and S. Mansourian, 2005. The Arguments for Protection Series – Beyond Belief: Linking Faiths and Protected Areas to Support Biodiversity Conservation , pp. 91-95; World Wide Fund for Nature, (ISBN 2-88085-270-6) Website of the Sacred Grove Restoration Project, Society for Ecological Restoration.

Fred H. 2005. The Meaning of Trees: Botany, History, Healing, Lore.

Gadgil, M. and Vartak, V.D. 1975. Sacred Groves of India: A Plea for Continued Conservation Journal of Bombay Natural History Society, 72: 314-320.

Gadgil, M., D. And Chandran S., 1998. Sacred Groves and Sacred Trees of Uttara Kannada , Lifestyle and Ecology, Edited by Baidyanath Saraswati. New Delhi: Indira Gandhi National Centre for the Arts.

Jayarajan, M. Sacred Groves of North Malabar , Kerala Research Programme on Local Level Development, Centre for Development Studies, Thiruvananthapuram (ISBN 81-87621-95-8).

Khumbongmayum, M.D., Khan, M.L., and Tripath, R.S, 2004. Sacred Groves of Manipur – Ideal Centres for Biodiversity Conservation , Current Science, Vol. 87, No. 4.

M. Amirthalingam, 1998. Sacred Groves of Tamil Nadu – A Survey, CPR Environmental Education Centre, Chennai, India, p. 191.

Martin G.J. 1995. Ethnobotany. A Methods Manual. People and Plants Conservation Manual. Chapman and Hall, London.

Ram Kumar Bhakat, 2003. Socio-religious and Ecological Perspective of a Sacred Grove from Midnapore District, West Bengal, Science and Culture (Sci. Cult.), Vol. 69, No 11-12, pp. 371-374 Database at the CPR Environmental Education Centre.

Rao B. Ravi Prasad, 2006. Conservation of Threatened Flora in Sacred Groves of Southern Andhra Pradesh , Symposium On National Biodiversity and Ecosystem Information Infrastructure (NBEII): Challenges and Potentials, Pune.

S.S. Dash, 2005. Kabi Sacred Grove of North Sikkim Current Science, Vol. 89, No. 3.

Upadhaya, K.; Pandey, H.N. 2; Law, P.S.; Tripathi, R.S; 2003 Tree Diversity in Sacred Groves of the Jaintia Hills in Meghalaya, Northeast India, Biodiversity and Conservation, Volume 12, Number 3, pp. 583-597(15)

Waghchaure, C.K.; Pundarikakshudu T.; Gunale, V. R.; Noshir H.; Birdi, Tannaz J., Sacred Groves of Parinche Valley of Pune District of Maharashtra, India and their Importance, Anthropology & Medicine, Volume 13, Number 1, April 2006, pp. 55-76(22).

8

Landslide Hazard Scenario and its Mitigation Strategy in Uttarakhand Himalaya in the Context of Environmental Management

Puran Ch. Joshi[1*] and **Narayan Singh**[2]

> *"Everything around us is in a state of changing, everything is either growing or diminishing and nothing is really stable. Geographical phenomena, both physical and human must be studied from that point of view."*

INTRODUCTION

According to this statement of Jean Brunhes nature plays a dramatic role in human life. Sometimes we get its favorable aspects and vice versa destructive one. The destructive aspects of nature occur in the form of natural hazard. When these spoil the cultural landscape and human lives they become disasters.

Disaster mitigation is the ongoing effort to lessen the impact disasters have on people and property. Fewer people and communities would be affected by natural disasters with the use of this process. Because of the varying degree of each natural disaster, there are different mitigation strategies for each. Present paper describes the landslide problem and its mitigation strategy in Uttarakhand Himalaya.

In the Himalayan region, landslides take place every year, and the nature and the factors, natural or manmade, responsible for generating these landslides are indeed diverse. Landslides are responsible for the loss of

1. **Dept of Geography, Dr. S.T.P. College Sitarganj, Dist. US Nagar 262 405, Kumaun University, Nainital (Uttarakhand), India.**

2. **Manager, CSR, Project, TERI, Dalash, Kullu, Himachal Pradesh, India.**

human lives and property in the Himalaya. About 60-70 million years ago, in the wake of the Cenozoic Era, mother earth gave birth to the Himalaya-world's highest and youngest mountain range. The variety of ecosystems that it supports is therefore, so fragile, such that even small disturbance triggers, changes that rapidly assume alarming proportions. The boundary thrusts that tectonically subdivide the Himalayan province into latitudinal zones are characterized by multiple splitting of rock-formations and high degree of crushing and shattering of rocks, and are thus, particularly vulnerable to extensive erosion and landslides. We can observe in table most of the landslides have been occurred in Uttarakhand around MBT and MCT.

Table 8.1: Some of the Major Landslides in Uttarakhand

Sl. No.	Year	Description of Landslide Events and Damages
1.	1803	Landslide damming near Srinagar, Flashfloods swept away one third of Srinagar.
2.	1857	Massive landslide blocked the flow of Mandakini river for three days.
3.	1868	Sher-ka-Danda landslide in Nainital damaged settlement.
4.	1880	Sher-ka-Danda landslide in Nainital, large debris avalanches killed 143 persons and a great loss of the property in Mallital.
5.	1893	Landslie on Brihi Ganga Formed 350 m high dam and large Gohna lake. This dam burst a year later and affected settlement aas far away as Srinagar.
6.	Aug 17, 1899	Landslide on Balia stream near Nainital buried brewery settlement.
7.	1956	Landslide damming on Dhauli Ganga River.
8.	1967	Landslide damming on Rishi Ganga River.
9.	1968	Landslide damming near Rini and Dhauli Ganga river.
10.	Jul 20,1970	Belakuchi landslide damming on Alaknanda river killed 55 persons, 142 animals perished, 101 villages affected.
11.	1977 and 1979	Khela landslide destroying Twaghat near Dharchula in Pithoragarh District.
12.	1978	Landslide damming on Bhagirathi river (Kanauldia Gad) damaged 2 motor bridges. 3 pedestrians bridges and 5 km stretch of mettaled Road.
13.	1979	Konth (Okhimath) landslide killed 39 persons.
14.	1983	Landslide destroyed Karmi Village in Bageshwar District.
15.	1986	Jakholi landslide in Tehri Garhwal killed 32 persons.
16.	Sep19, 1988	Kaliyasaur landslide in Alaknanda valley.
17.	1991	Landslide around Gopeshwar, 36 victims in six villages.
18.	Jul 1998	Landslide in Nainital on southern mountain side.

(Contd...)

Sl. No.	Year	Description of Landslide Events and Damages
19.	Aug 11/12 and, 1998	Landslide damming on Madhyamaheshwar river near monsoon in Okhimath area killed 101 persons, 29 villages affected, 820 houses damaged. 9752 people affected, 422 cattle heads perished.
20.	Aug 18 1998	Malpa landslide killed 207 persons including 60 pilgrims of Kailash Maansarowar Yatra, 5 huts and 5 houses people affected, 69 cattle heads perished.
21.	Mar. 28/29 1999	Numerous earthquake induced landslides noticed in Chamoli District.
22.	Oct. 20 1999	1999 Earthquake induced 47 new and 6 old landslides in Uttarkashi area killing hundreds of people and causing extensive damage to property.
23.	Aug. 2003	Uttarkashi, heavy loss of infrastructures.
24.	Jul 2004	Joshimath, heavy landslides hit Lambagarh area and washed away nearly 300 meter long road between Joshimath and Badrinath, 17 killed.
25.	August 03, 2004	Landslide at Tehri dam project, 9 killed.
26.	August 08, 2009	La, Chanchna villages of district Pithoragarh, 38 persons killed.

GENERAL GEOGRAPHY OF THE STUDY AREA

Uttrakhand extends from 28° 43′ N to 31° 27′ N longitude and 77° 34′ East to 81° 02′ E latitude. Uttarakhand borders Tibet to the north, Nepal to the east, and the states of Himachal Pradesh and Uttar Pradesh in the west and south respectively. The region is traditionally referred to as Uttarakhand in Hindu scriptures and old literature, a term which derives from the Sanskrit for Northern Country or Section, with an area of 53,566 km². Uttarkhand was a part of Uttar Pradesh before 9 November, 2000. It has 13 districts.

According to the 2011 census of India, Uttarakhand has a population of 10,116,752 comprising 5,154,178 males and 4,962,574 females, with 69.45% of the population living in rural areas. The state is the 20th most populous state of the country having 0.84% of the population on 1.69% of the land. The population density of the state is 189 people per square kilometre having a 2001-2011 decadal growth rate of 19.17%. The gender ratio is 963 females per 1000 males.

DIFFERENT BETWEEN DISASTER AND HAZARD

Hazard and disaster are closely related. A hazard is a natural event while the disaster is its consequence. A hazard is a perceived natural event, which threatens both life and property. A disaster is the culmination of such hazard. A hazard becomes a disaster when it hits an area affecting the normal life system. For example, the 2001 Gujarat earthquake killed many people in Ahmedabad when buildings collapsed because of their poor construction quality. In another earthquake of similar intensity in the USA during the same year, no one died as no building collapsed because of their better construction quality. The USA earthquake was considered a hazard while the Gujarat earthquake was considered a disaster due to the severe loss of life and property.

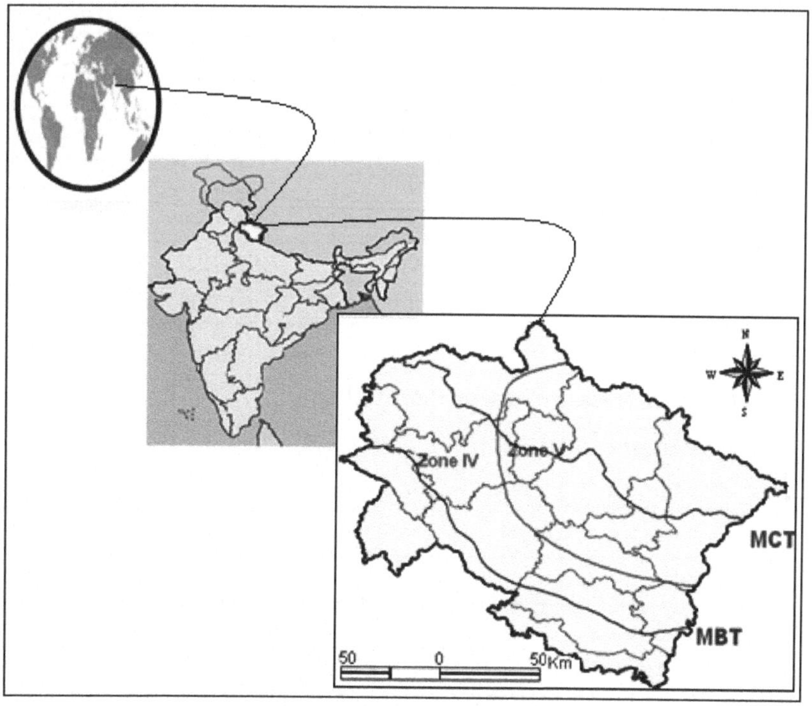

Fig. 8.1: Location Map of the Study Area

Economic Loss in Malpa Landslide

Table 8.2: Landslide Damage at Malpa (1998)

Name of Damaged Things	Detail
Person Dead	209
Animals	69
Houses	05
Huts (KMVN)	02
Huts (PWD)	02
Huts (Army)	01
Wodden Bridge	01
Cultivated Land	0.408ha
Barren Land	1.701ha

Source: Tehsil Office Dharchula.

Table 8.3: Loss of Economy in Malpa Landslide (1998)

Sl. No.	Particulars	Public Cost (Rs.)	Private Cost (Rs.)	Total Cost (Rs.)
1.	Livestocks	1,38,000	9,22,650	10,60,650
2.	Settlements	21,55,000	4,90,000	26,45,000
3.	Arable Land	-	60,430	60,430
4.	Barren Land	-	1,08,000	1,08,000
5.	Vegetation	-	28,500	28,5000
6.	Wodden Bridge	1,00,000	-	1,00,000
7.	Porter's Income	-	3,26,700	3,26,700
8.	Other Items	6,00,000	7,64,923	13,64,923
	Total	**29,93,000**	**27,01,203**	**56,94,203**

Source: Tehsil Office Dharchula.

Table 8.4: Human Loss in Malpa Landslide

Persons	Total No.
Kailash Mansarovar Pilgrims of twelfth group	60
Guides and workers of KMVN	05
Coolies of K.P	59
Labours of GREFF	09
Members of ITBP force	08
PWD labours	04
Members of 5 families of Malpa	16
Constables of UP police	03
Inhabitants of Gunji and Budhi village	32
Inhabitants of Dumling village	12
Hermit	01

Source: Tehsil Office Dharchula.

Similarly, a hazard such as a cyclone hits an unpopulated coast, it need not be considered as a disaster. However, it will be considered a disaster, if life and property are seriously damaged. For example in the year 1998, Central Himalaya was struck hard by landslides. Major incidences took place in Kali, Kaliganga and Madhyamaheshwar river valleys and the death toll in these crossed three hundred. These were one of the worst landslides, India has witnessed in the last century.

Reactivated Chautuladhar Landslide Near Tawaghat

Thus a hazard has a potential for a disaster. While hazards are inevitable, each hazard need not convert into a disaster. So natural hazards are events like earthquakes, volcanic eruptions, landslides, tsunamis, floods and drought-any physical event that happens naturally. They are caused by changes in the atmosphere, the earth's surface or the sea or other body of water. They can happen quickly, called a rapid onset hazard, or build up gradually, called a slow onset hazard. They can happen over smaller, local areas or affect countries, regions or the whole world – some even happen in space, on the sun for example.

Disaster is "an event concentrated in time and space in which a society or community undergoes severe damage and incurs such losses to its members and physical appurtenances that the social structure is disrupted and the fulfilment of all or some of the essential factors of the society is prevented" (UN Disaster Relief Office).

CONCEPTUAL FRAMEWORK OF LANDSLIDE DISASTER

Classification of Landslides

Landslides may be active, dormant or stabilized. They have been classified in many different ways due to their wide nature and variety. Some of these classifications are region specific, depending upon the geology of the region.

Any classification of landslides should provide a reasonably good method of identification of type of landslides. This would help in taking corrective action by instituting preventive and remedial methods for each established group of slope movement. For such a classification any good textbook may be referred to. In the present study landslides have been classified on the basis of material type and type of movement Table 1.1 (Varnes, 1978).

Material Type

The material involved in a landslide is classified into two groups, 'bedrock' and 'soil' Soil, which is generally unconsolidated sacrificial material, is further subdivided into 'debris' and 'earth' depending upon its texture.

Bedrock refers to earth materials that have lithified by some rock-forming process. Its strength depends on the rock type, degree of weathering, density and orientation of discontinuities that are generally planes of weakness in rock mass. For instance, if strong hard granite contains many fractures, it may be no stronger than a coarse grained soil.

Debris is composed of predominantly coarse grained soil or as mentioned above, can also include highly fractured bedrock. The strength of coarse grained soil is generally derived from friction between the grains. Woody debris such as high percentage of trees or logs, or other organic material, is sometimes incorporated with the inorganic debris.

Earth refers to predominantly fine grained soil (primarily silt & clay sized materials). The strength of fine grained soil is generally derived from cohesion, the chemical and electrical bonding between small particles of soil.

TYPES OF MOVEMENTS

Falls

Falls are abrupt movements of masses of geologic materials, such as rocks and boulders, which become detached from steep slopes or cliffs (Fig. 8.1). Separation occurs along discontinuities such as fractures, joints, and bedding planes and movement occurs by free-fall, bouncing, and rolling. Falls are strongly influenced by gravity, mechanical weathering, and the presence of interstitial water.

Topples

Toppling failures are distinguished by the forward rotation of a unit or units about some pivotal point, below or low in the unit, under the actions of gravity and forces exerted by adjacent units or by fluids in cracks (fig. 8.2).

Flows

There are five basic categories of rapid mass movement in which a combination flows that differ from one another in fundamental ways.

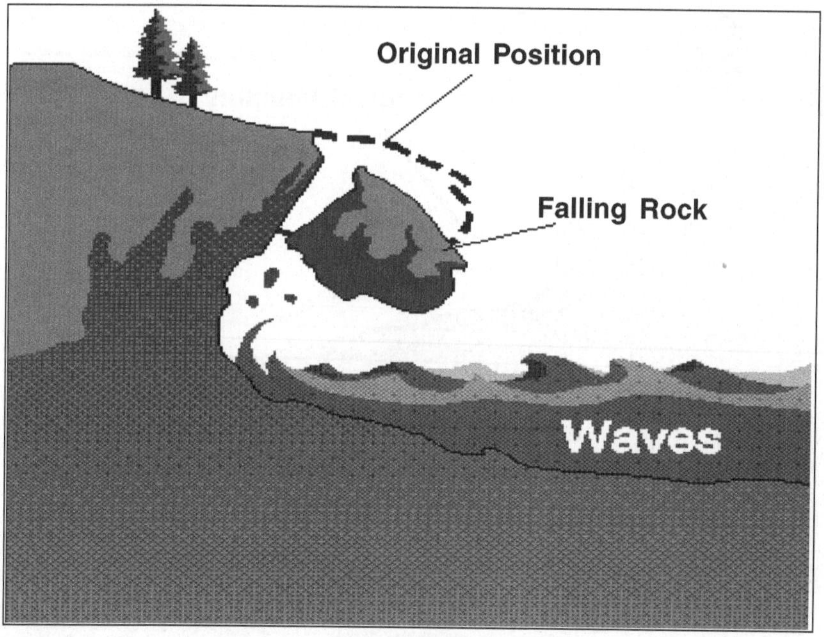

Fig. 8.2: Fall

Fig. 8.3: Topple

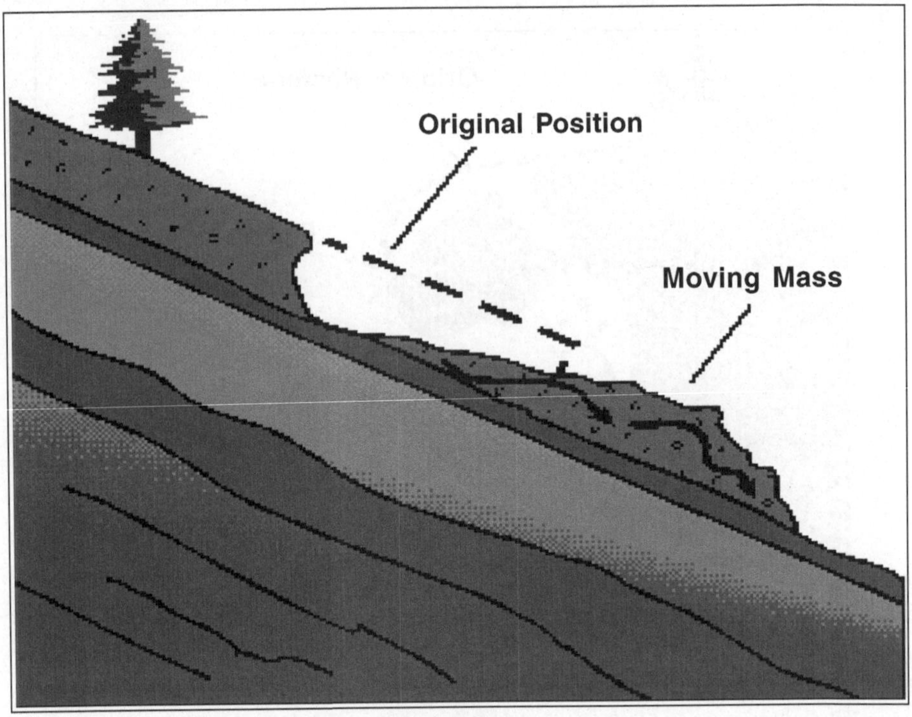

Fig. 8.4: Flows

(a) *Debris flow:* A debris flow is a form of rapid mass movement in which a combination of loose soil, rock, organic matter, air, and water mobilize as slurry that flows down slope. Debris flows include<50% fines. Debris flows are commonly caused by intense surface-water flow, due to heavy precipitation or rapid snowmelt that erodes and mobilizes loose soil or rock on steep slopes. Debris flows also (Fig. 8.4) commonly mobilize from other types of landslides that occur on steep slopes. Debris flows are nearly saturated and consist of a large proportion of silt- and sand-sized material. Debris-flow source areas are often associated with steep gullies, and debris-flow deposits are usually indicated by the presence of debris fans at the mouths of gullies. Fires that denude slopes of vegetation intensify the susceptibility of slopes to debris flows.

(b) *Debris avalanche:* This is a variety of very rapid to extremely rapid debris flow.

(c) *Earth flow:* Earth flows have a characteristic "hourglass" shape. The slope material liquefies and runs out, forming a bowl or depression at the head. The flow itself is elongate and usually occurs in fine-grained materials or clay-bearing rocks on moderate slopes and under saturated conditions. However, dry flows of granular material are also possible.

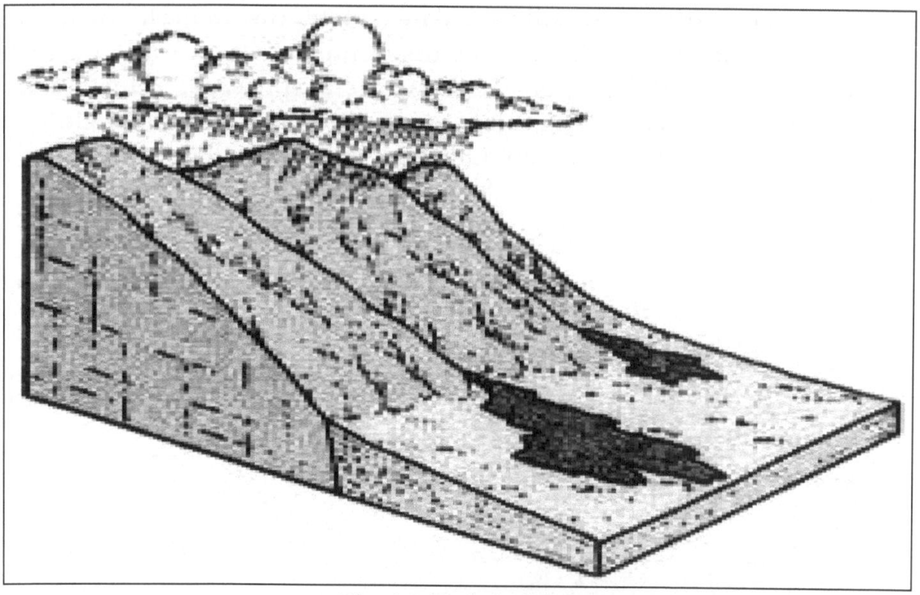

Fig. 8.5: Debris flow

(d) *Mudflow:* A mudflow is an earth flow consisting of material that is wet enough to flow rapidly and that contains at least 50 per cent sand, silt, and clay-sized particles. In some instances, for example in many newspaper reports, mudflows and debris flows are commonly referred to as "mudslides."

(e) *Creep:* Creep is the imperceptibly slow, steady, downward movement of slope-forming soil or rock (Fig. 8.5). Movement is caused by shear stress sufficient to produce permanent deformation, but too small to produce shear failure. There are generally three types of creep: (*i*) seasonal, where movement is within the depth of soil affected by seasonal changes in soil moisture and soil temperature; (*ii*) continuous, where shear stress continuously exceeds the strength of the material; and (*iii*) progressive, where slopes are reaching the point of failure as other types of mass movements. Creep is indicated by curved tree trunks, bent fences or retaining walls, tilted poles or fences, and small soil ripples on ridges.

Lateral Spreads

Lateral spreads are distinctive because they usually occur on very gentle slopes or flat terrain. The dominant mode of movement is lateral extension accompanied by shear or tensile fractures. The failure is caused by liquefaction, the process whereby saturated, loose, cohesionless sediments (usually sands and silts) are transformed from a solid into a liquefied state. Failure is usually triggered by rapid ground motion, such as that experienced during an earthquake, but can also be artificially induced. When coherent material, either bedrock or soil, translate, rotate, disintegrate, or liquefy and rests on materials that liquefy, the upper units may undergo fracturing and extension and may then subside flow. Lateral spreading in fine-grained materials on shallow slopes is usually progressive. The failure starts suddenly in a small area and spreads rapidly. Often the initial failure is a slump, but in some materials movement occurs for no apparent reason. Combination of two or more of the above types is known as a complex landslide.

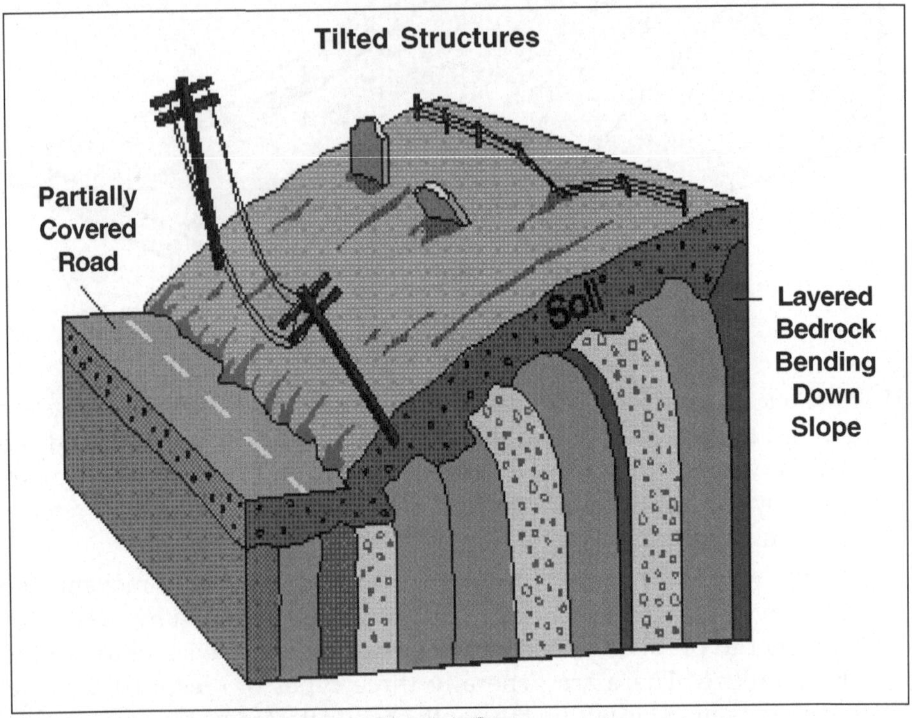

Fig. 8.6: Creep

Slides

Although many types of mass movements are included in the general term "landslide," the more restrictive use of the term refers only to mass movements, where there is a distinct zone of weakness that separates the slide material from more stable underlying material. The two major types of slides are rotational slides and translational slides.

(a) *Rotational slide:* This is a slide in which the surface of rupture is curved concavely upward and the slide movement is roughly rotational about an axis that is parallel to the ground surface and transverse across the slide.

(b) *Translational slide:* In this type of slide, the landslide mass moves along a roughly planar surface with little rotation or backward tilting. A *block slide* is a translational slide down slope as a relatively coherent mass.

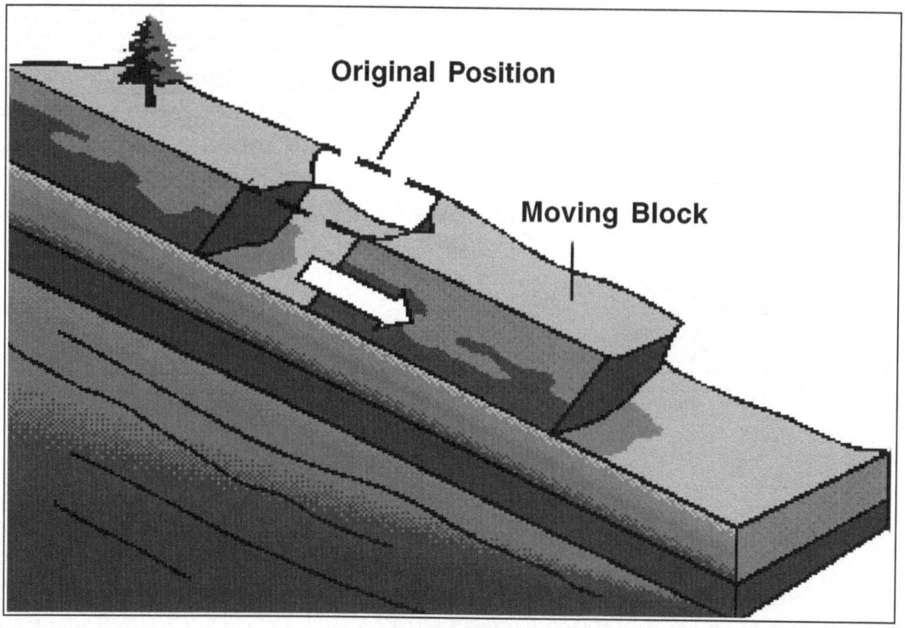

Fig. 8.7: Slide

Table 8.5: Classification of Slope Movements (Adapted from Varnes, 1978)

Type of Movement			Bedrock	Type of Material Engineering	Soils
				Predominantly coarse material	Predominantly fine material
Falls			Rock fall	Debris fall	Earth fall
Topples			Rock topple	Debris topple	Earth topple
Slides	Rotational	Few Units	Rock slump	Debris slump	Earth slump
	Translational	Many Units	Rock slide	Debris slide	Earth slide
Lateral Spreads			Rock spread	Debris spread	Earth spread
Flows			Rock flow (deep creep)	Debris flow (soil creep)	Earth flow (soil creep)

FACTORS CAUSING LANDSLIDES

Hills and mountains have been sculptured over years by violent eruptive formations and slow processes of erosion. They are not permanent and everlasting. Surface of the land is made by nature from decay and our fertile plains are formed by ruins of our mountains. Landslides, denudation and other associated processes of erosion have to be accepted as part of the natural process. They are intractable being a function of gravity and time.

Despite growing scientific knowledge of landslides, their threat continues to increase due to increasing development in vulnerable terrain; construction activity such as laying new roads; global climate changes that result in violent and severe weather and deforestation. Landslides and other "ground failures", worldwide cost more lives and more money each year than all other natural disasters combined. Despite their seemingly less impact, landslides cost to a nation like India more than 100 million US$ annually in restoration work and economic losses.

Landslide and Blocked Road Near Nainital

Influencing factors, where landslides occur, can be divided into two sets, permanent and variable or triggering factors. Permanent factors are characteristics of the landscape which remain unchanged or very little from a human perspective. The steepness of a slope or the type of rock, for example, presents changes only with the passage of long periods of time. Permanent factors such as rock type and slope steepness can be recognized and identified for specific landslides after their occurrence. By examining existing landslides in an area, it is possible to recognize how permanent factors contributed to these slope failures. Identifying conditions and processes promoting past instability makes it possible to use these factors to estimate future landslides (Varnes, 1985).

Variable factors are landscape characteristics that change quickly as a result of some triggering event. Ground vibration due to earthquakes, a rapid rise in groundwater levels, and increased soil moisture due to intense precipitation are examples of variable factors. It is often necessary to be present at the time when a landslide occurs or shortly thereafter to assess these factors. Due to the lack of long-term records relating landslide activity to historic earthquakes, storms, or other initiating factors, permanent factors are usually used to estimate landslide hazard. As such, identifying landslide areas is not an accurate science and leads, in general, to depicting hazard-prone areas based on estimation. At best, landslide and landslide susceptible areas can be identified along with expected triggering events.

There are various causes of landslides. Landslides are caused by natural (geological, material, geomorphologic, rainfall, gravity, tectonic) as well as anthropogenetic (road construction, deforestation, overgrazing) factors. Seismic activity in mountains also results in considerable landslide movement. On some slopes, heavy monsoon rainfall often in association with cyclonic disturbances, results in considerable landslide activity. On 8 August 2009 the landslide which occurred at La-Jhenkla, Chachna villages of Pithoragarh district, was the result of a cloudburst. Total 38 persons lost their lives. This landslide was triggered by the clodburst. In the Himalaya, landsliding involves a variety and combination of processes, including falls, topples avalanches, slides, and flows. Rapid tectonic uplift and the intense fluvial and glacial incision produce long steep slopes that are prone to failure. Slope failure in the Himalaya is commonly due to under cutting of slopes by fluvial erosion, shaking during earthquakes, and in the monsoon-influenced areas by the heavy rainfall leading to saturation and erosion of slopes. However landsliding may have been increased in many regions due to human activity, such as slope modification for construction activity, deforestation, terracing, and agricultural activities etc. Climatic change may also be responsible for unusually severe rainstorms that trigger landslides. In general the following are the causes of slope failure:

(a) **Gravity:** The gravitational force of the earth is responsible for downward movement of an object, without applying any external force. Thus mass movement consequently occurs more frequently on steep slopes than on shallow ones. It's a fact that gravity constantly act on a slope, landslide only occurs when the stress produced by the force of gravity exert the resistance of the material.

(b) **Water:** Water plays a key role in slope failures. This effect can occur in the form of intense rainfall, snowmelt, changes in ground-water levels, and water level changes along coastlines, earth dams, and the banks of lakes, reservoirs, canals, and rivers. In the Himalayan region landslides are frequently triggered by rainfall. In the study area almost 80 per cent annual precipitation (1796.5mm) is concentrated during the monsoon season. The unprotected rain soaked soil often with clay, talcose, quartzitic material becomes unstable.

(c) **Seismic Activity:** Many mountainous areas that are vulnerable to landslides have also experienced at least moderate rates of earthquake occurrence in recorded times. The occurrence of earthquakes in steep landslide-prone areas greatly increases the likelihood of landslides, due to ground shaking alone or shaking- caused dilation of soil materials, which allows rapid infiltration of water. The lesser Himalaya in general and the northeastern Kumaun Himalaya in particular are highly prone to seismic movements. This region falls in ZoneV (Very high damage risk zone, where the seismic intensity can reach upto IX or more in MSK scale) of the seismic zonation map of India prepared by Ministry of Urban Affairs, GOI, New Delhi1997. A number of rock falls, slips and landslides have been initiated in the study area due to these activities, causing extensive damage to various masonry structures and civil constructions.

(d) **Road construction:** The most important anthropogenic factor causing landslides is road construction. The stability of Himalayan slopes have been, to a large extent, jeopardized by construction of road which invariably involves steep and deep back cutting in to hills. These cutting involve tremendous release of stress, setting in a process of progressive failure. The network of roads in the Himalayan region is approximately 50,000 km long, many of these roads have been unimaginatively planned and their construction very cruelly executed, leading to destabilization of hillsides and production of colossal amount of debris. It has been calculated that 600 cub meter of debris per kilometer of road is produced annually by landslides and rockfalls, causing about 24 × 106 cub meter of sediment to slide down the slope (Valdiya 1985). After the roads are built, they are recurrently ravaged by landslides and rock falls during rains. Along the Dehradun-Tehri road, there are ten landslides in every kilometer. Each of which generates 500-cub meter of debris. Most of roads in Himalayan region have been unscientifically constructed. For example, Panar-Ghat road sections (Distt. Pithoragarh) is constructed parallel to North Almora Thrust.

(e) **Deforestation:** The relation between 'deforestation' and 'slope instability' has been a subject of considerable research. Most of the landslides occur due to extensive deforestation for urbanization. The deforestation brings problem of erosion and soil movement. Stripped off the protective vegetal cover, the ground is no longer capable of absorbing rain water, so that much of precipitation runs off, eroding the hill slopes at furious pace and flooding the alluvial plains. Overgrazing on the hill slope is also a cause of slope instability.

Transverse faults are responsible for the great mass movement in Himalaya. Himalaya represents a highly sensitive ecosystem that is naturally

Landslide at Mangti Village

poised for disaster. Although triggered by a wide variety of factors, mass movements in this terrain are controlled mainly by the geotectonic set-up of rocks. The Precambrian sedimentary and metamorphic rocks of the Higher and Lesser Himalaya have experienced severe folding, faulting and shattering during successive deformational phases of the Himalayan orogeny. These highly deformed rocks are deeply dissected by streams and rivers. Neotectonic activity has accelerated the pace of erosion and mass movement in this zone. The subtropical climate characterized by abundant and seasonally intense rainfall is responsible for the formation of a thick mantle of weathered rocks. Extensive human activity in the region has caused intensive erosion and triggered slope failures. The consequences are endemic and locally large landslides are registered, particularly in the zones of active faults and thrusts.

According to an estimate of Valdiya in 1985 about more than 44,000 km long roads are spread over the Himalayan region. It has been calculated that 550 cub metre of debris per kilometer of road is produced annually by landslides and rockfalls, causing about 24 × 106 cub metre of sediment to slide down the slopes (Valdiya, 1985). About 40,000 to 80,000 cub metre of debris is required to be removed in the construction of just one km long road (Valdiya, 1985). Ten landslides found in every kilometer along the Dehradun-Tehri road, each of which estimated to generate 500 cub meter of debris. The observations made by Patnaik (1981) revealed that at the rate of 411 cub metre per kilometer per year the Border Roads Organisation clears debris from Tanakpur-Tawaghat road.

Landslide at Tintola Village

MITIGATION STRATEGY

Development agencies are funding the construction of an increasing number of infrastructures in mountainous regions as access to outlying districts moves up the development agenda. Infrastructure is important as a first step towards sustainable development and these regions, despite their inhospitable terrain, are often home to large populations of subsistence farming communities. The regions are therefore very important socially and economically, while requiring sympathetic development because of the fragile nature of their environment. A substantial number of developing countries and emerging nations occupy regions with difficult mountainous or steep hilly terrain, where geotechnical hazards tend to be severe and road construction costs are high. The most severe geotechnical hazards encountered on road networks in these terrains are those associated with landsliding of natural slopes. Governments face a major problem in balancing reasonable construction and maintenance costs with how best to allocate scarce resources within such areas.

Policies may be needed to control or restrict development in specific areas. Where slope instability cannot be overcome satisfactorily or where it provides other environmental benefits a presumption against development may be appropriate. In other areas, built development may not be appropriate unless adequate and environmentally acceptable slope stabilisation measures are included in the development proposal.

Local Plan development proposals should ensure that land use is appropriate in the light of any known landslide risk. As well as the consideration needed for new development, where there are risks to existing development, proposals may include specific action on land stabilisation or coast protection to reduce those risks or to enable appropriate beneficial use of unstable slopes.

It is experienced that a large proportion of planning applications are for minor extensions to existing buildings and for garages and for changes of use. Where such "small developments" are situated on potentially unstable slopes, as identified in the landslide assessment, they would normally require a slope stability report. Since these are largely situated adjacent to existing property and generally unlikely to pose a significant threat to slope stability, it may be appropriate, in considering an application for planning permission, for them not to be subject to this requirement provided that there is no evidence of current instability and that the site is not to be significantly disturbed, i.e. that:

- cuts and fills are limited in depth and any deep temporary excavations for surface or foul drains or other services are limited to short lengths across the slope;
- provision is made for free drainage of groundwater within the slope and for inspection and facility for future works for maintenance of flows;
- surface drainage is not restricted or diverted;
- drainage from the proposed development is collected and conveyed in flexible piped systems; and
- any existing retaining walls are not removed or altered.

However, the need to satisfy the Regulations that landsliding, in so far as it can reasonably be foreseen, shall not threaten the security of a building may require the submission of a slope stability report to the building control authority.

Whilst a local planning authority is entitled to rely on the expert advice provided by a developer in relation to slope instability, it is recommended that a check development is that of the developer, the decision on the planning merits may not require the local planning authority to check design assumptions and calculations. However, there will remain a need for the local authority or an approved inspector to check designs submitted for approval under the Regulations.

RECOMMENDATIONS

Ban on blasting for road construction and slope cutting for constructional purpose, as the blasting affects the fragile rocks of this area prone to landslide, blasting also opens the cracks or joints of the rocks, which further facilitate landslide.

1. An afforestation drive should be initiated in entire valleys.
2. Rain gauges should be installed in upper the higher himalaya so that rainfall could be monitored regularly.
3. Proper drainage network and suitably designed retaining walls should be constructed in all the places where road cutting has rendered the slopes unstable.
4. A drainage network planning needs to be initiated for the entire landslide prone village in order to flush out the additional rain water and minimize the seepage into fragile rocks through their cracks. Local labour could be employed for annual maintenance of the drainage network.
5. One geotechnical investigation unit needs to be set up to collect regularly geotechnical data of unstable slope etc. and for taking suitable remedial measures to control the vulnerable landslides.
6. The monitoring of some of the active landslide needs to be undertaken every year using high resolution satellite data.
7. Proper instrumentation need to be installed to monitor the movement of active landslides.
8. Use all the data available for the management in a danger prone area. Use the geographic map to check the gravity of danger.
9. Select those places where the probability of landslides and avalanche is considerably low.
10. Do not allow ice pocket to be formed on the roof or on the construction site. To remove the weight of ice, the tilt of roof must be greater than 50° when they are constructive.
11. The construction of enormous buildings on deep and weak slopes of hills should be stopped. If it is necessary to construct the building then the rules must be followed with attention.
12. It would be of great dangers if the hill which is situated under village is cut off.
13. Strong walls should be constructed on the lower part of the hills so that it can act like a strong base and help the hills to stand tall.
14. These should be good outlet arrangement for the rain walls to follow else the water will seep into the hill and make it weak.
15. The overgrazing of cattle should be controlled or else the upper layers of the hills will get destroyed hence leading to the soil erosion.

16. The building should not be constructed at the bank of any dry, short or long river.

Landslides are natural phenomena which often have detrimental consequences. Landslide hazards can be systematically assessed by using different factors and methods. Movements and landslide predisposing factors will be similar to those verified in the past, we are able to predict that future slides occurring in a non-specified time span.

The entire terrain of the study area is the morphological expression of complex and on going geological processes operating in the area. These processes have rendered the rocks of the area in a shattered state, which, as such, are very susceptible to slide. Deforestation, blasting for road, dam and tunnel construction and unplanned slope modification by villagers has further enhanced the susceptibility of slope failure.

Deforestation has resulted in removal of natural anchoring of soil and jointed rocks by tree roots. Unplanned modification of hill slopes has considerably disturbed the angle of rest of slope forming mass. Added to this is the continuous blasting in rocks which, in turn, generates shock waves to open the closed joints of rocks on even to develop new planes of failure in rocks. These shock waves might also have triggered a few landslides in the region, particularly along the Dhauliganga valley where construction work for Hydroelectric Power Projects are going on. Shock waves trigger landslides as they shake the ground in all directions and thus disturb the angle of rest of slope forming mass. But, in most cases, hydrological factors seem to be the prime causative force and that is why the proper drainage network for and afforestation in the region has been recommended.

REFERENCES

1. Bhandari, R.K., (1998): Eco Development in the Garhwal Himalaya with Particular Reference to Field Study and Monitoring of Landslides and Development of Innovative Central Measures Report DOEn.
2. Bhandari, R.K., Gupta, C., (1985): Problems of Landslides in the Himalaya and Future Directions; In- J.S. Singh (Edts.) *Environmental Regeneration in Himalaya, Concepts and Strategies, Gyanodaya Prakashan, Nainital.*
3. Encardio Rite (2003): Landslides and Role of Instrumentation in Mitigation of Their Effect, Encardio Rite Electronics Pvt. Ltd., Lucknow.
4. Pandey, R.K., Tolia, R.S., Sharma, R., Pathak, J.K. (1999): Landslide Problem in Uttarakhand. International Conference on Disaster Management Cooperative Networking in South Asia 28-30 November 1999, New Delhi.
5. Pant, C.C. and Sharma, A.K., (2002): Landslide Hazard Evalution and Zonation in North Western Nainital Hill, Uttaranchal Lesser Himalayas, In- C.C. Pant and A.K. Sharma (Edts.) *Aspect of Geology and Environment of the Himalaya, Gyanodaya Prakashan Nainital.*

6. Patnaik, N., (1981): Role of Soil Conservation and Afforestation for Flood Moderation, in Inter. Con. on Flood Disaster, December, 1981. *Ind. Natl. Sci. Acad. New Delhi (Mimeograph)*
7. Pnadey, R.K., (1998): Okhimath Lndslide 1998: Some Experience. Res. *Monograph No. 7, DMMC*, Dehradun.
8. Pnadey, R.K., (2006): Landslide Problem in Uttaranchal, India: Issues and Challenges, *Disaster Prevention and Management*. Vol. 15, pp. 247-255.
9. Rautela, P. and Paul, S.K., (2001): August 1998 Landslide Tragedies of Central Himalaya (India); Learning from Experience, *International Journal of Environmental Studies* Vol. 58, pp. 343-355.
10. Rautela, P., Pandey, R.K., (2005): Traditional Inputs in Disaster Management: The Case of Amparav, North India, *International Journal of Environmental studies* Vol. 62, No. 5, pp. 505-515.
11. Valdiya, K.S., (1985): Accelerated Erosion And Landslide Prone Zones in the Central Himalayan Region. In- J.S. Singh (Edts.) *Environmental Regeneration in Himalaya, Concepts and Strategies. Gyanodaya Prakashan, Nainital.*
12. Valdiya, K.S., (1988): Tectonics and Evolution of the Central Sector of Himalaya. *Phil. Trans, R. Soc. London*. Vol. 326, pp. 151-175.
13. Varnes, D.J., (1978): "Slope Movement and Process" in Landslide: Analysis and Control, In- R.L. Schuster and RJ Krizek (edts.) *Landslides, Analysis and Control, Special Report, Washington DC (National Academy of Science)*, pp. 12-33,.
14. Varnes, D.J., (1984): *Landslide Hazard Zonation: A Review of Principles and Practice.* UNESCO France. pp. 63.

9

Allelopathy
A Tool for Weed Management

Jyoti Pandey[1]; Sumit Chaturvedi[2] and Narayan Singh[3]

INTRODUCTION

In traditional agroforestry systems, farmers grow agricultural crops along with various multipurpose trees on boundaries between agricultural fields. With the increasing recognition of agroforestry as an alternative land use, many scientists have focused their attention on trees. These trees contribute to sustainability of food production and are essential for the survival of local population. Trees, especially fast-growing multipurpose species (MPTS), are becoming an integral part of intensive commercial agroforestry models introduced in recent times. Most of these tree species are exotics of small to medium size, amenable to repeated pruning management and ideally suited for small farm conditions. Among them eucalyptus have succeeded as a preferred species for agroforestry and farm forestry interventions throughout the country (Sachan, 2006).

Weed infestation in agricultural fields results in huge economic losses and low quality crop yields (Appleby *et al.*, 2000). Worldwide, a large amount of money is spent every year to control them. In India about 45 per cent crop loss is caused due to weeds in agriculture production which is worth of

1. **Research Scholar, Department of Forestry and Environmental Science, Kumaun University, Nainital (Uttarakhand), India.**

2. **Assistant Professor, College of Agronomy, GBPUA& T, Pantnagar, Udham Singh Nagar (Uttarakhand), India.**

3. **Manager, TERI, CSR, Project, Dalash, Kullu, Himachal Pradesh, India.**

Rupees 20,000 million annually. A successful establishment of a weed in any ecosystem is attributed to its high growth rate, high reproductive potential, wide adaptive nature and above all interference by resource depletion and allelopathy (Kohli and Rani, 1994). A weed possesses various toxicological effects on ecosystem. Weeds may also harbour insects and pathogens adding more complications to their control. The control of weeds can be achieved through several means such as mechanical, chemical, biological and cultural; the use of synthetic herbicides is common and provides an effective method. Unfortunately, the use of synthetic herbicides may affect the environment and human health, and is also leading to increasing herbicidal resistance among many weed species. Agriculture worldwide is currently using about 3 million tons of herbicides annually, and herbicide-resistant weeds have become more prolific, which has further expanded the use of herbicides (Shibayama, 2001). Therefore, efforts to develop alternative means of weed control, which are not only eco-friendly, but also cost effective and bioefficaceous are needed. In this direction, efforts to utilize allelopathy and natural plant products for effective weed management are being made.

GENERAL REVIEW OF ALLELOPATHY

Allelopathy is generally associated with interaction between living plants, a significant role in plant-plant interaction. Growing environmental and public health concern from the use of agricultural chemicals (pesticides) in agriculture has stimulated interest in the search for new and environmentally safe technologies for effective inhibition of weeds (Rice, 1994). Allelopathy refers to the beneficial or harmful effects of one plant on another plant, both crop and weed species, from the release of bio-chemicals, known as allele-chemicals, from plant parts by leaching, root exudation, volatilization, residue decomposition, and other processes in both natural and agricultural systems. Also refers to the inhibition of growth of one plant by chemical compounds that are released into the soil from neighboring plants. Allelopathy is generally associated with interaction between living plants, a significant role in plant-plant interaction. Growing environmental and public health concern from the use of agricultural chemicals (pesticides) in agriculture has stimulated interest in the search for new and environmentally safe technologies for effective inhibition of weeds.

CONCEPTS AND FACTS

The term was first introduced by Molisch (1937) to refer biological interaction between all types of plants including micro organisms. According to Rice (1994) he defined allelopathy as the effect (both positive and negative) of one plant on the growth of another plant through the release of chemical compound into the environment. The International Allelopathic Society defined allelopathy as follows "Any processes involving secondary metabolites produced by plants, micro organism, viruses and fungi that influence the growth and development of agricultural and biological systems (excluding animals) including positive and negative effects" (Torres et al., 1996). So allelopathy is the direct influence of a chemical released from one living plant on the development and growth of another plant. Allelopathy offers a great potential for weed management. Rice (1995) discussed the applied aspect of allelopathy i.e. employing allelopathy in natural weed management. The term allelopathy is derived from two Greek words "alleon" meaning mutual and "pathos" meaning harm. Allelopathic properties have been reported for many species, especially trees (Table 9.1).

Table 9.1: Some Examples of Agroforestry Tree Species Reported to have Allelopathic Effects

	Compounds	Representing Plants
Phenolic compounds	3, 4-Dihydroxybenzoic acid	Delonix regia
	3, 4-Dihydroxybenzaldehyde	Delonix regia
	3, 4-Dihydroxycinnamic acid	Delonix regia
	3, 5-Dihydroxybenzoic acid	Delonix regia
	Gallic acid	Celtis laevigata
	Gentisic acid	Celtis laevigata
	Scopoletin	Celtis laevigata
	Scoploline	Celtis laevigata
Alkaloids	Caffeine	Coffea Arabica
	Mimosine	Leucaena leucocephala
	Pyridine- 3, 4- diol	Leucaena leucocephala
Terpenoid	Abscisic acid	Festuca species
	Pinene	Salvia leucophylla
	Cineole	Salvia leucophylla
	Champhor	Salvia leucophylla

ALLELOPATHY IN NATURAL WEED MANAGEMENT

Allelopathy may be a successful tool to manage weed infestation in agricultural production, if it can be exploited appropriately in a rotational cropping system (Khanh *et al.*, 2005a). However, in the case of trees, it is difficult to apply the concept of rotation; therefore, enhancing weed suppression by trees itself through litter fall and isolation of natural plant product may be among the most feasible means of controlling weeds. The isolation and identification of allelochemicals responsible for weed suppression by trees may be helpful for understanding the chemical interactions of trees and other plant communities. Allelopathic suppression of weeds is receiving greater attention in recent years as a possible alternative for weed management. Numerous crops have been investigated for allelopathic activity towards weeds. A suppressive effect on weed, possibly mediated by the release of allelopathic compounds has been reported for a wide range of temperate and tropical crops. These include alfalfa (*Medicago sativa*), barley (*Hordeum vulgare*), clovers (*Trifolium* species, *Melilotus* species), brassica, eucalyptus, sesamum, tobacco, oats, rye, sorghum, sunflower and wheat (Narwal *et al*., 1998). Allelopathy can be used in weed management in different ways. The first is by selecting an appropriate crop variety or incorporating an allelopathic character into a desired crop variety. The second way is by applying crop residues and straw as mulches or growing an allelopathic variety in a rotational sequence that allows residues to remain in the field. The third way is use of allelochemicals as natural herbicides (Rice, 1995).

ALLELOCHEMICALS AS NATURAL HERBICIDES

The compounds from some plants have ability to produce natural plant products called allelochemicals that affect many weed species by inhibiting their germination and growth or simply the chemicals that impose allelopathic influences. They may be largely classified as secondary plant metabolites, which are generally considered to be those compounds (such as alkaloids, phenolics, flavonoids, terpenoids, and glucosinolates) which do not play a role in primary metabolic processes essential for a plant's survival, and are produced as offshoots of primary metabolic pathways. In contrast to primary metabolism, which comprises several hundreds of low molecular weight compounds, tens of thousands of secondary substances are known today, but only a limited number has been implicated as allelochemicals. They are present in virtually all plant tissues, including leaves, flowers, fruits, stems, roots, rhizomes, seeds and pollen. They may be released from plants into the environment by means of four ecological processes: volatilisation, leaching, root exudation, and decomposition of plant residues. Several chemicals can be released together and may exert toxicities in an additive or synergistic manner. The concentration of a single substance in field situations is generally below its inhibitory threshold. Allelopathic interferences often result from the joint action of several different compounds. The term was originally coined by Whittakar (1970). Putnam (1983, 1988) termed allelochemicals as nature's own herbicides. Duke et al. (2000) discussed that natural compounds have several benefits over synthetic compounds. For example, natural compounds may have novel structure due to diversity of molecular structure. This diversity is because synthetic chemists have been biased toward certain types of chemistry. They have had almost no interest in water-soluble compounds (Steve Duke, personal communication). Unlike a high proportion of synthetic pesticides, natural compounds are mostly water-soluble and non-halogenated molecules. Natural products relatively have short half-life and therefore considered safe of environmental toxicology standpoint (Duke et al., 2002). There is a need to discover new herbicides since the number of herbicide-resistant weeds is increasing and conventional synthetic herbicides are becoming less and less effective against the resistant weed biotypes

(Bhowmik 2000; Duke et al., 2002). Duke et al. (2000) discussed the approaches needed to select sources of natural products for the discovery of potential herbicides. These are:

1. obtain pure compounds from other laboratories;
2. obtain previously unexploited biological material; and
3. employ ethno biological and/or chemical ecology data to select material. Understanding the ecological and physiological aspects of a compound has two main approaches:
   (i) allelopathy, e.g. sorgoleone; and
   (ii) sequestering of a compound by a species to avoid autotoxicity, e.g. artemisinin (Duke et al., 2000; Tellez et al., 1999).

Some of the natural products exploited as commercial herbicides are triketone, cinmethylin, bialaphos, glufosinate and dicamba. Bialaphos, a microbially or iginated herbicide, has limited use in Japan. A natural fatty acid, pelargonic acid and maize gluten (a by-product of the maize-milling process) are mainly used in organic farming and have limited use in USA (Bhowmik, 1992; Duke et al., 2000). Natural plant products may provide clues to new and safe herbicide chemistry (Duke, 1986; Nimbal et al., 1996b). Therefore, modifying these natural products could give more active and selective herbicides. One of the first phytotoxic compounds to be implicated in higher plants was 1, 8- cineole (Muller and Muller, 1964). Cinmethylin was developed as a herbicide and commercially used for weed control for a short period of time. It controls many annual grasses and suppresses many broadleaf weed species (Bhowmik, 1988). Its structure is similar to the structure of 1, 4-cineole. A second natural herbicide is AAL-toxin, a natural metabolite produced by *Alternaria alternate* f. sp. lycopersici, the pathogen that causes stem canker of tomato (*Lycopersicum esculentum* Mill.) (Abbas et al., 1995). The phytotoxic effects of AALtoxin were tested on 86 crop and weed species (Abbas et al., 1995). Monocots were generally immune to its effects. Black nightshade, *Datura stramonium* L. (jimsonweed), all species of tomatoes tested, and several other broadleaf weed species were susceptible at low doses. Other broadleaf species were susceptible but only at higher doses. Differential selectivity of species to AAL-toxin should be exploited for selective weed control. Recently, mesotrione, a HPPD inhibitor, has been developed as a herbicide for selective weed control in corn (Bhowmik and Zhang, 2003). This herbicide chemistry was discovered from a natural compound from lemon bottlebrush (*Callistemon citrinus* Splendens). There is not much success in discovering natural herbicides from higher plants (Heisey, 1999). Some examples of synthetically derivatized benzoic acid metabolites from plants are dicamba and chloramben. The compounds having potential herbicidal activity but not commercially used are artemisinin, sorgoleone and ailanthone.

Pyrethrins extracted from a species of Chrysanthemum is also a models for developing new pesticides. Cinmethylin derived from the natural product cineol of certain desert plants. By modifying these allelochemicals, the end product could be more active, selective, or persistent. In a review of the potential use of allelochemicals as herbicides, Putnam (1988) listed 6 classes of allelochemicals isolated from over 30 families of terrestrial and aquatic plants. These classes are alkaloids, benzoxazinones, cinnamic acid derivatives, cyanogenic compounds, ethylene and other seed germination stimulants, and flavonoids. All these chemicals possess actual or potential phytotoxicity.

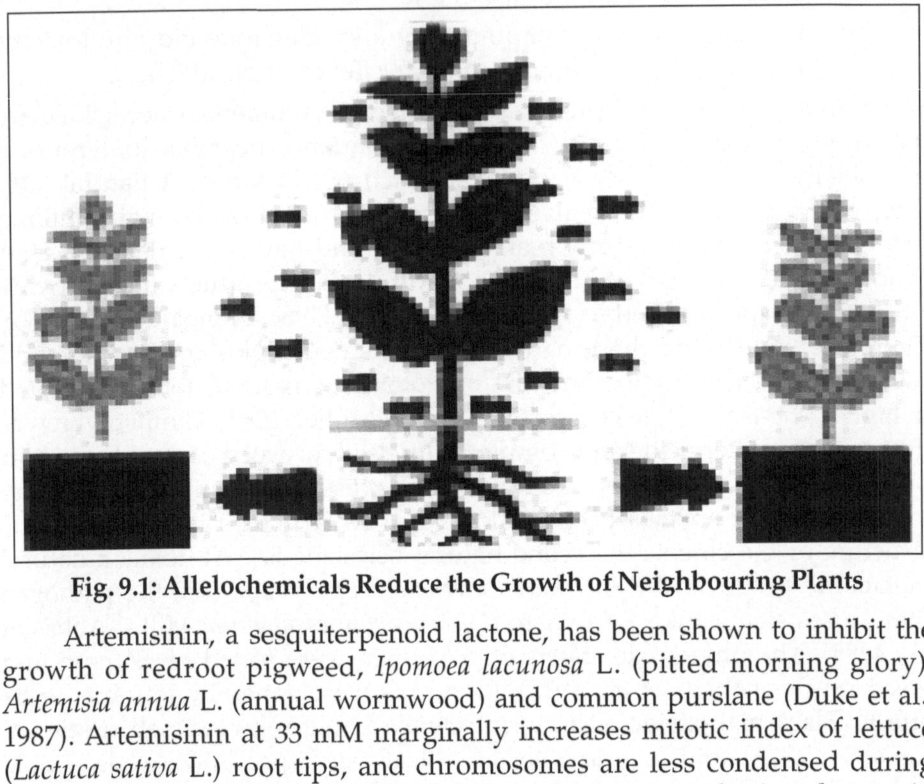

Fig. 9.1: Allelochemicals Reduce the Growth of Neighbouring Plants

Artemisinin, a sesquiterpenoid lactone, has been shown to inhibit the growth of redroot pigweed, *Ipomoea lacunosa* L. (pitted morning glory), *Artemisia annua* L. (annual wormwood) and common purslane (Duke et al., 1987). Artemisinin at 33 mM marginally increases mitotic index of lettuce (*Lactuca sativa* L.) root tips, and chromosomes are less condensed during mitosis. Duke et al. (1987) concluded that artemisinin is a selective phytotoxin with herbicidal activity similar to cinmethylin (Bhowmik, 1988). Although the exact mode of action is still unknown, Dayan et al. (1999) suggested that it is somewhat selective and might have a novel mode of action. Attempts have been made to use artemisinin as the basis for discovering new herbicides (Duke et al., 2001). Lydon et al. (1997) reported that the phytotoxic activities of annual wormwood cannot be solely explained by artemisinin. The dichloromethane extracts of annual wormwood leaves, which contain artemisinin, inhibited seed germination and seedling growth of redroot pigweed more strongly than did similar amounts of artemisinin alone. Furthermore, aqueous extracts without artemisinin had a similar activity to that of artemisinin alone. This illustrates the significance of joint action of allelochemicals in mixtures (Inderjit et al., 2002). Einhellig (1995) suggested that most allelopathic activities are due to the presence of several compounds in a mixture. The concentration of each compound in a mixture might be significantly less than the concentration of individual compounds needed to cause growth inhibition.

Heisey (1996) isolated a quassinoid compound, ailanthone, from bark and foliage of tree-of-heaven (*Ailanthus altissima* (Mill.) Swingle). The compound reported to possess pre- and post-herbicidal activity in greenhouse trials. Ailanthone exhibited a strong herbicidal activity when sprayed on soil before the seed germination. It, however, also had dramatic effects when sprayed onto seedlings after their emergence from soil. Although, not yet commercially exploited, Heisey (1996) advocated the use of ailanthone as potential herbicide due to its efficacy compared to widely used herbicides such as glyphosate and paraquat. Ailanthone is not commercially used as herbicide because of its rapid degradation in soil. Although weed species present at the time of spray may get killed, others may emerge once ailanthone disappears from the soil (Heisey, 1999). Multiple applications throughout the growing season of the crop could be a solution, but certainly would not be cost effective or feasible.

Allelochemicals are reported to be present in practically all plant tissues, including leaves, flowers, fruits, stems, roots, rhizomes and seeds. Chemical substances of plants come in contact with rain water, dew and mist and released in aqueous form as leachates and come in environment through volatilization, adsorption and microbial action. The effects of these allelochemicals are species specific and concentration dependent. Many of these allelochemicals are phytotoxic and have potential of herbicides. These could be used directly for weed control and also can be used to manufacture new herbicides rather than chemicals. The allelopathic compounds are tannins, phenolic acids, terpenoides etc. Davis (1982) identified juglone, quinine from walnut trees. Later on Cheema (1988) identified nine allelochemicals (benzoic, chlorogenic, ferulic, p-hydroxy benzoic, vanillic, p-coumaric, gallic and caffeic acids) in sorghum herbage while some unknown compounds were also present in the residual sample. Perveen (2000) found caffeic, ferulic, syringic and vanillic acid from sorghum plant extract through thin layer chromatographic technique. Anjum and Bajwa (2005) isolated annuionone from aqueous extract of sunflower leaves. The compound tested as natural herbicide against weeds and found a potent plant growth inhibitor that can be exploited for the development of herbicide model.

INHIBITORY EFFECT OF ALLELOCHEMICALS

Several allelochemicals act jointly to inhibit growth in laboratory and field conditions. The mechanism and mode of action of allelochemicals action were described by many scientists. Several modes of action for allelochemicals are involved in the inhibition and modification of plant growth and development (Einhelling, 1986). Einhellig and his group first reported the phytotoxic activity of sorgoleone (Einhellig, 1995; Einhellig and Souza, 1992). Sorgoleone and its analogues are structurally similar to plastoquinone (Duke et al., 2001).Sorgoleone inhibited the evolution of O_2 during photosynthesis in potato (*Solanum tuberosum* L.) and in common groundsel (*Senecio vulgaris* L.) (Nimbal et al., 1996a). Nimbal et al. (1996b) carried out a study on sorgoleone using triazine-susceptible potato and redroot pigweed thylakoids. Sorgoleone was a competitive inhibitor of atrazine binding sites. Sorgoleone also inhibited the photosystem II electron transport reactions (Gonzalez et al., 1997). Gattas-Halak et al. (1999) reported that sorgoleone influences the cell multiplication cycle by inhibiting the number of cells in prophase, metaphase, and anaphase stages. In theory, sorgoleone is considered as an efficient herbicide because of its potential to inhibit electron transfer between QA and QB at the reducing site of photosystem II (Czarnota et al., 2001). When applied at a rate of 0.6 kg ai/ha, sorgoleone significantly inhibited growth of several broadleaf and grass species. The most affected weeds (>80% inhibition) were black nightshade, redroot pigweed and *Ambrosia artemisiifolia* L. (common ragweed). Comparatively, lesser affected (>40% inhibition) weeds were *Cassia obtusifolia* L. (sicklepod), large crabgrass and *Abutilon theophrasti* Medik. (velvet leaf). Sorgoleone was applied to 14-day-old seedlings and data were collected 10 days after treatment. Although, sorgoleone is more active in vitro in inhibiting PS II when compared to atrazine, it is considered a weak herbicide due to its physicochemical properties and short environmental half-life (Streibig et al., 1999; Duke et al., 2000). Allelopathic agents influenced plant growth by affecting various physiological processes such as cell division and cell elongation, phytoharmone induced growth, membrane permeability, mineral uptake, stomatal uptake, photosynthesis and respiration (Rice, 1984).

Fig. 9.2: Inhibitory Allelopathic Effect

RESEARCH STRATEGIES AND POTENTIAL APPLICATIONS

The basic approach used in allelopathic research for crops has been to screen both crop plants and natural vegetation for their capacity to suppress weeds. Allelopathy, plant origin, production, and identification of allelochemicals must be established as well as persistence in the environment over time in concentrations sufficient to affect plant species. In the laboratory, plant extracts and leachates are commonly screened for their effects on seed germination, with further isolation and identification of allelochemicals from greenhouse tests and field soil confirming laboratory results. Interactions among allelopathic plants, host crops, and other non-target organisms must also be considered. Furthermore, allelochemistry may provide basic structures or templates for developing new synthetic herbicides. Studies have elucidated specific allelochemicals involved in weed suppression, including benzoxanoids in rye; diterpenoid momilactones in rice; tabanone in cogongrass; alkaloids and flavonoids in fescue; anthratectone and naphthotectone in teak (*Tectona grandis*); abscisic acid beta-d-glucopyranosyl ester in red pine; cyanamide in hairy vetch; and a cyclopropene fatty acid in hazel sterculia (*Sterculia foetida*). Incorporation of allelopathic traits from wild or cultivated plants into crop plants through traditional breeding or genetic engineering methods could also enhance the biosynthesis and release of allelochemicals. Genetic basis of allelopathy has now been demonstrated in winter wheat and rice. Specific cultivars with increased allelopathic potential are known in both these crops. An allelopathic crop can potentially be used to control weeds by planting a variety with allelopathic qualities, either as a smother crop, in a rotational sequence, or when left as a residue or mulch, especially in low-till systems, to control subsequent weed growth. For example, in one study, rye mulch had suppressive effects on pigweed and common purslane, but had no effects on velvetleaf and common lambsquarters. A fall cover crop of forage radish had weed suppression effects on the following season's crop. In a multiseason field study, when applied as a soil amendment, mustard seed meal derived from white mustard (*Sinapis alba*) was effective for weed suppression in organic sweet onion, but crop injury was also significant. Alternatively, application of allelopathic compounds before, along with, or after synthetic herbicides could increase the overall effect of both materials, thereby reducing application rates of synthetic herbicides.

AQUEOUS EXTRACTS FOR WEED CONTROL

The water extract of many *Eucalyptus* species were used in various study. They contain a number of allelochemicals which are more effective and economical to control the weeds of crops. Putnam (1984) reported that *Eucalyptus* species released volatile compounds such as benzoic, cinnamic and phenolic acids, which inhibit growth of crops and weeds growing near to it. Water extract of *Eucalyptus grandis* significantly reduce weed establishment Schumann *et al.* (1995). Various doses and concentration of Sorghum water extract has been used in different experiments and encouraging results were obtained regarding weed control specially lambsquarters, wild medic, broad leaves dock, fumitory, fields bindweed, cannery grass and wild oat (Cheema *et. al.*. 2003c). The aqueous extract of sun flower leaves inhibited broad leaved weeds especially broadleaf dock and lambsquarters and resulted up to 75% reduction in their dry weight as compared to control (Anjum and Bajwa, 2005). Narwal (2001) were found reduction in weed population especially lambsquarters by tissue leachates of *Brassica napus* and several *Brassica* species. Certain Brassica release sufficient quantities of allelochemicals which can completely inhibit the germination of green foxtail and redroot pigweed (Holtz, 2001). Some attempts have been reported on application of aqueous extracts of allelopathic plants on crops for weed suppression. In one study, an extract of brassica (*Brassica napus*), sorghum, and sunflower was used on rain-fed wheat to successfully reduce weed pressure. When an allelopathic plant water extract was tank-mixed with atrazine, a significant degree of weed control was achieved in wheat with a reduced dose of herbicide. Sunflower residues with a preplant herbicide (Treflan®) enhanced weed suppression in broad bean.

Sasikumar *et al.* (2001) observed that the different species of eucalyptus had differential effect on various plant processes. The bioassay with leaf extract showed germination inhibition with all four species of eucalyptus; however the dry matter accumulation was affected by *Eucalyptus camaldulensis* and *Eucalyptus microtheca* only. Xuan *et al.* (2002) conducted a laboratory experiment and found that the germination of *Monochoria vaginalis, Echinochloa oryzicola* and *Cyperus defformis* was significantly reduced at concentration of 125 and 150g of alfalfa pellets. Qasem (2002) extract of leaf and stem extract of various medicinal trees were highly toxic to both weed such as *Amaranthus retroflexus* and *Chenopodium murale* and it can both prevented seed germination and growth.

Humaid and Warren (1998) studied the allelopathic effect of aqueous extract of 10, 20, 30, 40, 50, and 60g. dry mesquite(*Prosopis juliflora*) leaves in a liter of distilled water on seed germination and early growth of bermudagrass (*Cynadon dactylon*) at 30° C , the final germination percentage, germination rate and GT50 were significantly reduced with increase in concentration. Both radicle and plumule length were also significantly retarded. Ferguson et al. (2004) reported that wood chips of 13 different tree species have inhibitory effect on germination and seedling growth of lettuce seeds. Extracts from wood chips of red maple, swamp chestnut oak, red cedar and sweet bay were significantly inhibited the germination and seedling growth. The affect of these four species were more than the other nine species studied the use of aqueous extract of *Eucalyptus camaldulensis* L.

leaves not only inhibited the seed germination but also reduce the fresh and dry weight of field bindweed (*Convolvulus arvensis*), barley (*Hordeum vulgare*), London rocket, wild safflower, wild oat and common lambsquarters (*Chinopodium album*), (Khan *et al.*, 2008). Asharfi *et al.* (2008), found allelopathic influence of *Azadiracta indica* L. (neem) on tropical weeds for water-soluble fractions which suppress the germination and growth of root and shoot of all tropical weed species. Khan and Marwat (2005) in a laboratory bioassay studied the allelopathic effect of aqueous leaf extract of *Prosopis juliflora* and *Eucalyptus camaldulensis* and bark extract of *Acacia nilotica* at the concentration of 150g/l and observed that the germination percentage, seedling length (mm) and biomass yield (mg/plant) of crop and weeds such as Ipomoea species, *Asphodelus tenuifolius, Brassica campestris* and *Triticum aestivum* were significantly affected or reduced by extract as compared to control. *Prosopis juliflora* and *Eucalyptus camaldulensis* had more inhibitory effect as compared to Acacia species.

Khan *et al.* (2009) worked in laboratory to see the difference between two methods (Sandwich method and Homogenate sandwich method) on root and hypocotyls length of lettuce seed. The result showed that both root and hypocotyls length was significantly reduced, but there was no significance difference between two methods and the effect was concentration dependent. Babu and Kandasamy (1997) reported that fresh and dried leaf leachate of Eucalyptus globules Labill have significantly suppress the germination and seedling growth of *Cyperus rotundus* and *Cynodon dactylon*. Xaun *et al.* (2004) in a bioassay study observed the germination and seedling growth of some specific crop bean, alfalfa, raddish, rice and *weeds Echinochloa crus-galli, Monochoria vaginalis* were significantly affected due to different concentration of leaf and bark extract of neem. The allelopathic influence of Kava (50, 25, 12.5, 6.3, 3.2, and 1.6g/l) on barnyard grass, *Monochoria* and Knotgrass. Noguchi *et al.* (2008) reported that aqueous extract of red pine needle have significantly reduce the root and shoot growth of lettuce, rye grass, alfalfa timothy, *Digitaria sanguinalis* and *Echinochloa crusgalli*. The growth of all the weeds were reduced with increased in concentration from 0.001 to 3mM.

Javaid *et al* (2006) reported that the germination of *Phalaris minor* was adversely affected due to dry leaf extract of *Eucalyptus citriodora, Mangifera indica, Syzgium cumini, Azadirachta indica* and *Alstonia schloris*. Aqueous extract of all the employed concentration of *Alstonia schloris, Azadirachta indica, and Eucalyptus citriodora* proved highly effective resulting in significant reduction of 43-100% in final germination of the target species. Aqueous extract of *Mangifera indica* and *Syzgium cumini* proved less effective whereas highest concentration of 8% exhibited significant negative impact against the germination of *Phalaris minor.* Manikandan and Rejula (2008) reported that leaf and bark extract of *Terminalia* species have inhibitory effect on growth of *Cassia occidentalis* and *Crotolaria retusa*. The leaf extract was found to have more inhibitory effect than bark extract. Chung *et al.* (2003) studied the allelopathic effect of various rice a variety by using their different parts such as leaves, hulls and straw. The germination and growth of barnyard grass was significantly reduced by rice varieties. The highest inhibition rate was found in Danganeuibangu (76.9%) in straw extract, dongobyeo (74%) in leaves and Bark (31.1%) in the hull. CUBA 65-v-58 (38.6%) had the highest inhibition on barnyard grass. Khanh *et al.* (2007) reported that the germination of major paddy weeds such as barnyard grass, lettuce and Indian joint vetch were significantly reduced due to the allelo-chemicals present in plants. Javaid *et al.* (2006), studied the herbicidal effect of aqueous root and shoot extract of three allelopathic crops such as sorghum, sunflower and rice at the concentration of 5, 10, 15, 20 and 25% on Parthenium found that shoot length and seedling biomass have insignificant effect while germination and root length were significantly reduced by extracts of all the test crops.

Shafique *et al.* (2005) observed that the aqueous extract of *Azadirachta indica* has significantly reduced the germination of weeds and crop plants. Higashinakasu *et al.* (2004) reported that the aqueous extract of *Brachiaria decumbens* at different stages of life cycle from different plant parts have inhibitory effect on germination, root and shoot growth of seven crops and weed species. Ashrafi *et al.* (2007) conducted an experiment in laboratory and applied water extract from 4 to 20 g/100ml of water of all Barley parts which significantly reduced the hypocotyls length. Hypocotyls weight, radicle weight, radicle length and seed germination of wild barley up to 79%. Fujii *et al.* (2004), studied the allelopathic effect of leaf litter leachates of tree species such as *Tamarindus indica, Gliricidia sepium* and *Piper betle* with sandwich method and found that the strongest inhibitory effect on radicle and hypocotyls elongation of lettuce of seeds, Sharma *et al.* (2000) studied the effect of aqueous extract of popular on germination and growth of *Phalaris minor* and found the reduction in all the parameters of *Phalaris minor* was more as compared to control. Aqueous extract of fresh and dry leaves of *Eucalyptus citriodora* reduce the seed germination, root shoot length of wild oat at 25% concentration (Kohli *et al.*,1998).

VOLATILE OILS FOR WEED CONTROL

The natural plant product i.e.: volatile essential oil is an important allelocompound of plants. Many species of plants have volatile oil such as *Eucalyptus* species and through various metabolic processes, decay processes it entered into the environment and affect the neighboring plant. They have relatively quicker degradation in the environment (Romagni *et al.* 2000). Terpenoids, particularly monoterpenes and sesquiterpenes, are the main components of essential oils and are often responsible for their inhibitory activity. Muller and Muller (1964) have reported lesser vegetation in the vicinity of purple sage owing to the presence of volatile compounds such as terpenes. Kohli and Singh (1991) reported that the essential oil from hybrid eucalypt (*Eucalyptus tereticornis* Sm.) inhibit the growth of lentil seedlings. Kohli *et al.* (1998) reported that the germination per cent, seed vigour, radicle and plumule length of *Parthinium hysterophorus* was inhibited due to *Eucalyptus globulas* and *Eucalyptus citriodora* oil when applied concentration of 10, 20 and 30 nl/cm^3.

Singh *et al.* (2005) in a bioassay study with *Eucalyptus citriodora* oil reported that seed germination, seedling length, chlorophyll content and respiratory activity of *Parthenium hysterophorus* were decreased with increased concentration of eucalypt oil from 0.2-5.0 nl/ml. and germination was completely inhibited at 5.0nl/mj concentration. The germination of *Raphanus sativus*, wheat, *Amaranthus virdis, and Echinochloa crus-galli* were retarded due to allelopathic effect of *Eucalyptus citriodora* oil. Maximum inhibition was observed in *Amaranthus virdis* whereas least affect was seen on *Raphanus sativus*. Based on germination response, dose response curve was generated and LC_{50} was calculated. LC_{50} was maximum for *Raphanus sativus* and minimum for *Amaranthus virdis* (Batish *et al.* 2004). Singh *et al.*(2009) studied the allelopathic effect of *Artemisia scoparia* oil and its main constituent on three important weeds *Avena fatua, Phalaris minor* and *Cyperus rotundus*, and observed that the germination, seedling growth and dry weight was significantly reduced. The inhibitory affect of Artemisia oil was found to be more on germination than â- myrcene. The growth was decline with increase in concentration. Among the three species the inhibitory effect was more on *Cyperus rotundus*. The H_2O_2 content was increased with increase in concentration with both respectively. Accumulation of H_2O_2 in *Cyperus rotundus* roots further enhanced lipid per oxidation thus resulting in oxidative stress, and leading to disruption of metabolic activities in the cell.

Batish *et al.* (2007) observed that the use of eucalypt oil significantly decrease the emergence and earlier growth of little seed canary grass at very low concentration. Singh *et al.* (2001) while studying the herbicidal activity of two volatile monoterpene cineole and citronellol (eucalyptus) on *Ageratum conyzoides* for weed management observed that the germination, speed of germination and seedling growth were significantly reduced from 0 to 6nl/cc concentration. Tworkoski (2002) conducted a laboratory experiment to determine the herbicidal effect of plant derived oil and found that the 1%v/v from plant were most phytotoxic and caused electrolytic leakage resulting in cell death of common lambsquarters.

Azirak and Karaman (2008) studied that the allelopathic effect of some essential oil plants (*Mentha spicata, Carum carvi, Origanum onites*) at 3, 6, 10 and 20 µl concentration on weed species like *Amaranthus, Centaurea* species, *Sinapis arvensis* etc.) And showed that germination was significantly inhibited by all plants species. Verdeguer *et al.* (2009) studied the activity of *Eucalyptus camaldulensis* and *Eriocephalus africanus* against *Amaranthus hybridus* and *Portulaca oleracea*. *Eucalyptus* completely inhibited the germination and seedling growth of both weeds. While the essential oil of *Eriocephalus africanus* showed activity similar to that of *Eucalyptus camaldulensis* on *Amaranthus hybridus*, but it was not so effective against *portulaca oleracea*. The knaweed is capable of displacing natives monoculture (Fig. 9.1). Phytotoxins produced by invasive exotic plants such as spotted knapweed may explain the remarkable success of some of these plants when transported to a new continent. The "novel weapons hypothesis" for plant invasions proposes that some invasive plants produce novel chemicals that are more effective against neighboring species in their new environment than in their native environment (Callaway and Aschehoug 2000; Callaway and Ridenour 2004). While species in the native environment may have evolved resistance to the phytotoxins, species in the new environment have only recently come into contact with the phytotoxins and may not have had time to evolve resistance.

Allelopathy in *Centaurea maculosa*

Fig. 9.3: Spotted knapweed (*Centaurea maculosa*) populations. In its native European habitat, spotted knapweed (*center of photograph*) coexists with numerous other plant species (*left panel*). In its introduced range of North America, spotted knapweed is capable of displacing natives and forming dense monocultures (*right panel*).

Lack of allelochemical resistance in the new range may give some exotic plants a competitive advantage, allowing them to displace native species. To examine the effects of spotted knapweed root exudates on native North American plants, Ridenour and Callaway (2001) used activated carbon to adsorb organic compounds in the soil. Activated carbon reduced the negative effect of spotted knapweed on Idaho fescue (*Festuca idahoensis*), suggesting that chemicals in spotted knapweed root exudates may give knapweed a competitive advantage over native species. To isolate and characterize these allelo compounds released in spotted knapweed root exudates, plants were grown in sterile liquid media under laboratory conditions (Bais et al. 2002). A bioassay was developed in which media from spotted knapweed cultures was applied to other plants, and effects of the media were recorded over time. Media containing knapweed exudates inhibited the growth and germination of several plant species, suggesting the presence of phytotoxins. To determine which compound(s) in the exudates were responsible for the phytotoxic activity, the media was extracted with organic solvents and fractionated by high performance liquid chromatography (HPLC). These fractions were used in a similar bioassay and the phytotoxic activity was found to be confined to one chromatographic fraction containing a single peak, suggesting that a single compound was responsible for the phytotoxicity. The active fraction was analyzed by nuclear magnetic resonance (NMR) and mass spectrometry (MS) to identify the specific compound of interest.

Allelopathic characteristics are more likely to occur in crop predecessors or "wild types" that have evolved in the presence of allelopathic and competitive influence from other species, while the currently used cultivars would be expected to have diminished or reduced allelopathic capacity. Therefore, it is possible to enhance weed suppressive potential of crop cultivars or to transfer allelopathic characteristics from wild types or unrelated plants into commercial crop cultivars through conventional plant breeding methods or other genetic recombination strategies. Research on cucumber and rice germplasm has found large differences in allelopathic potential among accessions.

USE OF ALLELOPATHIC PLANTS IN COMPANION CROPPING

It is possible to utilize a companion plant that is selectively allelopathic against certain weeds and does not interfere appreciably with crop growth (Putnam, 1978). Rice (1984) lists a number of crop species whose presence or leachates have been shown to have inhibitory effects on a number of weeds. The list includes beets (Beta vulgaris), lupin (Lupinus sp.), corn, wheat, oats, peas, buckwheat (Fagopyrum esculentum), hairy vetch (Vicia villosa Roth.), millet (Panicum sp.), barley (Hordeum vulgare L.), rye, and cucumber. Weeds in cropping systems are most often considered to be detrimental. However, the interaction of weeds with crops may be positive. In a study where controlled densities of wild mustard (Brassica campestris L.) were interplanted with broccoli (Brassica oleracea var. Premium crop), crop yield increased by as much as 50% compared with broccoli planted alone (Jimenez-Osornio et al., 1987).

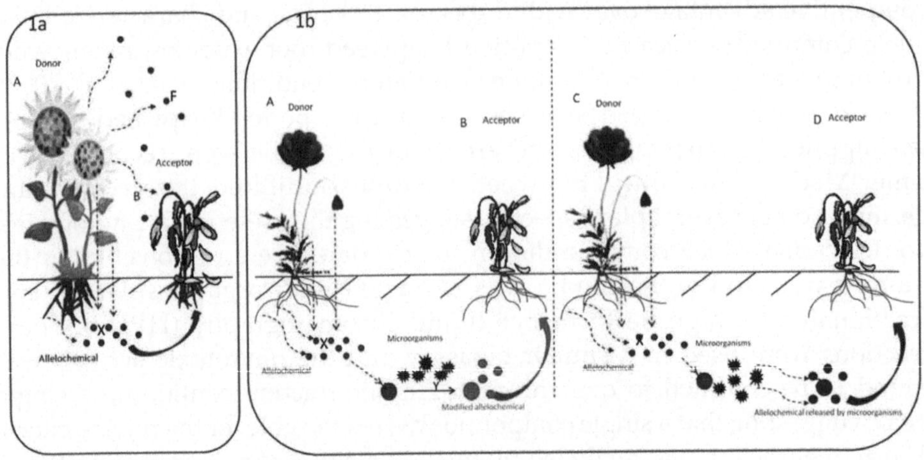

Fig. 9.4: Allelopathy Through Roots

PLANT RESIDUE MANAGEMENT

Utilising residue allelopathy as a management tool may be one of the more readily applicable uses of allelopathy in agro-ecosystems. Of all the possible strategies involving allelopathy for weed control, management of selectively toxic plant residues is the most successful, effective and readily available (Lovett, 1990; Putnam, 1988). Management methods might include incorporating allelopathic crops in crop rotation, applying phytotoxic mulches, and cover cropping with allelopathic plants or smother crops. Plant residue management may also overcome the negative effects of plant residues, and meet the increased demand for conservation and no-tillage farming systems. An et al. (1996) simulated allelopathic phenomena caused by decaying plant residues. Their theoretical analyses revealed that decomposing plant residues may either inhibit or stimulate plant growth, and that inhibition may be confined to a limited period, ie. the most severe inhibition by plant residues occurs at the early stages of residue decomposition, whereas at later stages the inhibition declines while stimulation gradually emerges. The inhibition and stimulation periods can be manipulated through a wide variety of management means. This approach has significant potential. For example, by analysing risk situations with respect to residue retention, a crop manager may avoid the inhibitory period of decaying residues, thus minimising their negative effects and await the stimulatory effect to crop plants, thereby enhancing the benefits of residue retention on the soil. By extending the inhibitory period of decaying residues and enhancing its effects, weeds may be controlled.

There are several studies which show a number of compounds in plants showing various impacts on other plants as given in Table 9.2. Allelopathy therefore have a bright future prospects to control weed growth without causing damage to the environment and people and superior over the chemical herbicides being a natural plant products and provide services at low cost. It is economically and ecologically beneficial tool for managing weeds.

Table 9.2: Examples of Allelopathy from Published Research

Allelopathic Plant	Impact
Rows of black walnut interplanted with corn in an alley cropping system.	Reduced corn yield attributed to production of juglone, an allelopathic compound from black walnut, found 4.25 m (~14 ft) from trees.
Rows of Leucaena interplanted with crops in an alley cropping system.	Reduced the yield of wheat and turmeric but increased the yield of maize and rice.
Lantana, a perennial woody weed pest in Florida citrus.	Lantana roots and shoots incorporated into soil reduced germination and growth of milkweed vine, another weed.
Sour orange, a widely used citrus rootstock in the past, now avoided because of susceptibility to citrus tristeza virus.	Leaf extracts and volatile compounds inhibited seed germination and root growth of pigweed, bermudagrass, and lambsquarters.
Red maple, swamp chestnut oak, sweet bay, and red cedar.	Wood extracts inhibited lettuce seed as much as or more than black walnut extracts.
Eucalyptus and neem trees.	A spatial allelopathic relationship if wheat was grown within 5 m (~16.5 ft).
Chaste tree or box elder	Leachates retarded the growth of pangolagrass, a pasture grass, but stimulated the growth of bluestem, another grass species.
Mango	Dried mango leaf powder completely inhibited sprouting of purple nutsedge tubers.
Tree of heaven activity similar to glyphosate.	Ailanthone, isolated from the tree of heaven, has been reported to possess non-selective postemergence herbicidal paraquat.
Rye, fescue, and wheat	Allelopathic suppression of weeds when used as cover crops or when crop residues are retained as mulch.
Broccoli	Broccoli residue interferes with growth of other cruciferous crops that follow Jungle rice Inhibition of rice crop.
Forage radish	Cover crop residue suppression of weeds in the season following the cover crop.
Jerusalem artichoke	Residual effects on weed species.
Sunflower and buckwheat	Cover crop residues reduced weed pressure in fava bean crop.

(Contd...)

Allelopathic Plant	Impact
Tifton burclover	Growth inhibition in wheat and autotoxicity in burclover.
Sunn hemp	Growth inhibition of smooth pigweed and lettuce and inhibition of vegetable seed germination.
Desert horsepurslane (*Trianthema portulacastrum*)	Growth promotion of slender amaranth (*Amaranthus viridis*)
Rhazya stricta	Growth inhibition of corn
Rough cocklebur (*Xanthium strumarium*)	Growth inhibition of mungbean
Garlic mustard	Inhibition of arbuscular mycorrhizal fungi colonizing on sugar maple.
Barbados nut (*Jatropha curcas*)	Extracts of leaves and roots inhibited corn and tobacco.
Chicory	Inhibition of Echinochloa crusgalli and Amaranthus retroflexus
Swallow-worts	Invasive species in northeastern United States and southeastern Canada; inhibited several weed species.
Vogel's tephrosia (*Tephrosia vogelii*)	Growth inhibition of corn and three narrow-leaf weed species.
Green spurge	Inhibition of chickpea.
Crabgrass	Inhibition of corn and sunflower but no inhibition of triticale when dry crabgrass residue was incorporated into soil.
Silver wattle (*Acacia dealbata*)	Inhibition of native understory species in northwest Spain.
Sticky snakeroot (*Ageratina adenophora*)	Volatiles were inhibitory to plants in non-native ranges but not inhibitory toplants in the native range.
Santa Maria feverfew (*Parthenium hysterophorus*)	Aqueous extracts had inhibitory effects on cereal crops.
Teak wood	Leaf extracts inhibited jungle rice and sedge, but not cultivated rice.
Rabbitfoot grass	Leaf extracts and mulch inhibited wheat

REFERENCES

Abbas, H.K., Tanaka, T.K., Duke, S.O., Boyette, C.D., 1995. Susceptibility of Various Crop and Weed Species to AAL-toxin, a Natural Herbicide. Weed Technol. 9, 125-130.

An, M., Johnson, I.R. and Lovett, J.V. 1996. Allelopathy J. 3, 33-42.

Anjum, T. and R. Bajwa. 2005. A Bioactive Annuionone from Sunflower Leaves. *Phytochemistry* 66: 1919-1921.

Appleby, A.P., Muller, F., Carpy, S. 2000. Weed Control in Muller F., (Ed) Agrochemicals. Wiley-VCH, New York: 687-709.

Ashrafi, Z.Y., Rahanavard, A., Sadeghi, S., Hassan, M.A., and Mashhadi, H.R. 2008. Study of the Allelopathic Potential of Extracts of *azadirachta Indica* (neem). *Journal of Biological Sciences.* 8(3): 57-61.

Ashrafi, Z.Y., Sadeghi, S., and Mashhadi, H.R. 2007. Allelopathic Effects of Barley (*hordeum vulgare*) on Germination and Growth of Wild Barley (*H. spontaneum). Pak. J. Weed Sci. Res.* 13(1-2): 99-112.

Azirak, Sebile., Karaman, Sengul., 2008. Allelopathic Effect of Some Essential Oils and Components on Germination of Weed Species. *Plant Soil Science.* 58: 88-92.

Batish, Daizy R.; Setia,N.; Singh, H. P. and Kohli, R. K. 2004. Phytotoxicity of Lemon-scented Eucalypt Oil and its Potential Use as a Bioherbicide. *Crop Protection* 23(6): 1209-1214.

Batish, D.R., Singh, H.P., Setia, N., Kohli, R.K., Kaur, S. and Yadav, S.S. 2007. Alternative Control of Littleseed Canary Grass Using Eucalypt Oil. Agron. Sustain. Dev. 27, 171-177.

Bhowmik, P.C. Zhang, C.X. 2003. Potential Use of Mesotrione in Controlling Annual Weed Species in Maize (Zea mays). The 19th Proceedings of the Asian-Pacific Weed Science Society Conference in Press.

Bhowmik, P.C., 1988. Cinmethylin for Weed Control in Soybeans, Glycine max. *Weed Sci.* 36, 678-682.

Bhowmik, P.C., 1992. Annual Grass Weed Control. *Mass Weed Sci. Res. Results* 11, 77-80.

Bhowmik, P.C., 2000. Herbicide Resistance: A Global Concern. Med. Fac. Landbouww. Univ. Gent. 65/2a, 19-30.

Babu, C.R., Kanadasamy, O.S., 2008. Allelopathic Effect of Eucalyptus Globules Labill. on Cyperus Rotundus L. and Cynodon Dactylon L. Pers. *J. of Agronomy and Crop Science.* 179: 123-126.

Bais, H.P., Walker, T.S., Stermitz F.R., Hufbauer R.A., and Vivanco J.M. 2002. Enantiomeric-dependant Phytotoxic and Antimicrobial Activity of (±)-catechin: A Rhizosecreted Racemic Mixture from Spotted Knapweed. *Plant Physiol.* 128: 1173-1179.

Callaway, R.M., and Aschehoug, E.T. 2000. Invasive Plants versus Their New and Old Neighbours: A Mechanism for Exotic Invasion. *Science* 290: 521-523.

Callaway, R.M., and Ridenour, W.M. 2004. Novel Weapons: Invasive Success and the Evolution of Increased Competitive Ability. *Front. Ecol. Environ.* 2: 436-443.

Cheema, Z.A. 1988. Weed Control in Wheat Through Sorghum Allelochemicals. Ph.D. Thesis, Department of Agronomy, University of Agriculture Faisalabad, Pakistan.

Cheema, Z.A., A. Khaliq and M. Mubeen. 2003c. Response of Wheat and Weeds to Foliar Application of Different Plant Water Extracts. *Pakistan J. Weed Res.* 9(1-2): 89-97.

Chung, I.M. Kim, K.H. Ahn, J.K. Lee, S.B. Kim S.H. and Hahn, S.J. 2003. Comparison of Allelopathic Potential of Rice Leaves, Straw, and Hull Extracts on Barnyardgrass. *Agronomy Journal* 95: 1063-1070.

Czarnota, M.A., Paul, R.N., Dayan, F.E., Weston, L.A., 2001. Further Studies on the Mode of Action, Localization of Production, Chemical Nature, and Activity of Sorgoleone: A Potent PS II Inhibitor Produced in Sorghum spp. Root Exudates. *Weed Technol.* 15, 813-825.

Davis, E.F. 1982. The Toxic Principle of *Juglan nigra* as Identified with Synthetic Juglone and its Toxic Effects on Tomato and Alfalfa Plants. *Am. J. Biol.* 15: 620-621.

Dayan, F.E., Hernandez, A., Allen, S.N., Moraces, R.M., Vroman, J.A., Avery, M.A., Dudai, N., Mayer, A.M., Putievsky, E., Lerner, H.R., 1999. Essential Oil as Allelochemicals and Their Potential Use as Bioherbicides. *J. Chem. Ecol.* 25, 1079-1089.

Duke, S.O., Dayan, F.E., Rimando, R.M., Scharder, K.K., Aliotta, G., Oliva, A. and Romagni, J.G. 2002. Chemicals from Nature for Weed Management. *Weed Science.* 50: 138-151.

Duke, S.O., 1986. Naturally Occurring Chemical Compounds as Herbicides. *Rev. Weed Sci.* 2, 15-44.

Duke, S.O., A.M. Rimando, S.R. Baerson, B.E. Scheffler, E.Ota and R.G. Belz. 2002. Strategies for the Use of Natural Products for Weed Management. *J. pesticide Sci.* 27: 298-306.

Duke, S.O., Dayan, F.E., Ramagni, J.G., Rimando, A.M., 2000. Natural Products as Sources of Herbicides: Current Status and Future Trends. *Weed Res.* 40, 90-111.

Duke, S.O., Scheffler, B.E., Dayan, F.E., 2001. Allelochemicals as Herbicides. In: Bonjoch, N.P., Reigosa, M.J. (Eds.), First European OECD Allelopathy Symposium: Physiological Aspects of Allelopathy. GAMESAL, SA, pp. 47-59.

Duke, S.O., Vaughn, K.C., Croom, E.M., Elsohly, H.N., 1987. Artemisinin, a Constituent of Annual Wormwood (Artemisia annua) is a Selective Phytotoxin. *Weed Sci.* 35, 499-505.

Einhellig, F.A. 1986. Mechanism and Mode of Action of Allelochemicals. In: The Science of Allelopathy. (Ed): Putnam, A.R. and C.S. Tang. New York. pp. 171-187.

Einhellig, F.A., 1995. Allelopathy: Current Status and Future Goals. In: Society, Washington, DC, pp. 1-24.

Einhellig, F.A., Souza, I.F., 1992. Phytotoxicity of Sorgoleone Found in Grain Sorghum Root Exudates. *J. Chem. Ecol.* 18, 1-11.

Ferguson, J.J., Rathinasabapathi, B., and Gal, M. 2004. A Method to Screen Weed-suppressing Allelochemicals in Florida Biomass. *Proc. Fla. State Horti. Soc.* 117: 231-233.

Fujii, Y., Shibuya, T., Nakatani, K., Itani, T., Hiradate, S., Parvez, H.M., 2004. Assesment Method for Allelopathic Effect from Leaf Litter Leachates. *Weed Biology and Management.* 4: 19-23.

Gattas-Hallak, A.M., Davide, L.C., Souza, I.F., 1999. Effect of Sorghum (Sorghum Bicolor L.) Root Exudates on the Cell Cycle of the Bean Plant (Phaseolus vulgaris L.) Roots. *Gen. Mol. Biol.* 22, 95-99.

Gonzalez, V.M., Kazimir, J., Nimbal, C., Weston, L.A., Cheniae, G.M., 1997. Inhibition of a Photosystem II Electron Transfer Reaction by the Natural Product Sorgoleone. *J. Agric. Food Chem.* 45, 1415-1421.

Heisey, R.M., 1996. Identification of an Allelopathic Compound from Ailanthus Altissima (Simaroubaceae) and Characterization of its Herbicidal Activity. *Am. J. Bot.* 83, 192-200.

Heisey, R.M., 1999. Development of an Allelopathic Compound from Tree-of-heaven (Ailanthus Altissima) as a Natural Product Herbicide. In: Cutler, H.G., Cutler, S.J. (Eds.), Biologically Active Natural Products: Agrochemicals. CRC Press, Boca Raton, FL, pp. 57-68.

Higashinakasu, K.; Yamada, K.; Shigemoru, H. and Hasegawa, K. 2004. Effect of Seed Exudates of Several Plant Species during Germination Stage. *Weed Biology and Management*. 4: 171-175.

Holtz, G.P. 2001. Brassica Cover Crop for Biological Weed Control in no Tillage. Ph.D. diss. Ohio State University, Columbus.

Humaid, I. Al and Warrag, M.O.A. 1998. Allelopathic Effects of Mesquite Foliage on Seed Germination and Seedling Growth of Bermudagrass. *Journal of Arid Environments*. Vol. 38(2): 237-243.

Inderjit, Striebig, J., Olofsdotter, M., 2002. Olofsdotter, m. Joint Action of Phenolic Acid Mixtures and its Significance in Allelopathy Research. *Physiol. Plant* 114, 422-428.

Javaid, A.; Shafique, S. and Shafique, S. 2006. Herbicidal Potential of Aqueous Leaf Extract of Allelopathic Trees Against *Phalaris minor. Pakistan Journal of Weed Science and Research*. 12(4): 339-346.

Javaid, A.; Shafique, S.; Bajwa, R. and Shafique, S. 2006. Effect of Aqueous Extract of Allelopathic Crops on Germination and Growth of *Parthenium hysterophorus* L. *South Journal of Botany* 72: 609-612.

Jimenez-Osornio, J.J. and Gliessman, S.R. 1987. In "Allelochemicals: Role in Agriculture and Forestry" Edited by G.R. Waller. American Chemical Society, Washington, DC. pp. 262-274.

Khan, M.A.; Hussain, I. and Khan, E.A. 2008. Allelopathic Effects of *Eucalyptus* on Germination and Seedling Growth of Wheat. *Pakistan Journal of Weed Science Research*. 14(1-2): 9-18.

Khan, M.A.; Hussain, I. and Khan, E.A. 2008. Suppressing Effect of Eucalyptus Camaldulensis L. on Germination and Seedling Growth of Six Weeds. *Pakistan Journal of Weed Science Research* 14 (3-4): 201-207.

Khan, A.L., Hamayun, M., Hussain, J., Khan, H., Abdullah, H., Gilani and Kikuchi. 2009. Assessment of Allelopathic Potential of Selected Medicinal Plants of Pakistan. *African Journal of Biotechnology* Vol. 8 (6), pp. 1024-1029.

Khanh, T.D., Xuan, T.D. and Chung, I.M. 2007. Rice Allelopathy and the Possibility for Weed Management. Annals of Applied Biology ISSN 0003-4746.

Khanh, T.D., Chung, I.M., Xaun, T.D. and Tawata, S. 2005a. The Exploitation of Crop Allelopathy in Sustainable Agriculture Production. *Journal of Agronomy and Crop science,* 14 (3-4): 201-207.

Kohli, R.K., Singh. D., 1991. Allelopathic Impact of Volatile Components from Eucalyptus on Crop Plants. Biologia Plantarum. 33, 6 475-483.

Kohli, R.K; Batish, D. and Singh, H.P. 1998. Eucalyptus Oil for the Control of *Parthenium hysterophorus* L. *Crop Protection* 17: 119-122.

Kohli, R.K; Rani, D., 1994. Parthenium Hysterophorus- A Review. Research Bulletin of the Punjab University (Science). 44(1-4), 105-149.

Lovett, J.V. 1990. In "Alternatives to the Chemical Control of Weeds." Edited by C. Bassett, L.J. Whitehouse and J.A. Zabkiewicz. Rotorua, New Zealand. pp. 57-65.

Lydon, J., Teasdale, J.R., Chen, P.K., 1997. Allelopathic Activity of Annual Wormwood (Artemisia Annua) and its Role of Artemisinin. *Weed Sci.* 45, 807-811.

Manikandan, M. and Rejula, M. 2008. Identification of Allelochemicals from *Terminalia Chebula. An International Multi-Disciplinary Journal.* Vol. 2 (3) pp. 306-314.

Molisch, H. 1937. Der Einfluss einer Pflanze auf die andere- Allelopathic. Fisher, Jena.

Muller, W.H., Muller, c.h., 1964. Volatile Growth Inhibitors Produced by *Salvia* Species. Bull. Torr. Bot. Club 91, 327-330.

Narwal, S.S. 2001. Crop Allelopathy for Weed Management in Sustainable Agriculture. 1st European Symposium Vigo, Spain, June 21-23, 2001. pp. 107-127.

Narwal, S.S., M.K. Sarmah and J.C. Tamak. 1998. Allelopathic Strategies for Weed Management in the Rice-wheat Rotation in North-Western India. In: Allelopathy in Rice, 25-27 Nov. 1996. Manila (Phillippines): International Rice Research Institute (ed.) M. Olofsdotter, IRRI Press, Manila.

Nimbal, C.I., Pedersen, J.F., Yerkes, C.N., Weston, L.A., Weller, S.C., 1996a. Phytotoxicity and Distribution of Sorgoleone in Grain Sorghum Germplasm. *J. Agric. Food Chem.* 44, 1343-1347.

Nimbal, C.I., Yerkes, C.N., Weston, L.A., Weller, S.C., 1996b. Herbicidal Activity and Site of Action of the Natural Product Sorgoleone. *Pest Chem. Physiol.* 54, 73-83.

Noguchi, H.K., Fushini, Y. and Shigemori, H. 2009. An Allelopathic Substance in Red Pine Needles (*Pinus densiflora*). *Journal of Plants Physiology.* 166, 442-446.

Perveen, Z. 2000. Identification of Allelochemicals in Sorghum (*Sorghum bicolor L.*) and Their Effects on Germination and Seedling Growth of Wheat. M.Sc. Thesis. Department of Agronomy, University of Agriculture Faisalabad, Pakistan.

Putnam, A.R. and Duke, W.B. 1978. Ann. Rev. Phytopath. 16, 413-51.

Putnam, A.R. 1984. Allelopathic Chemicals: Can Natural Plant Herbicides help Control Weeds. Weeds Today, 15: 6-8.

Putnam, A.R., 1983. Allelopathic Chemicals: Nature's Herbicide in Action. *Chem. Eng. News* 4, 34-45.

Putnam, A.R., 1988. Allelochemicals from Plants as Herbicides. *Weed Technol.* 2, 510-518.

Qasem, J. R. 2002. Allelopathic Effect of Selected Medicinal Plants on *Amaranthus Retroflexus* and *Chenopodium Murale. Allelopathy Journal* 10(2): 105-122.

Rice, E.L. 1984. "Allelopathy." 2nd Ed. Academic Press, New York. 421 pp.

Rice, E.L., 1994. Overview of Allelopathy: Allelopathy in Agriculture and Forestry. (Ed.) S.S. Narwal and P. Tauro, Scientific Pub. Jodhpur India. p. 1-21.

Rice, E.L., 1995. Biological Control of Weeds and Plant Diseases: Advances in Applied Allelopathy. University of Oklahoma Press, Norman, OK.

Ridenour, W.M., and Callaway, R.M. 2001. The Relative Importance of Allelopathy in Interference: The Effects of an Invasive Weed on a Native Bunchgrass. *Oecologia*, 126: 444-450.

Romagni, J.G., Allen, S.N., Dayan, F.E., 2000. Allelopathic Effects of Volatile Cineoles on Two Weedy Plant Species. *J. Chem. Ecol.* 26, 303-313.

Sachan , M.S. 2006. Structure and Functioning of Traditional Agroforestry Systems Along an Altitudinal Gradient in Garhwal Himalaya. Ph.D. Thesis. H.N.B. Garhwal University, Srinagar Garhwal, Uttranchal, India.

Sasikumar, K.; Vijayalkshmi, C. and Prathiban, K.T. 2001. Allelopathic Effect of 4 *Eucalyptus* Species on Red gram (*Cajanus cajan* L.) *Journal of Tropical Agriculture.* 39: 134-138.

Schumann, A.W.; Little, K.M. and Eccles N.S. 1995. Suppression of Seed Germination & Early Seedling Growth by Plantation Harvest Residues. *South African Journal of Plant and Soil,* 12: 170-172.

Shafique, S.; Bajwa, R. and Javaid, A. 2005. Biological Control of *Parthenium* IV. Suppressive Ability of Aqueous Leaf Extracts of Some Allelopathic Trees Against Germination and Early Seedling Growth of *Parthenium hysterophorus. Pakistan Journal of weed Science Research.* 11: 75-79.

Sharma, N.K., Samra, J.S., Singh, H.P., 2000. Effect of Leaf Litter of Poplar on Phalaris Minor Weed. *Allelopathy Journal.* 7(2): 243-253.

Shibayama, H. 2001. Weeds and Weed Management in Rice Production in Japan. *Weed Biology and Management.*

Singh, H.P., Batish, D.R., Kohli, R.K., and Arora, K. 2007. Arsenic-induced Root Growth Inhibition in Mung Bean (*Phaseolus aureus* Roxb.) is due to Oxidative Stress Resulting from Enhanced Lipid Peroxidation. *Plant Growth Regul.* 53: 65-73.

Singh, H.P.,Kaur, S. and Mittal, S. 2009. Essential Oil of Artemisia Scoparia Inhibits Plant Growth by Generating Reactive Oxygen Species and Causing Oxidative Damage. *J. Chem Ecol.* 35: 154-162.

Singh, H.P.; Batish, Daizy R., Setia, N. and Kohli, R.K. 2005. Herbicidal Activity of Volatile Oils from *Eucalyptus citriodora* Against *Parthenium hysterophorus. Annals of Applied Biology.* 146: 89-94.

Streibig, J.C., Dayan, F.E., Rimando, A.M., Duke, S.O., 1999. Joint Action of Natural and Synthetic Photosystem II inhibitors. *Pestic. Sci.* 55, 137-146.

Tellez, M.R., Canel, C., Rimando, A.M., Duke, S.O., 1999. Differential Accumulation of Fumonisins and Related Compounds in a Ducksalad Bioassay. *Phytochemistry* 33, 779-785.

Torres, A., R. M. Oliva, D. Castellano and P. Cross. 1996. First World Congress on Allelopathy. A Science of the Future. SAI (University of Cadiz). Spain, Cadiz. p. 278.

Verdeguer, M., Blazquez, M.A., Boira, H., 2009. Phytotoxic Effects of Lantana Camara, Eucalyptus Africanus Essential Oils in Weeds of Mediterranean Summer Crops. *Biochemical Systematics and Ecology.* 37: 362-369.

Whittakar, R.H. 1970. The Biochemical Ecology of Higher Plants. In: Chemical Ecology (ed.) E. Sondheimer and J.B. Simeone, New York Academic Press. pp. 43-70.

Xuan, T.D., Tsuzuki, E., Uematsu, H., and Terao, H. 2002. Effect of Alfalfa (*Medicago sativa* L.) Pellets on Weed Control in Rice. *Allelopathy Journal* 9(2):195-203.

Xuan, T.D.; Eiji, T.; Hyroyuki, T.; Mitsuhiro, M.and Chung, I. M. 2004. Evaluation on Phytotoxicity of Neem to Crop and Weeds. *Crop Protection* 23: 335-345.

10

Global Warming and Climate Change
Impact and Strategies for its Mitigation

Altamash Bashir*; Mumtaz Majeed***
Hilal A. Rather**; Abrar Y Wani****; M. Amin Ahangar**

ABSTRACT

Global warming and climate change refer to an increase in average global temperatures. The gases with special optical properties that are responsible for climate warming include carbon dioxide (Co-2), chlorofluorocarbons (CFCs), methane (Ch4), ozone (O3), Carbon monoxide (CO), Water vapour (H2O) and nitrous oxide (N2O). These gases are collectively called as green house gases (GHGs). Climate change on the planet Earth is inevitable. It was only because of this change that the earth became suitable for human beings. But in the recent past this rate of change has been triggered due to tremendous increase in human population, industrial processes, fossil fuel combustion, and changes in land use, such as deforestation. Observed changes in temperature, precipitation, snow cover, sea level and extreme weather conditions confirm that global warming is a reality. Continuation of historical trends of greenhouse gas emissions will result in additional warming over the 21st century. Current projections point to a global

* Ph.D. Scholar, Faculty of Forestry and Environmental Management, P.O. Box 4400 28 Dineen Drive, University of New Brunswick Fredericton, NB E3B 5A3, CANADA.

** Sher-e-Kashmir University of Agricultural Sciences and Technology, Faculty of Forestry, Kashmir, 191 211, J & K, India.

*** Forest Department Kashmir, J & K, 190 001, India.

**** Punjab Agricultural University, College of Agricultural Engineering, Ludhiana, Punjab, 141 027, India.

increase of 2.0°F to 11.5°F (1.1°C to 6.4°C) by 2100. Forests play an important role in minimizing the effects of global warming by sequestration of carbon globally. As globally important storehouses of carbon, forests play a critical role in influencing the Earth's climate mitigating the effects of global warming. The Earth's forests serve as crucial carbon sinks due to their ability to absorb greenhouse gases. While climate change now appears unavoidable, hence the need to adapt to climate change has become inevitable and for that purpose various strategies have to be executed. Adaptation has the potential to reduce adverse impacts of climate change and to enhance beneficial impacts. In this reference cooperation among different international agencies for emission reduction has to be followed strictly that too at the stipulated time, introducing carbon credits and managing multifunctional forests, offer opportunity for carbon sequestration, biodiversity conservation and benefit to the society. In years to come more substantial short as well as long term reduction standards of emission need to be achieved. Poorer countries tend to be more seriously affected by climate change, yet have reduced assets and capacities with which to adapt, therefore these countries require special attention to get rid of the negative impacts of climate change. A balance, however, between development and climate change mitigation and adaptation needs to be found. Hence, there is a need of exploring strategies of integration between the climate change plans and development plans in the global south.

Keywords: Global warming, Climate change, GHGs, Carbon sequestration, Carbon credits and Forests.

INTRODUCTION

Climate Change: A Global Concern

Global warming and climate change refer to an increase in average global temperatures. Natural events and human activities are believed to be contributing to an increase in average global temperatures and climate change (Shah 2009). The scientific community has reached a strong consensus regarding the science of global climate change, that the world is undoubtedly warming and warming is largely due to the emissions of carbon dioxide and other greenhouse gases from human activities including industrial processes, fossil fuel combustion, and changes in land use, such as deforestation (Fig 10.1). Continuation of historical trends of greenhouse gas emissions will result in additional warming over the 21st century. Current projections point to a global increase of 2.0°F to 11.5°F (1.1°C to 6.4°C) by 2100. The global warming will also cause additional sea-level rise that will gradually inundate coastal areas and increase beach erosion and flooding from coastal storms, changes in precipitation patterns, increased risk of droughts and floods, threats to biodiversity, and a number of potential challenges for public health.

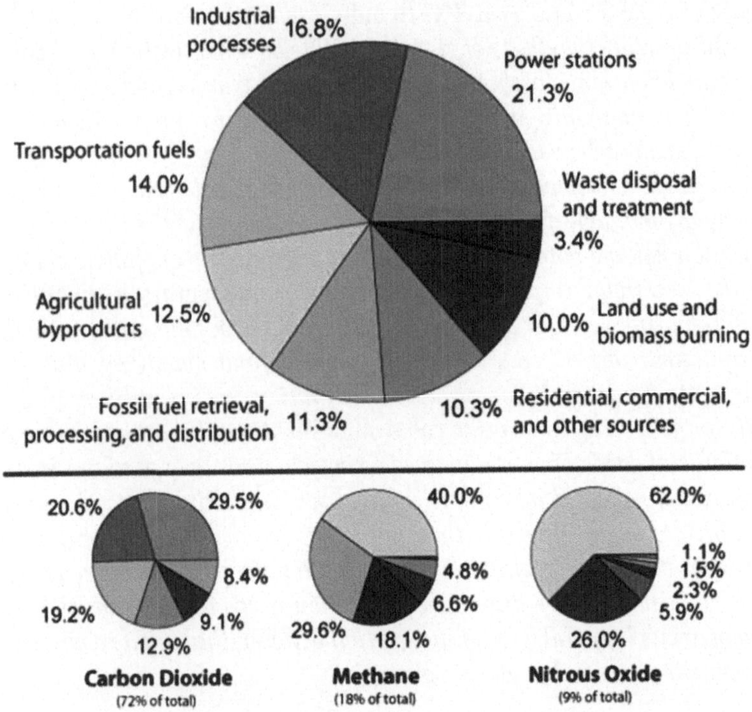

Fig. 10.1: Annual Greenhouse Gas Emissions by Sector

Global warming and climate change is the greatest crisis collectively faced by the human-kind; unlike other crisis, it is global in nature, threatens the very survival of civilization and promises to throw up only losers over the entire international socio-economic fabric and addressing climate change is no simple task, to protect ourselves, our economy, and our land from the adverse effects of climate change, we must ultimately dramatically reduce emissions of carbon dioxide and other greenhouse gases. To achieve this goal we must fundamentally transform the way we power our global economy. Such a transformation will require society to engage in a concerted effort, over the near- and long-term, to seek out opportunities and design actions to reduce greenhouse gas emissions

The latest estimate by the Intergovernmental Panel on Climate Change (IPCC) shows that a business as usual scenario will lead to an increase in global mean temperature of about 1°C above the present value by the year 2025 and 3°C before the end of the next century. There are many greenhouse gases (Table 10.1) which could adversely affect the world's climate but most steadily increasing gases are carbon-dioxide, methane, chlorofluorocarbons and nitrogen oxides. It has been estimated that carbon dioxide accounts for about 50% of the global warming effect which is followed by methane which contributes 20% of total GHGs and nitrous oxide 6% to total green house effects (Houghton 1997: 251). However, (Kumar 2002) reported that carbon dioxide contributes about 50%, chlorofluorocarbons 20%, methane 16%, ozone 8% and nitrous oxide 6% to total green house gases (GHGs).

Table 10.1: Contribution to Global Warming by Greenhouse Gases and Human Activities (% of Global Warming)

Sector	Carbon dioxide	Methane	Ozone	Nitrous oxide	Chiorofluocarbons	% Warming by Sector
Energy Direct	35	3	X	4	X	49
Indirect	X	1	6	X	X	
Deforestation	10	4	X	X	X	14
Agriculture	3	8	X	2	X	13
Industry	2	X	2	X	20	24
% warming by gas	50	16	8	6	20	100

Why to Scare Global Warming and Climate Change

Scientists all over the world are making predictions about the ill effects of Global warming and connecting some of the events that have taken place in the past few decades as an alarm of global warming. The effect of global warming is increasing the average temperature of the earth. A rise in earth's temperatures can in turn root to other alterations in the ecology, including an increasing sea level and modifying the quantity and pattern of rainfall. These modifications may boost the occurrence and concentration of severe climate events. The variations due to global warming and climatic change in different sectors have been discussed under the following sub-headings.

Effects on Environment: Global warming is expected to cause changes in the overall distribution and intensity of events, such as changes to the frequency and intensity of heavy precipitation. Broader effects are expected to include glacial retreat, Arctic shrinkage, and worldwide sea level rise. Some effects on both the natural environment and human life are, at least in part, already being attributed to global warming. A 2001 report by the IPCC suggests that glacier retreat, ice shelf disruption such as that of the Larsen Ice Shelf, sea level rise, changes in rainfall patterns, and increased intensity and frequency of extreme weather events are attributable in part to global warming (Climate Change 2001). Other expected effects include water scarcity in some regions and increased precipitation in others, changes in mountain snow pack, and some adverse health effects from warmer temperatures (McMichael *et al.*, 2006). It is also predicted that future climate changes will include further global warming, sea level rise and a probable increase in the frequency of some extreme weather events. Ecosystems are seen as being particularly vulnerable to climate change.

Effects on Agriculture: Global warming has affected agricultural yield directly because of alterations in temperature and rainfall, and indirectly through changes in soil quality, pests and diseases. As the temperatures rise conditions will become more favorable for pests such as grasshoppers to complete a number of reproduction cycles, thereby increasing their population. A study published in "Science" suggest that, due to climate change, "southern Africa could lose more than 30% of its main crop, maize, by 2030. In South Asia losses of many regional staples, such as rice, millet and maize could raise upto 10%" (Lobell *et al.*, 2008). (Samra and Sharma 2002) reported that if there is an increase of 0.5° C in mean temperature in Punjab, Haryana and Uttar Pradesh there would be a reduction in productivity of wheat crop by 10 per cent. Much of Latin America, from Mexico to Argentina, could see decline in crop yields (Bhardwaj *et al* 2003). Extreme weather conditions such as high temperature, heavy rainfall, floods, droughts, etc. will also affect crop production. Temperatures in developing countries, which are predominantly located in lower latitudes, are already closer to or beyond thresholds at which further warming will reduce rather than increase agricultural capacity, and these countries tend to have less capacity to adapt. Moreover, agriculture accounts for a much larger share of GDP in developing countries than in industrial countries, so a given percentage loss in agricultural potential would impose a larger income loss in a developing country than in an industrial country (Cline, 2007). Overall, global production would decline by 1 to 8 per cent which may lead to higher food prices and the increase in the number of people at risk of hunger (Lashof, 1993). (Cline 2007) finds that agricultural production in developing countries may fall between 10 and 25 per cent, and if global warming progresses unabated, India's agricultural capacity could fall as much as 40 per cent. Thus, policymakers should address this phenomenon now before the world's developing countries are adversely and irreversibly affected.

Effects on Forests and Wildlife: Ecosystems sustain the earth's entire storehouse of species and genetic diversity. Plants and animals in the natural environment are very sensitive to changes in climate. It has been estimated that each 1°C rise in temperature will displace the limits of tolerance of land species some 125 km towards the poles or 150 m vertically on mountains (Bhardwaj et al 2003). (Papadopal 2000) was of the view that in the 20-50yrs, the productivity of forests could drop by 40-100 per cent especially southern edge of species ranges due to insufficient water availability. In Boreal coniferous forests, climatic warming increases fire frequency and pest outbreak, which likely to decrease the average age, biomass and carbon storage (Rawat et al., 2003). In some US temperate forests, rapid climate change and accompanying extreme events, such as droughts, floods, and wind storms could lead to increased disease, insects, landslides and wildfires that could increase tree mortality and, in some cases, replace forests by grasslands. The key impact of global warming on wildlife is habitat displacement, e.g. ice giving way to water in polar bear habitat is just one example of this. Affected wildlife populations can sometimes move into new spaces and continue to thrive (Walters, 2009). Increasing global temperature means that ecosystems will change; some species are being forced out of their habitats because of changing conditions. Currently, studies have concluded that global warming may drive one quarter of all land animals and plants to extinction by 2050. The absolute worst case scenario that we are facing is a thrilling 1/3 to 1/2 of all plant and animal species facing extinction (Bhattacharya, 2009). The ecologically rich hot spots where potentially most damage would be done include places like South Africa's Cape Floristic Region, and the Caribbean Basin. These areas include a doubling of present carbon dioxide levels and rising temperatures that could eliminate 56,000 plant and 3,700 animal species in these hot spot regions (Handwerk and Hendwerk 2006).

Effects on Marine life and sea level rise: Corals are known as the tropical forests of the oceans and sustain diverse life forms. But due to global warming the rise in ocean temperatures cause bleaching in corals. Large stretches of the Great Barrier Reef in Australia have been damaged by bleaching. The Zooplanktons have also shown decline which in return resulted in reductions in number of fishes and sea birds that feed on these organisms. Similarly, reductions in phytoplankton caused by warmer sea temperatures have devastating effects on predators, such as seabirds and marine mammals, at the top of the food. The warming of oceans may also lead to migration of organisms along the east and west coasts. Heat-tolerant species, such as shrimp, will expand northward, while heat-intolerant species, such as clams and flounder, will retreat northward (Lindell, 2008). Coastal areas and small islands are the most threatened because of rises in sea level that global warming may cause. Increasing temperatures result in sea level rise by the thermal expansion of water and through the addition of water to the oceans from the melting of continental ice sheets.

STRATEGIES FOR CLIMATE CHANGE AND GLOBAL WARMING MITIGATION

A number of strategies have been formulated to mitigate the impacts of climate change and global warming. These strategies can be used independently or in combination to effectively control the growing menace of global warming and climate change.

Reduction in emission of GHG: Climate change arising due to the increasing concentration of greenhouse gases in the atmosphere since there pre-industrial times has emerged as a serious global environmental issue and poses a threat and challenge to mankind (Sharma *et al* 2006). The increased volumes of CO2 and other greenhouse gases released by burning of fossil fuels, land clearing and agriculture, and other activities are the primary sources of the human-induced component of global warming The prime task is to control present and future CO2 emissions and agree upon building up an optimum level of CO2 concentration (Rao 2006). Much of mitigation of Global warming is due to the reduction of common energy sources in favor of using renewable and sustainable energy. For example, instead of using fossil fuels that produce greenhouse gases, companies and nations can start creating policies that promote the use of wind or solar energy, thus reducing their impact on global warming. Improving vehicle fuel efficiency is one way to mitigate global warming as is the use of and promotion of energy resources such as nuclear power, hydrogen fuel cells, tidal power, and geothermal energy. (Lenton and cannel 2002) reported that maximum rate of global warming can be restricted to < 0.20 C/decade by restraining fossil fuel emission rates during the present century to < 0.030 C Gt carbon/yr. In years to come more substantial short as well as long term reduction standards of emission need to be achieved.

Forestry based mitigation options: The world's forests provide many important benefits: Home to more than half of all species living on land, a forest also helps slow global warming by storing and sequestering carbon.

RECOGNIZING FORESTS ROLE IN CLIMATE CHANGE AND CARBON SEQUESTRATION

Forests play an important role in minimizing the effects of global warming by sequestration of carbon globally. As globally important storehouses of carbon, forests play a critical role in influencing the Earth's climate. The Earth's forests serve as crucial carbon sinks due to their ability to absorb greenhouse gases. As a matter of fact drawing Co_2 out of the air and sequestering it into biomass is the only known practical way to remove large volumes of GHG from the atmosphere. The capability of forests to remove and store CO_2 from the atmosphere remains an important part of the global carbon balance. The environmental, social and economic benefits from forests provide additional reasons to protect them and enhance their management (Tuttle and Andrasko, 2006).

Measures to protect, restore, and sustainable manage forests offer significant climate change mitigation potential. Furthermore, forest-based measures can be an effective complement to abatement options focused on fossil fuel emissions. Forests play a major role in present and projected future carbon budget, since they store about 80% of all above ground and 40% of all below ground terrestrial organic carbon (Dixon *et al.*, 1994). (Perlack *et al.*, 1992-93) reported that in sub Saharan Africa reducing deforestation by half could power emissions to 21 million tonnes. Agro-forestry, if adopted at a rate of 2 to 4 % annually, could reduce annual carbon emission by about 38 to 68 million tonnes. Converting one-tenth of high and medium productivity land back to forest each year could result in the sequestration of about 11 to

18 million tones annually (Ravindranath and Somashekhar, 1995). Forest-based mitigation of global warming can occur by Conservation of existing forests - to avoid emissions associated with forest degradation or clearing. Sequestration by increasing forest carbon absorption capacity - occurring primarily by planting trees or facilitating the natural regeneration of forests, especially on marginal land and by making changes in forest management to increase biomass. (Houghton, *et al.,* 2000).

Substitution of sustainable produced biological products - substituting wood products for materials requiring energy-intensive production, such as aluminum or concrete, and substituting woody biomass for fossil fuels as an energy source. Properly designed and implemented, forest and land-use measures to mitigate climate change can result in other social and environmental benefits (e.g., protecting biodiversity and watersheds, promoting rural employment (IPCC, 2001).

Forest and land-use measures have the potential to reduce net carbon emissions by the equivalent of 10-20% of projected fossil fuel emissions through 2050. Worldwide, the greatest potential for carbon sequestration by forests exists in tropical and subtropical regions (IPCC, 2001: 9). In the present scenario role of forests is being viewed as inevitable. Hence 1997 Kyoto protocol specifically mentioned afforestation and reforestation as tools that can be used to reduce level of carbon dioxide from atmosphere (Bala *et al.,* 2004)

Introducing Carbon credits: Carbon credits are a key component of national and international attempts to mitigate the growth in concentrations of greenhouse gases (GHGs). One carbon credit is equal to one ton of carbon dioxide or in some markets carbon dioxide equivalent gases. The concept of carbon credits came into existence as a result of increasing awareness of the need for controlling emissions (IPCC 2007).The goal is to allow market mechanisms to drive industrial and commercial processes in the direction of low emissions or less carbon intensive approaches than those used when there is no cost to emitting carbon dioxide and other GHGs into the atmosphere. Since GHG mitigation projects generate credits, this approach can be used to finance carbon reduction schemes between trading partners and around the world. Carbon credits are a part of international emission trading norms. They incentivise companies or countries that emit less carbon. The total annual emissions are capped and the market allocates a monetary value to any shortfall through trading. Businesses can exchange, buy or sell carbon credits in international markets at the prevailing market price. India and China are likely to emerge as the biggest sellers and Europe is going to be the biggest buyers of carbon credits.

Role of international organisations: organisations associated with the environment can play an important role in planning, education and funding different nations for improving their environment. The main current international agreement on combating climate change is the Kyoto protocol, which came into force on 16 February 2005. The Kyoto Protocol is an amendment to the United Nations Framework Convention on Climate Change (UNFCCC). Countries that have ratified this protocol have committed to reduce their emissions of carbon dioxide and five other Green house gases, or engage in emissions trading if they maintain or increase emissions of these gases. The U.S Climate Change Science Programme is a group of about twenty federal agencies and US Cabinet Departments, all working together to address global warming. In July 2005 the U.S., China, India, Australia, as well as Japan and South Korea, agreed to the Asia-Pacific Partnership for Clean Development and Climate. The pact aims to encourage technological development that may mitigate global warming, without coordinated emissions targets. In an attempt to provide more opportunities for developing countries to adapt clean technologies, UNEP and WTO urged the international community to reduce trade barriers and to conclude the Doha trade round "which includes opening trade in environmental goods and services.

ADAPTATION TO CLIMATE CHANGE AND GLOBAL WARMING: AN IMMEDIATE REMEDY

Adaptation is a necessary strategy at all scales to complement climate change mitigation efforts because we cannot be sure that all climate change can be mitigated. Adaptation has the potential to reduce adverse impacts of climate change and to enhance beneficial impacts, but will incur costs and will not prevent all damages. Human and natural systems will to some degree adapt autonomously to climate change but planned adaptation can supplement autonomous adaptation. The need to adapt to climate change has become inevitable and for that purpose various strategies have to be executed, some of these strategies are listed below.

Geoengineering: Geoengineering is the deliberate modification of Earth's natural environment on a large scale to suit human needs. An example is greenhouse gases remediation which removes greenhouse gases from the atmosphere, usually through carbon sequestration techniques such carbon dioxide air capture. Solar radiation management reduces absorbed solar radiation, such as by the addition of stratospheric sulfur aerosols or cool roof techniques. To date, no large-scale geoengineering projects have been undertaken. Some limited tree planting (Fearnside, 1999) and cool roof projects are already underway, and ocean iron fertilization is at an advanced stage of research, with small-scale research trials and global modeling having been completed (Boyd, 2007).

STRATEGIES FOR AGRICULTURE

Agriculture of any kind is strongly influenced by the availability of water and as Climate change modifies rainfall, evaporation, runoff and soil moisture. So, more attention should be given to agriculture while formulating the strategies for climate change adaptation. The rising temperature may increase the frequency of droughts, which in turn results in moisture stress during flowering, pollination and grain-filling which is harmful to most crops and particularly to corn, soybeans and wheat. As a result, there is a need to develop crop varieties with greater drought tolerance. Due to the occurrence of droughts large scale scarcity of water for irrigation and other purposes like drinking will lead to instability and migration of living beings. Therefore, the strategy for water conservation and water rationing has to be followed effectively. The demand of water for irrigation is projected to rise in a warmer climate, bringing increased competition between agriculture already the largest consumer of water resources in semi arid regions and urban as well as industrial users. Falling water tables and the resulting increase in the energy needed to pump water will make the practice of irrigation more expensive. One strategy involves adapting urban areas to increasingly severe storms by increasing rain water storage (domestic water butts, unpaved gardens etc) and increasing the capacity of stormwater systems (and also separating stormwater from blackwater, so that overflows in peak periods do not contaminate rivers).

Managing Forests can help in adapting to climate change:

Trees can help offset or worsen global warming. As a tree grows, it absorbs CO2 at a rate that varies with species and age. Faster growing tress consume more, but longer-lived species "fix" the gas for longer periods. Once the tree is cut down the carbon is release into the atmosphere through natural decay or sped up through burning of organic materials (Robertson, 1997: 34). Most countries have already defined adaptation plans or projects, but few are considering forests role in adapting to climate change. We need to include forests in climate change adaptation policies for two reasons:

- Because they are vulnerable
- Because the play a key role in reducing the vulnerability of society to losses from climate change.

Our twin goals are to ensure that forestry policy and practice adequately address the need to protect forest-dependent livelihoods from adverse climate change and to ensure that adaptation strategies adequately incorporate improved forest management. There is an urgent need to protect forests, either through conservation or sustainable management. Climate change (including climate variability) coupled with degrading processes such as high deforestation rates will almost certainly affect the provision of goods and services from forests and, hence, hinder sustainable development.

Regarding climate change, sustainable management must include reducing the vulnerability of both the forest ecosystems and the social groups dependent on them. This implies a series of challenges ranging from understanding possible changes in forest ecosystems, to planning and implementing management measures aimed at reducing a specific vulnerability. Three strategies of forest management should be considered for adaptation measures: conservation, rehabilitation and forest plantations (Table 10.2). The examples presented in (Table 10.2) highlight the importance that forest management can have in reducing climate change vulnerability. Recent preliminary research has begun to determine the potential of such activities in the context of adaptation to climate change (IUCN, 2003). Concrete management practices should be designed according to specific site data and considering future climate scenarios.

Table 10.2: Examples of Forest Management Strategies as Adaptation Measures

Management Strategy	Potential Impact of Climate Change	Adaptation Measure
Conservation	Desertification increase	Watershed conservation
	Increase in fire events	Creation of fire barriers, collection and use of biomass
Rehabilitation	Greater exposure to torrential rains, reduced food security	Rehabilitation by agroforestry
	Change in structure and morphology of forest ecosystems	Selection of species and management practices considering future climate scenarios
Plantations	Landslide risk	Plantations with fast-growing species
	Exacerbation of impacts on ecosystems owing to increased fuelwood demand	Establishment of fuelwood orchards

ASSISTING DISADVANTAGED NATIONS

Many scientists, policy makers and the IPCC Fourth Assessment Report have agreed that disadvantaged nations, especially in the global south need more attention to the negative impacts of climate change. A balance, however, between development and climate change mitigation and adaptation needs to be found. It is important to recognize that if climate change phenomenon is not properly understood and coping strategies such as mitigation and adaptation are not adopted on timely manner, climate change impacts will exacerbate these pre-existing problems. Hence, there is a need of exploring strategies of integration between the climate change plans and development plans in the global south. Adaptation to climate change will be "ineffective and inequitable if it fails to learn and build upon an understanding of the multidimensional and differentiated nature of poverty and vulnerability (IDS

Bulletin, 2008). Poorer countries tend to be more seriously affected by climate change, yet have reduced assets and capacities with which to adapt. The world's largest historic emitter of greenhouse gases and with one of the highest levels of per capita emissions the United States has a responsibility to help the least developed countries face the threats brought on by global warming. And providing financial assistance for these countries to use in adapting to global warming's effects would be a responsible and sensible course of action that would also promote stability and prosperity abroad. Improving climate resilience and supporting adaptation will encourage capacity building, improve infrastructure, and thus promote economic growth. It will also enhance agricultural development and provide opportunities for clean-energy accessibility and reliability to help alleviate global energy poverty. Six billion people in the developing world have much more immediately at stake in the resolution of climate change. For everyone's sake, one cannot miss the chance to make these investments in their future and in ours.

CONCLUSION

Climate change arising due to the increasing concentration of greenhouse gases in the atmosphere since the pre-industrial times has emerged as a serious global environmental issue and poses a threat and challenge to mankind. A number of strategies have been formulated to mitigate the impacts of climate change and global warming. These strategies can be used independently or in combination to effectively control the growing menace of global warming and climate change. Adaptation is a necessary strategy at all scales to complement climate change mitigation efforts because we cannot be sure that all climate change can be mitigated. Forests can play a major role towards increasing the global carbon sequestration and also help in mitigating the adverse impacts of climate change if the world forests could be managed properly with due importance to afforestation and reforestation.

REFERENCES

Anup Shah , 2009 Climate Change and Global Warming Introduction, Global Issues, www.globaissues.org accessed on 11-01-2010.

Bala, N., G. Singh, P. Kumar and A.K. Sinha (2004). Role of Forests in Carbon Sequestration. Indian Forester, 6: 799-806.

Bhardwaj, S.D. and P. Panwar (2003). Global Warming and Climate Change- Effect and Strategies for its Mitigation. *Indian Forester*, (6) pp. 741-748.

Bhattacharya, S (2009). "Global Warming Threatens Millions of Species." Global Warming. pp no. 7-9. www.newscientist.com accessed on 1-01-2010.

Boyd, P.W. (2007). Mesoscale Iron Enrichment Experiments 1993-2005: Synthesis and Future Directions. *Science* 315: 612-617.

Bloomfield, J. (2000). The Potential Impacts of Global Warming on America's Forests; Critical Findings for Forest Lands from the First National Assessment of the Potential Consequences of Climate Variability and Change Complex Systems Research Center, Durham pp. 1-6.

Climate Change (2001). Impacts, Adaptation and Vulnerability. Contribution of Working Group II to the Third Assessment Report of the Intergovernmental Panel on Climate Change". www.grida.no accessed on 12-1-2010. pp. 1-45.

Climate Change (2007) Mitigation of Climate Change, Summary for Policymakers from IPCC Fourth Assessment Report". Working Group III, IPCC. pp. Item 25 and Table SPM.7, pp. 29-31. Retrieved 2007-05-10.

Cline, W.R. (2007) Global Warming and Agriculture: Impact Estimates by Country, www.newscientist.com accessed on 1-01-2010 pp.1-9.

Dixon, R.K., S. Brown, R.A. Houghton and A.M. Solomon (1994). Carbon Pools and Flux of Global Forests: ecosystems. *Science*, 263: 185-190.

Fearnside, P. (1999). Forests and Global Warming Mitigation in Brazil: Opportunities in the Brazilian Forest Sector for Responses to Global Warming Under the Clean Development Mechanism. Biomass and Bioenergy 16: 171-189.

Handwerk, B and B. Hendwerk (2009). "Global Warming Could Cause Mass Extinctions by 2050, National Geographic News. www.nationalgeographic.com. Accessed on 15-1-2010.

Houghton, J (1997) Global warming: The Complete Briefing. Camdridge University Press, Camdridge, U.K: 251.

Houghton, R.A., J.L. Hackler, and K.T. Lawrence. 2000. The U.S. Carbon Budget: Contributions from Land-Use Change. Science 285: 574.

IPCC. 2001. Technical Summary. In Climate Change 2001: Mitigation. Contribution of Working Group III to the Third Assessment Report of the Intergovernmental Panel on Climat eChange, Cambridge University Press: Cambridge, United Kingdom and New York, NY, USA.

IUCN, IISD, SEI-B & Intercooperation. 2003. Combining Disaster Risk Reduction, Natural Resource Management and Climate Change Adaptation in a New Approach to the Reduction of Vulnerability and Poverty. A Conceptual Framework Paper Prepared by the Task Force on Climate Change, Vulnerable Communities and Adaptation. Manitoba, Canada, IUCN.

Kumar,U. (2002).Global Warming and Green Houseeffect. *Agrobios* Newsletter, 1(7): 12-13.

Lashof, D. A. (1993). The Risks of Global Warming. *The Electricity Journal*. Vol. 10 (2) pp. 1-14.

Lental, T.M. and M.G.R. Cannell (2002). Climate Change, 52: 255-262.

Lindell, N (2008). A Discordant Sea: Global Warming and its Effect on Marine Populations. Geography, pp. 26-32.

Lobell DB, Burke MB, Tebaldi C, Mastrandrea MD, Falcon WP, Naylor RL (2008). "Prioritizing Climate Change Adaptation Needs for Food Security in 2030". *Science* 319 (5863): 607-10.

McMichael AJ, Woodruff RE, Hales S (2006). "Climate Change and Human Health: Present and Future Risks". *Lancet* 367 (9513): 859-69.

Papadopol, C.S. (2000). Impats of Climate Waming on Forests of Ontario: Option for Adaptation and Mitigation. *Forestry Chronicle*, 76(1): 139-149.

Perlack, R.D., R.L. Graham and A.M. Prasad (1992-93). Land Use Management and Carbon Sequestering in Sub-Saharan Africa. *J. Env. Systems*, 22(3) 199-210.

Poverty in a Changing Climate (2008).*IDS Bulletin* 39 (4): 2.

Rao, R. J 2006 Mitigation of Global Warming: *Journal of Governance and Public Policy*, Vol. 3,(1) Pages: 27-35.

Ravindranath, N.H. and B.S. Somashekhar (1995). Potential and Economics of Fprestry Options for Carbon Sequestration in India. *Biomass and Bioenergy*, 8: 323-336.

Rawat, V, S. Dhan and P. Kumar.(2003). Climate Change and its Impact on Forest Bio Diversity. *Indian Forester*, (6) pp. 787-798.

Robertson, L. (1997), Eugene Register-Guard, pp. 25-34.

Samara, J.S and P.D Sharma (2002). Safeguarding Natural Resources and Environment. *Indian Farming*, Nov. pp. 34-35.

Sharma, S., S. Bhattacharya and A. Garg (2006). Greenhouse Gas Emissions from India: A Perspective. *Current science*, Vol. 90, No. 3, pp. 22-31.

Tuttle, A and K. Andrasko (2006). Registries and Research: Climate Change Mitigation and Forestry in the United States. pp. 1-26, www.fao.org. Accessed on 2-2-2010.

Walters, J (2009). How is Wildlife Affected by Global Warming? Environmental Issues 1-9, www.sciencedirect.com accessed on 22-1-2010.

Index